AF594677

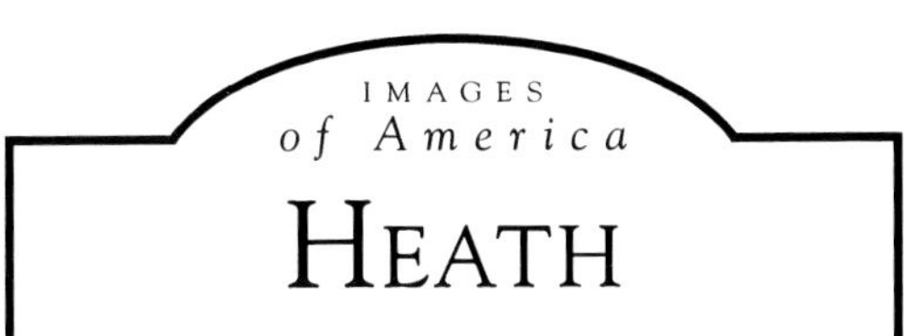
IMAGES
of America
HEATH

On the Cover: The Isbells, a prominent Heath family, gather on the front porch of their home in 1911. M.K. Isbell owned and operated a large general mercantile store in Heath, which sold everything from ladies' fashions to mules. From left to right are M.K. Isbell (father), Fay, Grady, Grace Isbell Vaughn and her daughter Lena, Frank, Mary, Anna, and Emma Lena Isbell (mother). (Courtesy of Fay Lofland.)

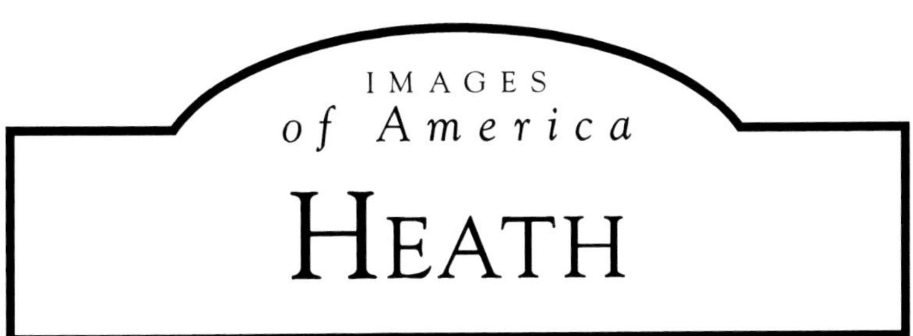

Austin Wells

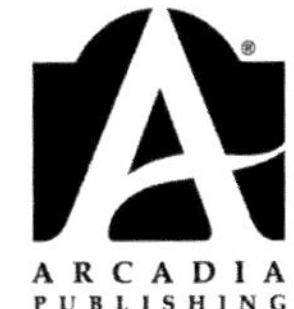

ISBN 978-1-4671-3349-4

Published by Arcadia Publishing
Charleston, South Carolina

Printed in the United States of America

Library of Congress Control Number: 2014959342

For all general information, please contact Arcadia Publishing:
Telephone 843-853-2070
Fax 843-853-0044
E-mail sales@arcadiapublishing.com
For customer service and orders:
Toll-Free 1-888-313-2665

Visit us on the Internet at www.arcadiapublishing.com

This book is dedicated to my awesome and loving parents, Dennis and Tommie Wells; my twin brother, Preston; and his wife, Victoria, all of whom have supported me wholeheartedly in my quest to uncover the history of my hometown of Heath. I also want to dedicate it to all of the longtime families who have called Heath their home for many, many years.

Contents

Acknowledgments

I want to start off by saying that I am no historian. In fact, I am merely a young writer who started this whole project with one goal in mind: to learn as much as I could about the history of the community I grew up in. I am proud to say that thanks to the large amount of support and knowledge of those that helped make this book a reality, I feel I have accomplished my goal and so much more. And I have so many to thank for that.

First, I would like to give big thanks to Clarice Isbell, Charlotte Krider, Bill and Jerry Way, Runell White, Ada Lou Myers, Reba Jett, Gale Terry, Mark Poindexter, Rosemary Klutts, Stephanie Galanides, Kim Dobbs, Jerry Deaton, Justin Holland, and Carolyn Francisco and the Rockwall County Historical Foundation, as well as anyone else who contributed to this book. Heath's history simply just could not be told without their wonderful pictures. Many thanks to Stacy Parks for welcoming me into the home of his late wife Sheri Stodghill Fowler Parks—a renowned author and Rockwall County historian who passed away from an extended battle with cancer in January 2015. The use of the workspace in her home proved a very valuable resource in terms of having a place to organize all the material found in the book. A special thanks to Sheri's wonderful mother, Patsy Stodghill, who was such a tremendous help and played a major role in helping me connect with longtime families in Heath and collecting the images in this book. Without her help, this book simply would not have become a reality.

I am very privileged to have been allowed the use of Fay Lofland's photo albums and scrapbooks. Many of the images and information used in this book came from them, and they were invaluable in helping to identify people and authenticating dates and events.

Thanks to Bob Chilton, Clarke Newman, and Lisa Blankenship with the Rush Creek Yacht Club for their contributions and assistance, as well as to the Rockwall County Historical Foundation.

Of course, I cannot say enough about Lily Watkins, Jeff Reutsche, and all the fine folks at Arcadia Publishing, who stuck by me through thick and thin and always seemed to know just what to say to keep me positive throughout this whole process. As someone who's new to the book publishing industry, I do not think I would have made it without their guidance and encouragement.

And to my Mom and Dad . . . thanks so much for believing I could write this book even when I felt overwhelmed by it all. Love you more!

Introduction

In 1840, a road was built from the city of Austin down to the intersection of the Red River and the mouth of the Kiamichi Creek. This road crossed over the East Fork of the Trinity River near the area that would eventually become known as Heath. It was due to this road that Heath gradually developed from a wilderness with a plentiful supply of duck, geese, wild turkeys, and the occasional pack of wolves to the open rural community it is today.

When immigrants and settlers learned of the rich black soil ripe for farming and the abundant supply of timber in the area, they set off to bring their families into Texas. One such pioneering family was the Heath family. In the spring of 1846, John O. Heath set out for Texas from his home in Simpson County, Kentucky, to visit friend and Kentucky neighbor Daniel Rowlett. Afterward, he decided to bring his family and settle in the area now named after his family. Heath brought his wife, Martha, and their first child, along with his brother-in-law C. L. Jones, and traveled down the Mississippi and the Arkansas Rivers by boat. They then travelled by ox and wagon into Mercer's Colony, a survey of land formed by Daniel Rowlett and located at the East Fork of the Trinity River. The Heath family built themselves a log cabin on the property, and John acquired the title to it on May 1, 1848, becoming one of the first to settle in the area.

The Heath family would soon be joined by Virginia native Sterling Rex Barnes, whose family also acquired a land grant for their home on 320 acres on the East Fork of the Trinity River at about the same time as the Heaths. Barnes eventually ended up operating the toll bridge crossing into Dallas from Heath known as Barnes Bridge. The Cary Cobb family also settled into the area that same year, near Rush and Yankee Creeks. Cary Cobb and Sterling Barnes (known as Judge Barnes after becoming justice of the peace in 1852) owned the only peach orchards in the area at the time. The Heath, Barnes, and Cobb families were very close, and in fact, Barnes, Heath, and Cobb would remain friends their whole lives.

The area initially went through several name changes before being named Heath. In 1849, John O. Heath established the area's first post office out of his log cabin home and called it Black Hills, thus providing one of Rockwall County's earliest settlements with its first name. The town was named Black Hills due to the blackness of the soil in the area. Heath served as the first postmaster of Black Hills until he and C.L. Jones opened a store near Rockwall and moved the post office into that location. The settlement then became Willow Springs because of the vast amounts of willow trees that grew in the area. It remained Willow Springs until 1886, when the town was called Heath after one of its earliest pioneers.

Not only did Heath go through several name changes, but the transformation of Texas from an independent territory to a state also meant the town transitioned into four different counties. In the 1800s, Heath was first a part of Nacogdoches County, then Henderson County, Kaufman County, and finally Rockwall County after the Heath family helped make known the petition requesting Rockwall to be made into a separate county.

While most of the Indians in the area had cleared out, during the late 1800s, buffalo could still be seen in Heath. The buffalo could be spotted roaming and grazing the prairie lands in the area of Darr Estates, and each day at sunset, they would cross the land to drink at the nearby creek. It has been said that children playing in the tall grass would be called in by a bell, warning them to clear the area and make way for the incoming buffalo herds. The creek where the buffalo drank became known as Buffalo Creek to commemorate their lasting legacy.

The first schools in the area were located on the Pinion farm and near the Baptist church, and in 1898 a cyclone destroyed the church. The building constructed to replace that church was the structure used for services until 1982.

From early 1900 to 1920, the town of Heath saw a great deal of growth and at one point had several businesses in operation, including a couple of barbershops and hardware stores, a bank, a blacksmith shop, a hamburger shop, drugstores, three cotton gins, and a general mercantile store. Mary Franklin donated the land for a new school building, and in 1902, the Heath Independent School District was formed. An L-shaped school building was erected where Heath City Hall now sits, near the intersection of Smirl and Laurence Drives. As time passed, new school buildings were put up, including a two-story wooden structure housing six classrooms and serving grades one through 10.

Throughout its early history, Heath suffered from a total of three fires that burned down several of the community's thriving businesses and homes. The fires, coupled with the harsh living conditions of the Great Depression, caused a significant decline in the growth of the town. Farming—a large part of daily life in the community—was no longer enough to support families unless the farm was rather large, and many residents left Heath to find work in larger cities. Ladies were involved in the PTA, Eastern Star, and the quilting club while many of the men were a part of the Woodmen of the World and the Heath Masonic Lodge and often participated in baseball tournaments and church activities.

In 1949, the Heath school system merged with the Rockwall Independent School District, and the Heath School was closed. However, the women in the community wanted to save part of the building, and their wish was granted. The part of the building that was kept was used for a variety of social and community events and even used as the headquarters for the local quilting club. Family reunions, fundraising events, and church socials from the three churches in Heath (Baptist, Methodist, and Church of Christ) were also held in the old school building.

The Town of Heath was officially incorporated in 1966, and Alvis Nash became the first mayor. At this time, Heath was just a small rural community with a population around 200, but this would soon change with the filling in of Lake Ray Hubbard and the construction of the Rush Creek Yacht Club in 1969. Promise of a quiet life down by the calm waters of the lake, together with the development of a new shopping center, helped attract more people into Heath, and by 1970, the population reached 520, with a total of 192 homes in the area, including Darr Estates, developed by longtime Heath settler Maon "Bill" Seabolt and family. The addition of all of these new buildings called for the formation of a volunteer fire department, and Bill Way became the first fire chief.

Heath continued to grow so much that by the 1990s the city needed new schools to accommodate its development. Amy Parks Heath Elementary was built in 1996, followed by Dorothy Smith Pullen Elementary and Maurine Cain Middle School in 1999. The Rockwall-Heath High School opened in 2005 and is located on FM 740.

Today, the city of Heath continues to grow, along with Rockwall County, with new developments being planned, including the Heath Golf and Yacht Club and the Lambert Addition. With its spacious lots, large modern homes, and rural atmosphere, the city of Heath in many ways pays homage to the quiet openness of its countryside, which helped attract many to its black hills all those years ago, while it strives for more growth and expansion.

One

Historic Places and Landmarks of Heath

Many might be surprised to know that during the very early 1900s, Heath had as many or more businesses than the city of Rockwall. However, even before those years in which Heath became a thriving community, it experienced steady growth beginning in the late 1800s, with several businesses and two schoolhouses operating in the area.

The community really began to take shape between the years of 1900 and 1920, with many businesses and even a new schoolhouse being built. Some of the businesses in operation during this time included two barbershops owned by a Mr. Gregory and Press Batcher; a furniture, hardware, and undertaker combination store first owned by McCoulskey, Bowen, and A. L. Martin and later Pete Darr; a local grocery store owned by Tom Wright and sometimes called the "chilie joint;" a drugstore owned by Dave Bryan that later became the famous landmark known as the Fred Laurence Drug Store, which remained in business until 1967 or 1968; cotton gins owned and operated by Bill Piper, John Vaughn, and the Hartman brothers; a blacksmith run by Roscoe Darr; a hamburger shop owned by Felix Darr; and a bank located on or near the site of the Brady Boys Country Store.

After a 1916 fire, the town began to see a decline. Three churches were located in the area: the Methodist church, Baptist church, and Church of Christ. In 1949, the school at Heath closed and merged with the Rockwall Independent School District. The old schoolhouse building was destroyed, although many of the ladies within the community voted to save the first floor of the school and use it as a community structure for family reunions, church socials, and fundraising activities. Heath incorporated in 1959, and after Lake Ray Hubbard filled in, the city saw more development, including Darr Estates and the Seabolt Addition.

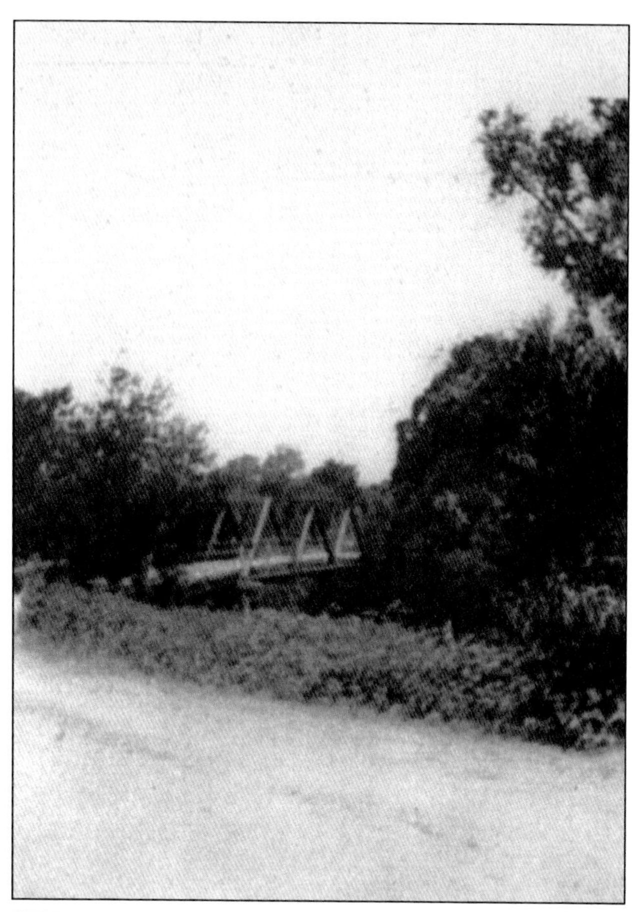

Sterling Rex Barnes began operating a toll bridge (pictured at left) across from his home on the banks of the East Fork of the Trinity River, near the present town of Heath, in 1854. The toll fees for the bridge, as set out in the commissioners' court minutes of Rockwall County in 1877, were as follows: 5¢ for footman, 10¢ for man and horse, 25¢ for horse and buggy, 40¢ for a two-horse wagon, 5¢ for loose horses, 3¢ for cattle, and 2¢ for sheep, hogs, or goats. Barnes continued to operate the bridge for 12 years until his death in 1866. Rockwall County eventually took over the operation of the bridge. In the image below, Kenny Terry draws a bow upon the Barnes Bridge. (Both, courtesy of the Rockwall County Historical Foundation.)

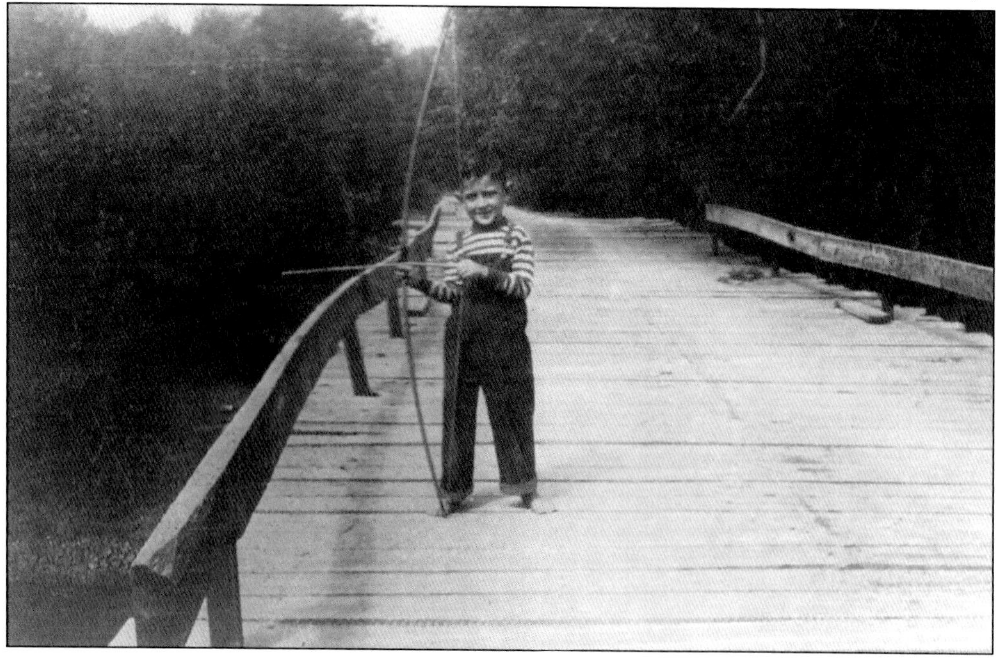

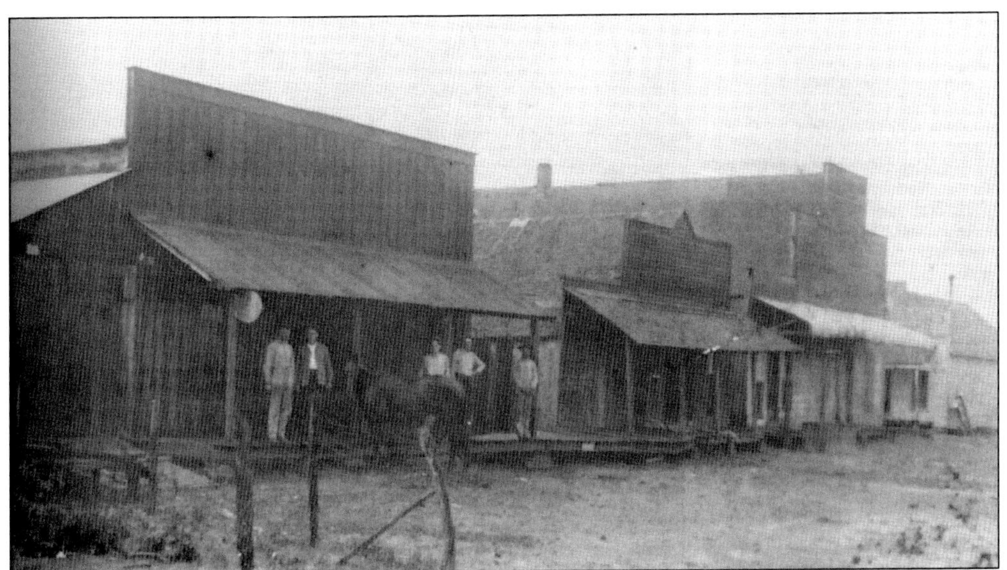

During the early 1900s, Heath was considered a thriving inland village, with many shops and businesses, including hardware stores, barbershops, banks, and a general mercantile store. Shown above is the McCoulskey-Bourne Hardware Company in Heath, which was later owned by L.L. "Pete" Darr. However, the town suffered a setback in its growth after a fire swept across the area in 1916 and burned many of the businesses. The town was rebuilt but two other fires occurred in later years. By 1936, only five businesses were still in operation, including Fred Laurence Drug Store, J.C. Gregory Barbershop, M.K. Isbell General Merchandise and Groceries and Filling Station, Heath Gin Company, and Taylor and Brooks Groceries and Meat Market and Filling Station. (Courtesy of the Rockwall County Historical Foundation.)

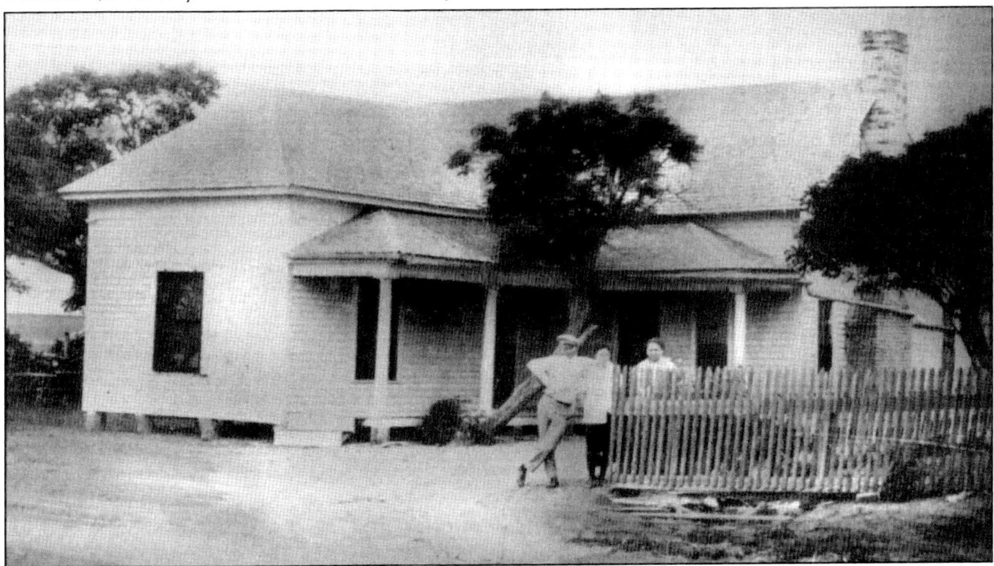

This photograph shows the homestead of Martha Lou Crawley, which is located on what is now Hubbard Drive. Crawley was married to Thomas David Lofland, who died of pneumonia January 3, 1898. Approximately eight years later, she married Robert Alfred Raburn, who was president of the Farmers Guaranty State Bank of Heath. He died at the age of 46 in 1911. (Courtesy of Fay Lofland.)

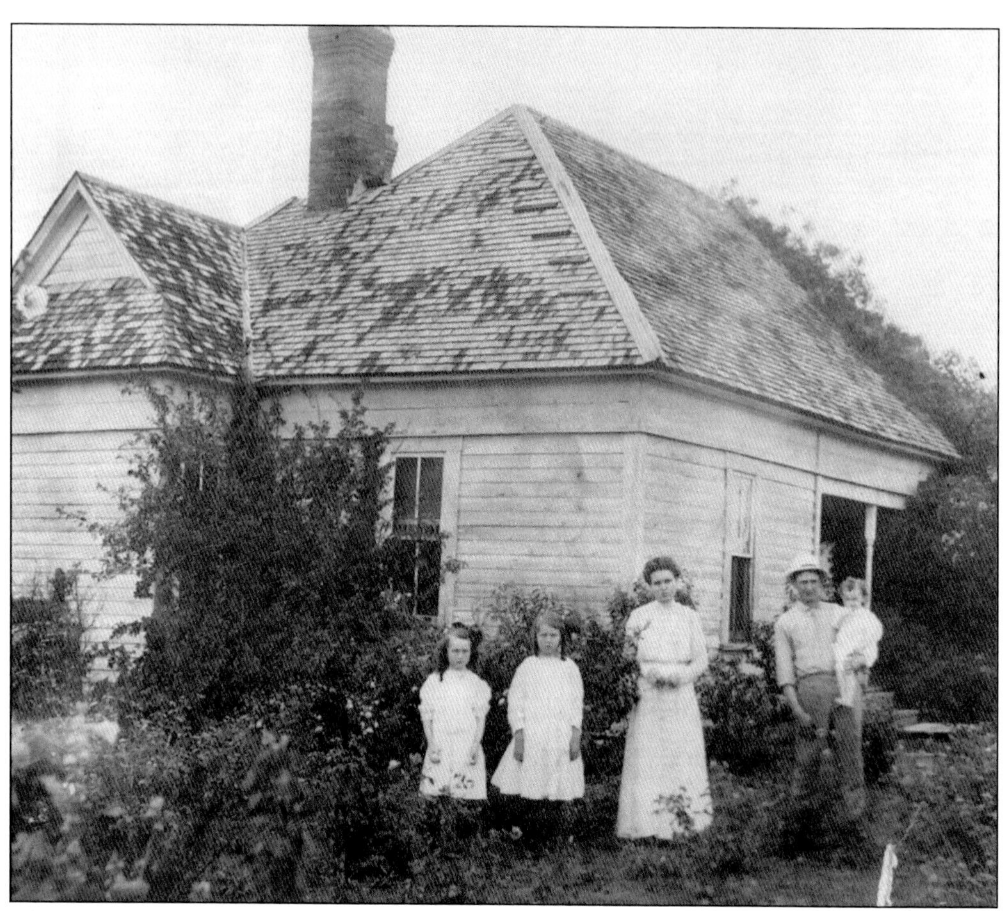

Above are, from left to right, Mary Isbell, Anna Isbell, Grace Isbell Vaughn, John Vaughn, and Lena Vaughn at the Vaughn home at Heath. John and his family moved to Heath in the early 1900s from Rome, Georgia. John and Grace were married by local Baptist minister J.T. Vance in his drugstore, which was located directly next door to her father's (M.K. Isbell) large general mercantile store in Heath. Below shows an advertisement for the Heath Gin owned by John Vaughn. James Thomas "Jim" Lofland acted as an assistant manager at the gin. John and Jim also operated a gin in Forney called the Forney Gin Company. (Courtesy of Fay Lofland.)

HEATH GIN CO.

JOHN VAUGHN, Mgr.
J. T. LOFLAND, Asst. Mgr.

5-80 LUMMUS EQUIPMENT
CAPACITY FIFTY BALES A DAY

Machinery of the highest type of efficiency. Service of the superior kind.

This institution is for the people of Heath and surrounding territory and we are always glad to serve you.

HEATH, TEXAS

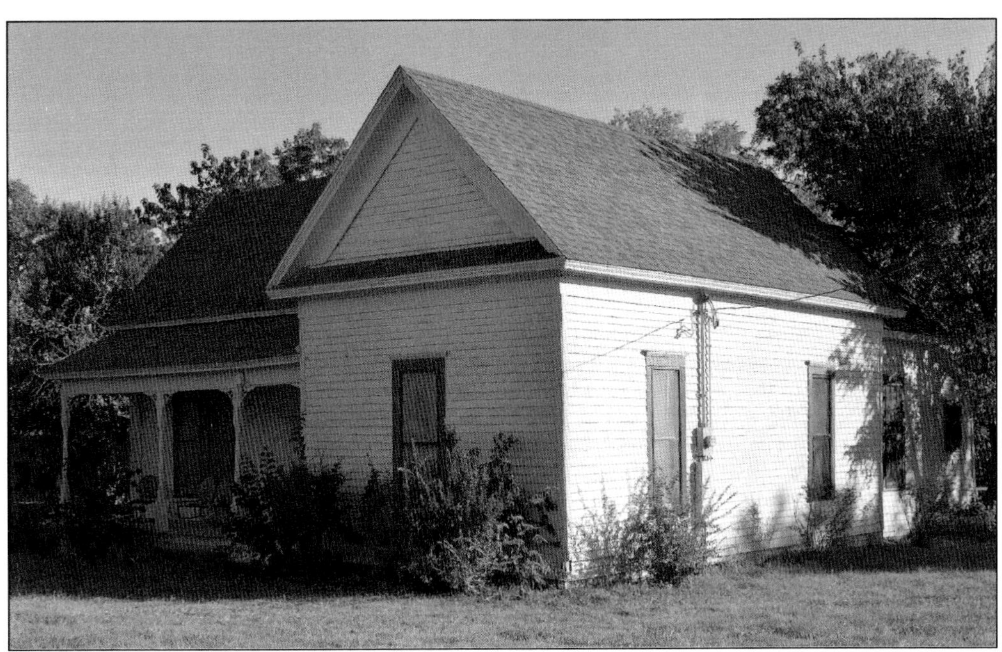

One of the oldest (if not the oldest) homes in Heath belonged to Jim Thomas and Fay Lofland and currently sits across the street from the old Methodist church building off FM 740 going toward Forney. The house was built in 1911, and it was their first and lifetime home. Fay Isbell and Jim Lofland married on June 29, 1913, when she was 18 and he was 20. At right is a receipt dated 1913 from L.L. Darr—dealer in hardware, undertaker supplies, and many other items—to J.T. Lofland depicting supplies bought for their home shown in the above image for a total of $161. Some of the items included one kitchen table, one dining table, six dining chairs, two rocking chairs, a dresser, a work stand, an iron board, a library table, one art square, and three rugs. (Above, photograph by author; both, courtesy of Fay Lofland.)

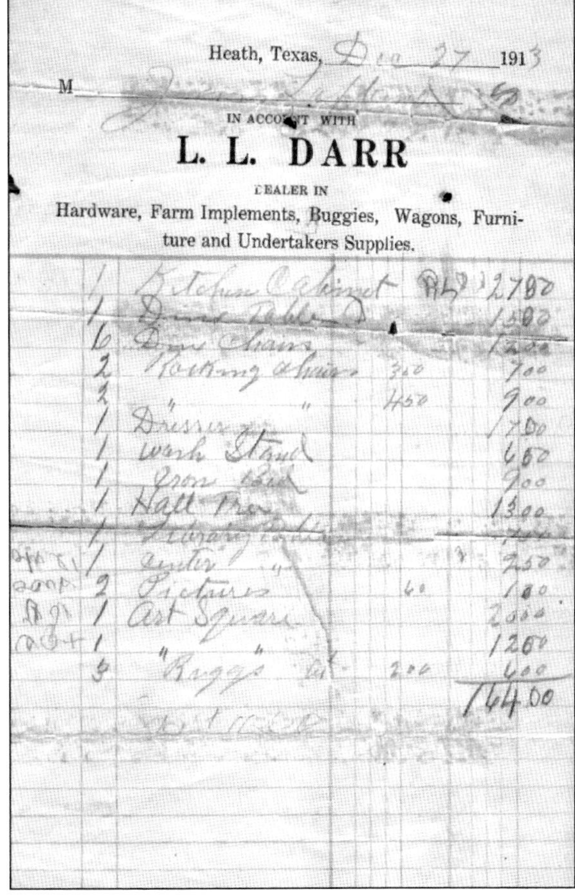

Heath, Texas, Dec 27 1913

M Jim Lofland

IN ACCOUNT WITH

L. L. DARR

DEALER IN

Hardware, Farm Implements, Buggies, Wagons, Furniture and Undertakers Supplies.

1	Kitchen Cabinet		27 00
1	Dining Table		15 00
6	Dining Chairs		12 00
2	Rocking chairs	3 50	7 00
2	" "	4 50	9 00
1	Dresser		17 00
1	Wash Stand		6 50
1	Iron Bed		9 00
1	Hall Tree		13 00
1	Library Table		[illegible]
1	[illegible] "		2 50
2	Pictures	60	1 20
1	Art Square		20 00
1	" "		12 00
3	Rugs at	2 00	6 00
			164 00

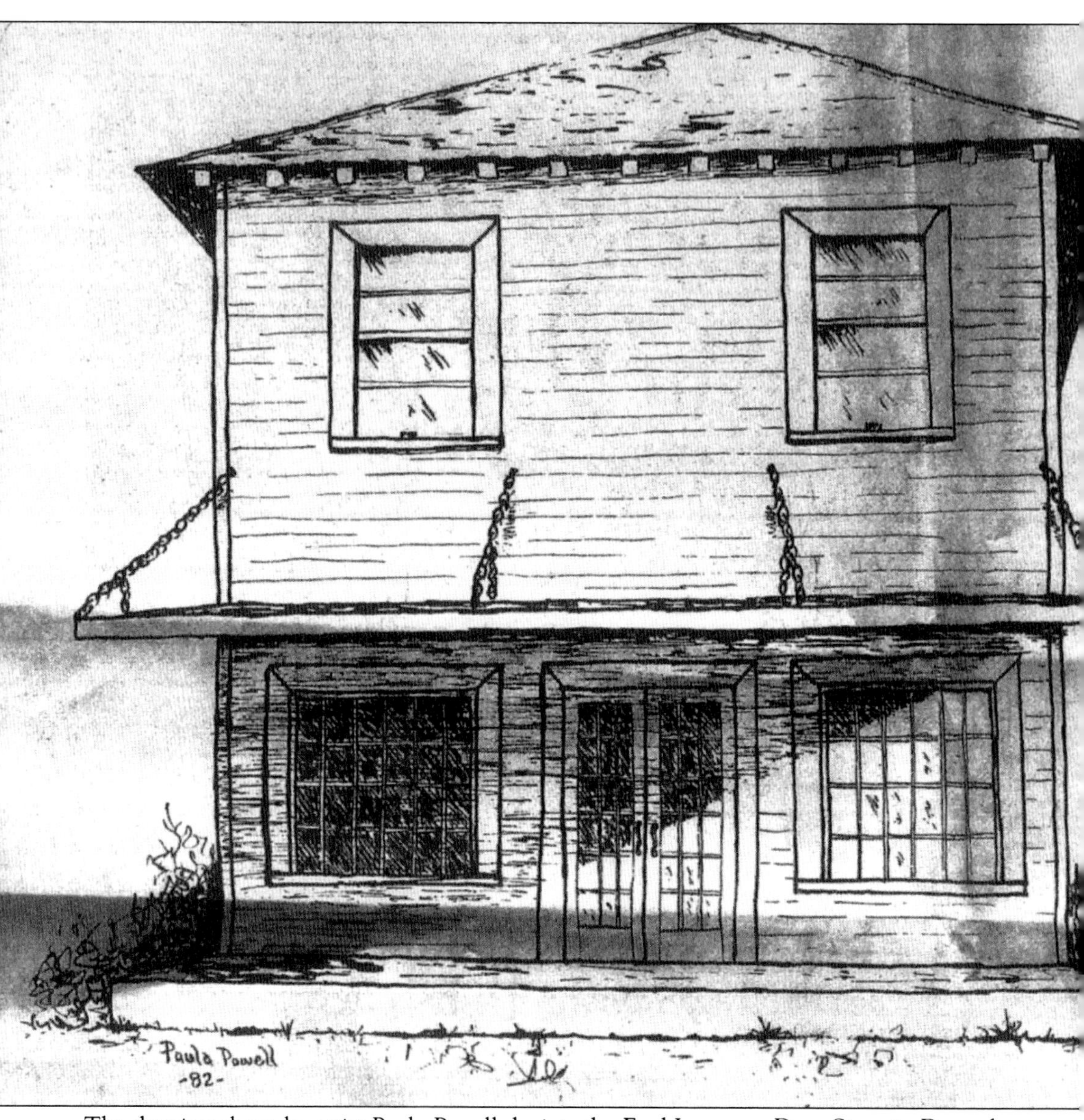

The drawing above by artist Paula Powell depicts the Fred Laurence Drug Store in December 1983. A longtime Heath landmark that was constructed around 1919, the two-story building stood at the southeast corner of FM 740 and FM 1140 and housed a drugstore, soda fountain, and an ice cream parlor, eventually evolving into a general merchandise store when Laurence began to supply the local families with other goods and services for their needs. Dr. F. M. McChristy helped establish the store and was manager and part-owner. His doctor's office was located inside the drugstore. Later, the store became the Bryan and Laurence Drug Store after D. S. Bryan and Fred Laurence took over ownership. The Heath Masonic Lodge occupied the entire second floor of the building for several years. (Courtesy of Clarice Isbell.)

D. S. BRYAN F. C. LAWRENCE

BRYAN & LAWRENCE

DRUGS AND DRUG SUNDRIES
COLD DRINKS

Whatever you need in Drugs or Drug Sundries you will find it here—and you will find it to be of the best quality and the price will be in your favor.

When in Heath don't fail to come to see us, we will be glad to se you. Our store is a friendly store.

HEATH, TEXAS

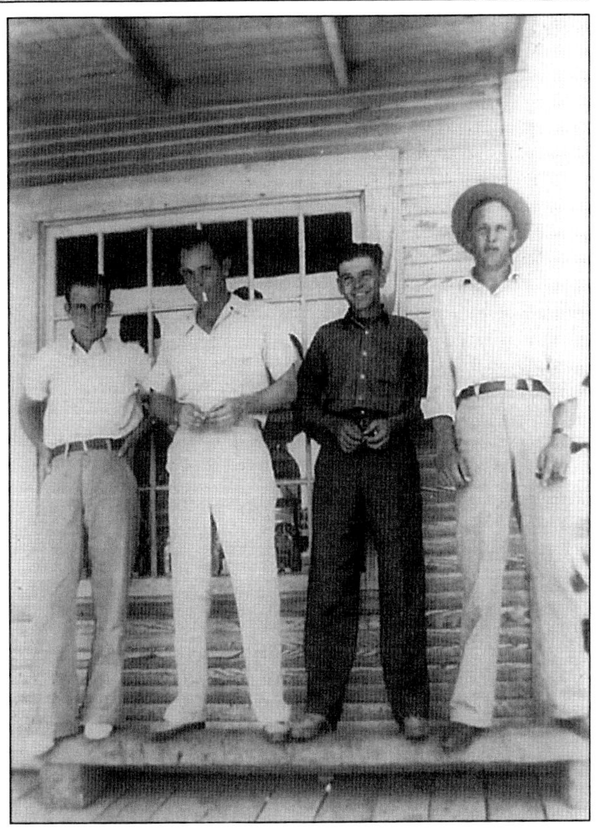

D.S. Bryan had been a businessman for many years in Heath and was later joined by Fred Laurence, who eventually became sole owner of the drugstore. The Laurence store stood as a landmark in Heath for many years until it was relocated to Forney in 1971 and remodeled into a private residence. Pictured above is an advertisement that ran for the store in a dated edition of the *Rockwall Success*. At right, from left to right, local residents Ivan Berry, Carl Pike, Woodrow Bryan, and Clifford Hall stand on the porch of the Fred Laurence Drug Store in Heath in 1941. One of the traditions of the Heath community involved the men of the town getting together on a daily basis to play Dominos on the front porch of the drugstore. During inclement weather, the game continued but was simply moved inside. (Above, courtesy of Fay Lofland; right, courtesy of the Rockwall County Historical Foundation.)

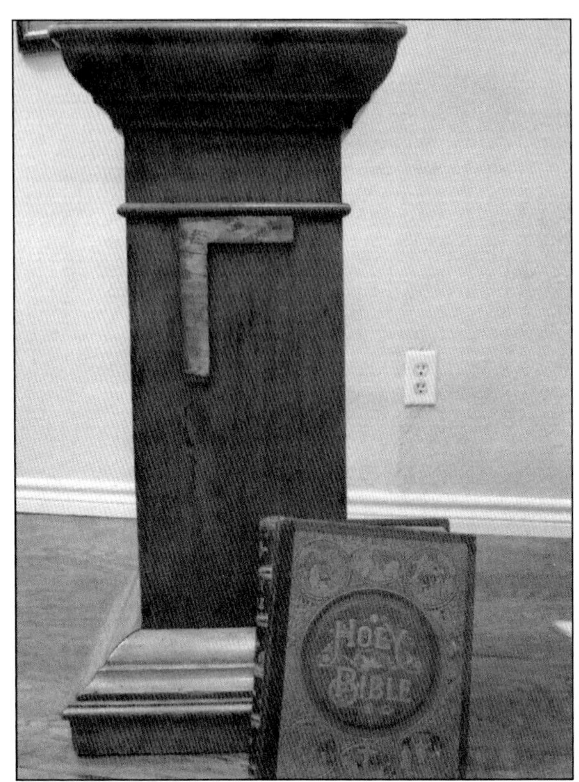

At left is one of the master stations and an old Bible belonging to Douglas R. Cullins, the last worshipful master of the E.C. Heath Masonic Lodge prior to its merger with the East Trinity Masonic Lodge No. 157 in 1968. Cullins was a constable in Heath for 17 years. The Bible was inherited by current Heath mayor pro tem Justin A. Holland, grandson of Cullins and member of the East Trinity Lodge. The E.C. Heath Lodge held its meetings on the second floor of the Fred Laurence Drug Store. (Both, photograph by author.)

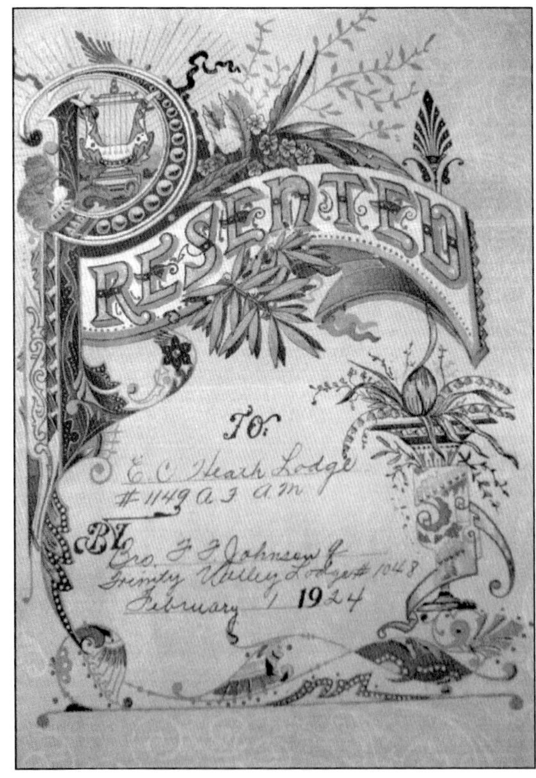

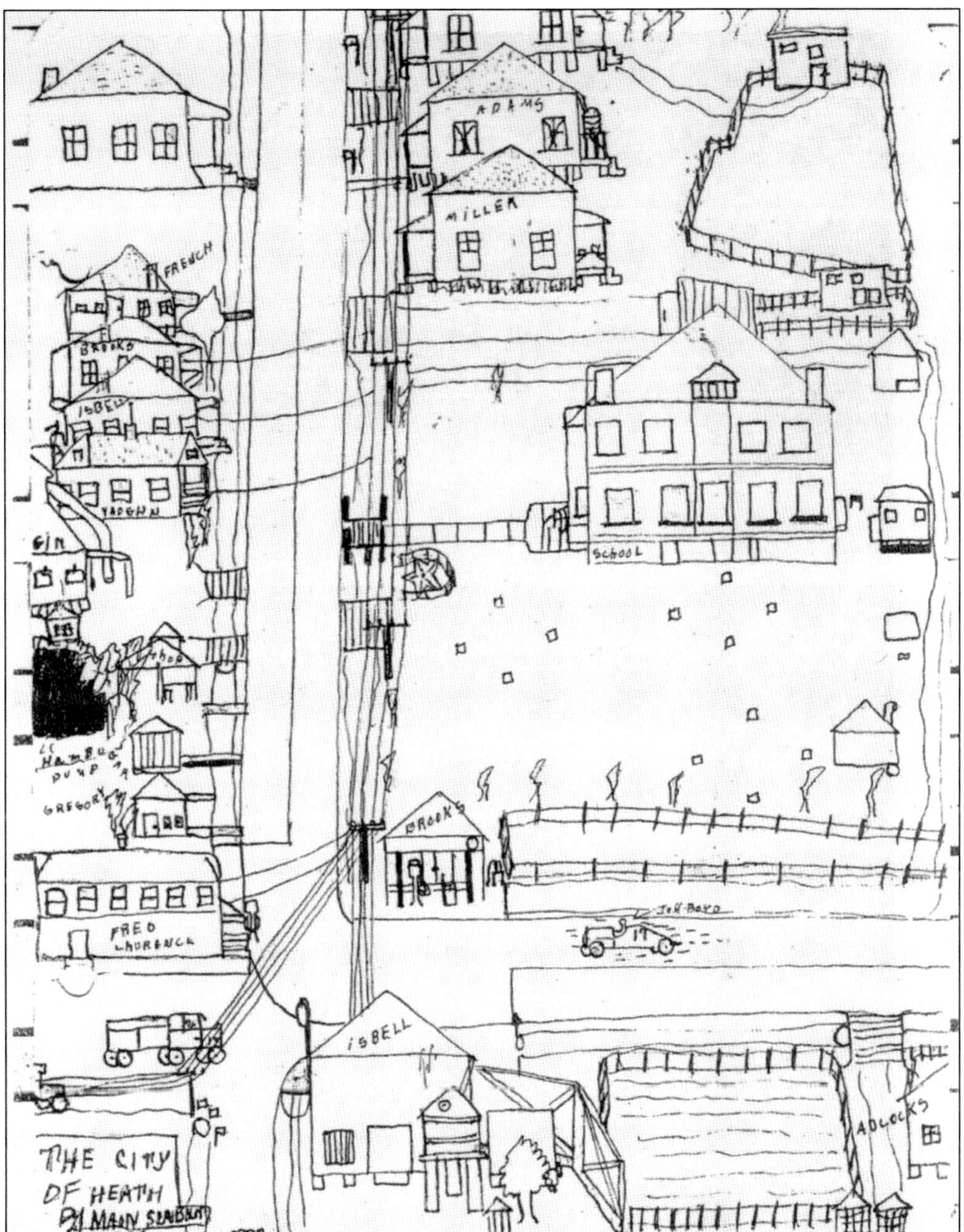

After looking at this drawing of Heath done in 1930 by 10-year-old Maon Seabolt, it is not too difficult to imagine that this creative-minded boy would eventually become the man who ended up developing Darr Estates on the property by the lake, which was owned by Maon's parents, Will and Rosa Lee Seabolt. The drawing depicts several homes and a couple of stores in Heath, including the Fred Laurence Drug Store. (Courtesy of Rosemary Seabolt Klutts.)

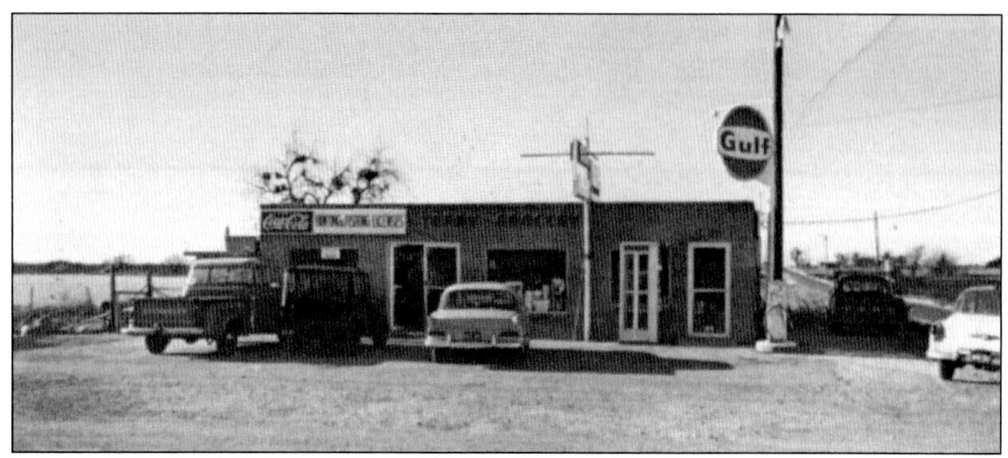

A general merchandise and grocery store has stood at the corner of Laurence Drive and FM 740 since M.K. Isbell established his store there. His daughter Anna and her husband, Ted Gardenhire, ran the store after his death. Later, J.H. "Rusty" Vaughn ran a similar business there that was destroyed by a fire of unknown causes. In 1966, Aileen and Waymond Terry built the store shown in the above image. Waymond was one of the first city councilman of Heath, and Aileen was a longtime city secretary who was well loved by all within the community. Others who have owned and operated stores on this property are Doris and Walter Cullins and Mike Brady. (Courtesy of the Rockwall County Historical Foundation.)

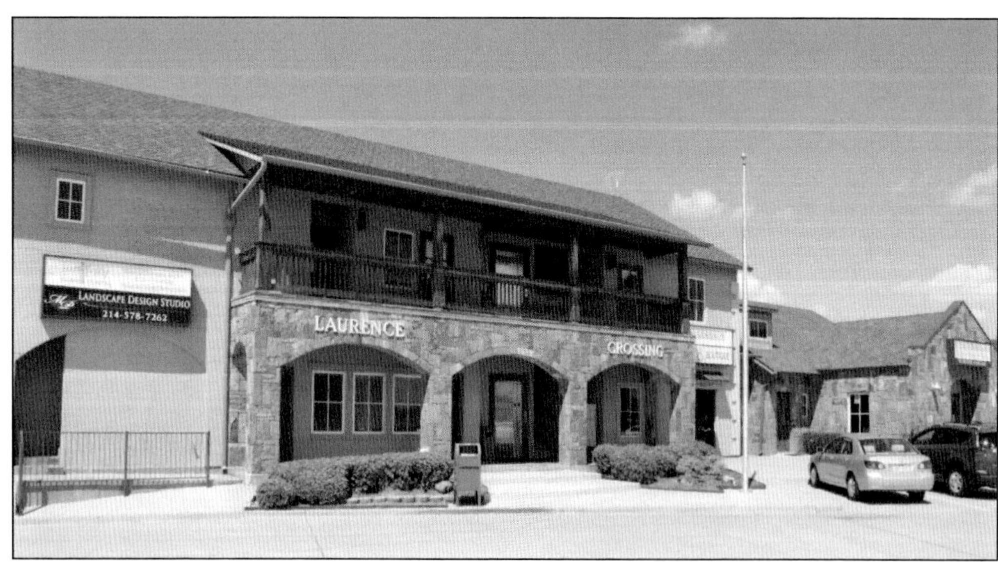

This image shows Laurence Crossing, which now exists where the Fred Laurence Drug Store and Masonic Lodge once stood. The structure houses several businesses, including a post office and Milanos Pizza.

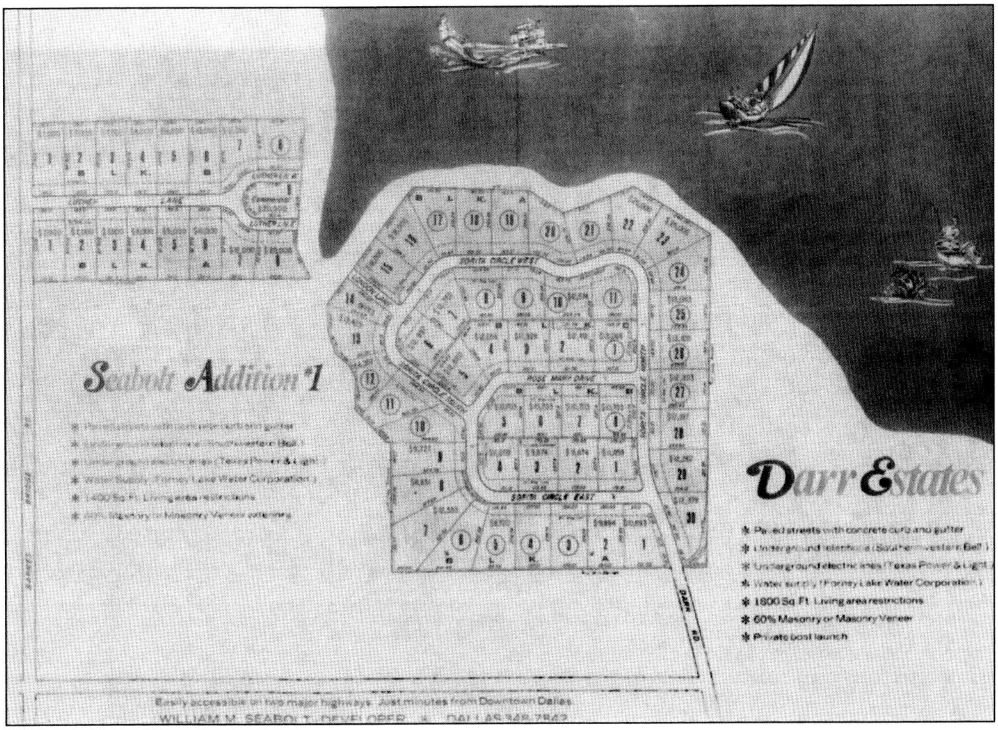

The plats shown here are for Darr Estates and the Seabolt Addition No. 1 and included paved streets with concrete curbs and gutters, underground electric lines supplied by Texas Power & Light, underground telephone (Southwestern Bell), water supply by the Forney Lake Water Corporation, and homes made up of 60 percent masonry exteriors and 1,400-square-foot living-area restrictions. Heath mayor Alvis Nash approved the platting of Darr Estates on October 9, 1967, and it was to be engineered by Harold Evans. The first lot was sold to a man named Jack Woodard on April 15, two years later. (Both, courtesy of Rosemary Seabolt Klutts.)

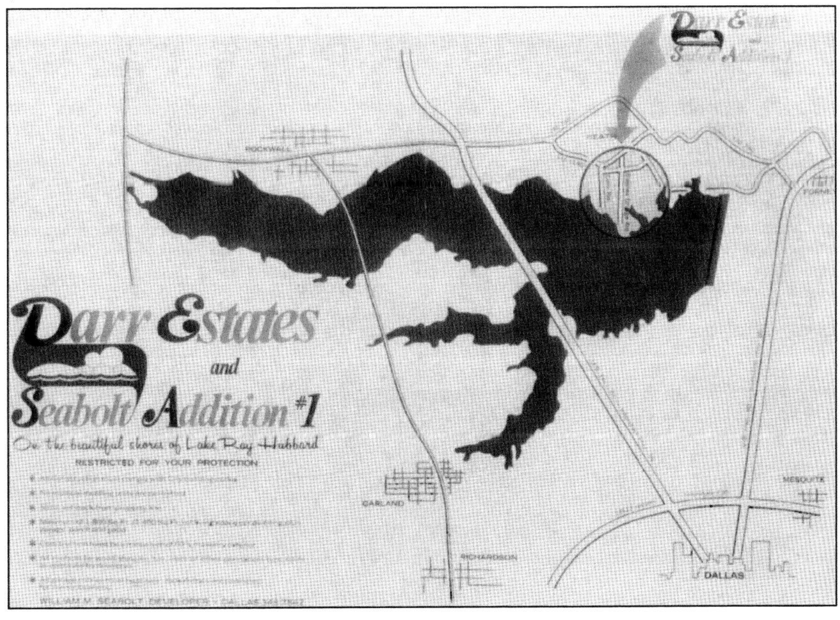

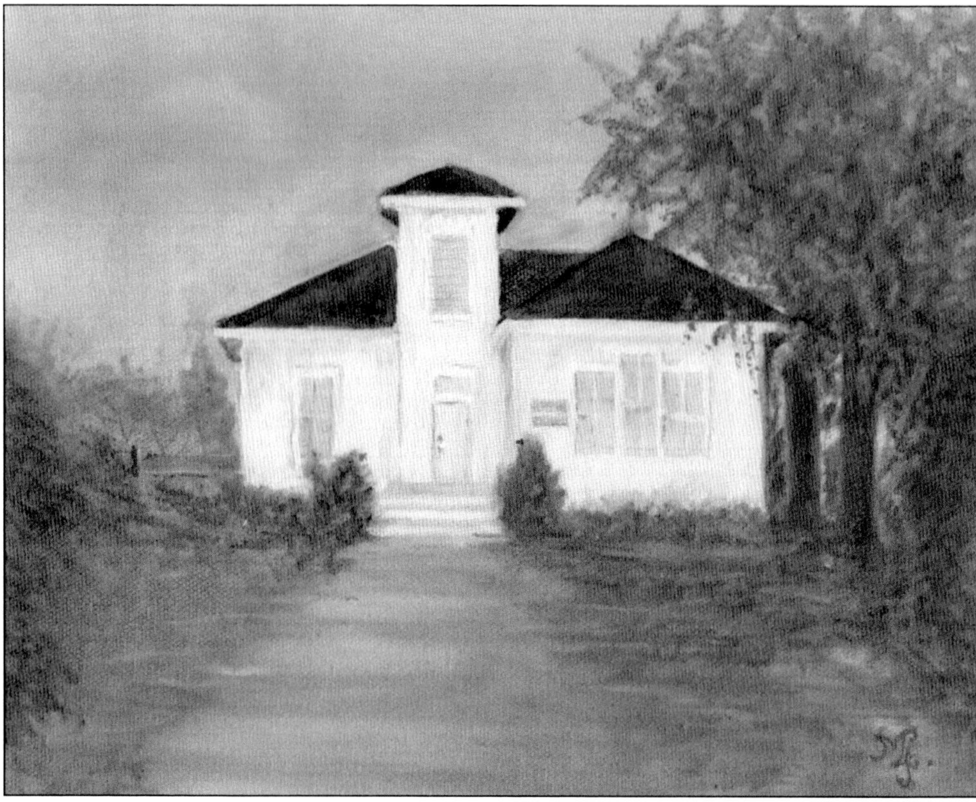

These images depict paintings of the First United Methodist Church (above) and Heath Baptist Church (below) back in late 1960s or early 1970s. A total of five churches are currently found in Heath, including the Church of Christ, Holy Trinity by the Lake Episcopal Church, and the more recently built Church of Jesus Christ of Latter-day Saints. The artist who did these paintings was Shirley Smirl, of the longtime Smirl family in Heath. (Both, courtesy of Clarice Isbell.)

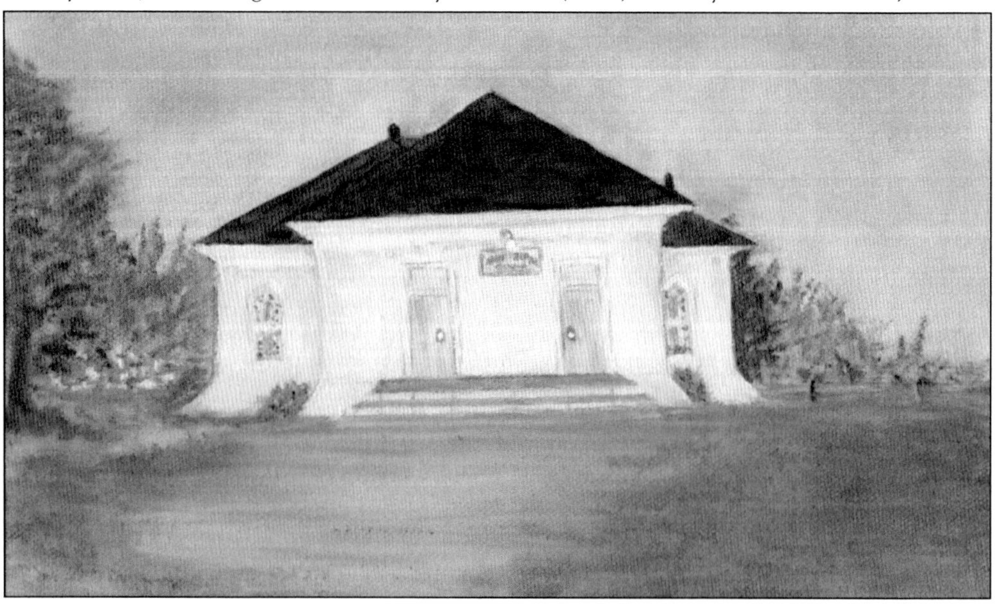

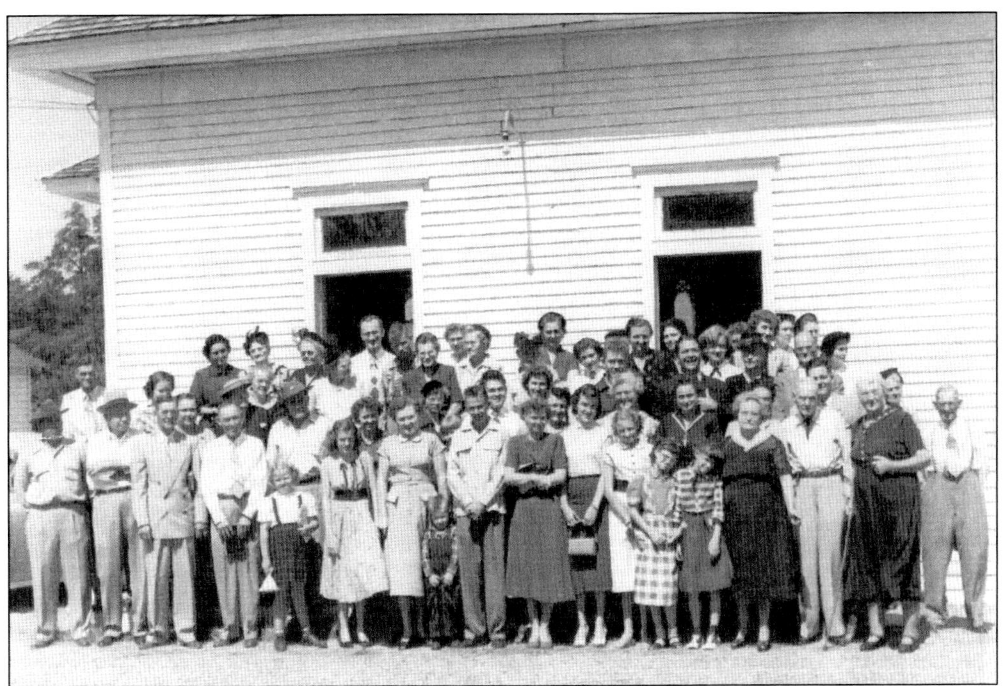

The Baptist church founders bought two acres of land for $55 from Dr. F.M. McChristy, and a church building was completed in 1894. The first service was held on May 26, 1894. On June 8, 1898, a cyclone destroyed the building, and a new one was constructed. That building—pictured above with church members—has been renovated, repainted, and reshingled over the years and is now Smirl Chapel (below). The church continued to meet in that structure until a new sanctuary, the present-day church building, was constructed. (Above, courtesy of the Rockwall County Historical Foundation; below, photograph by author.)

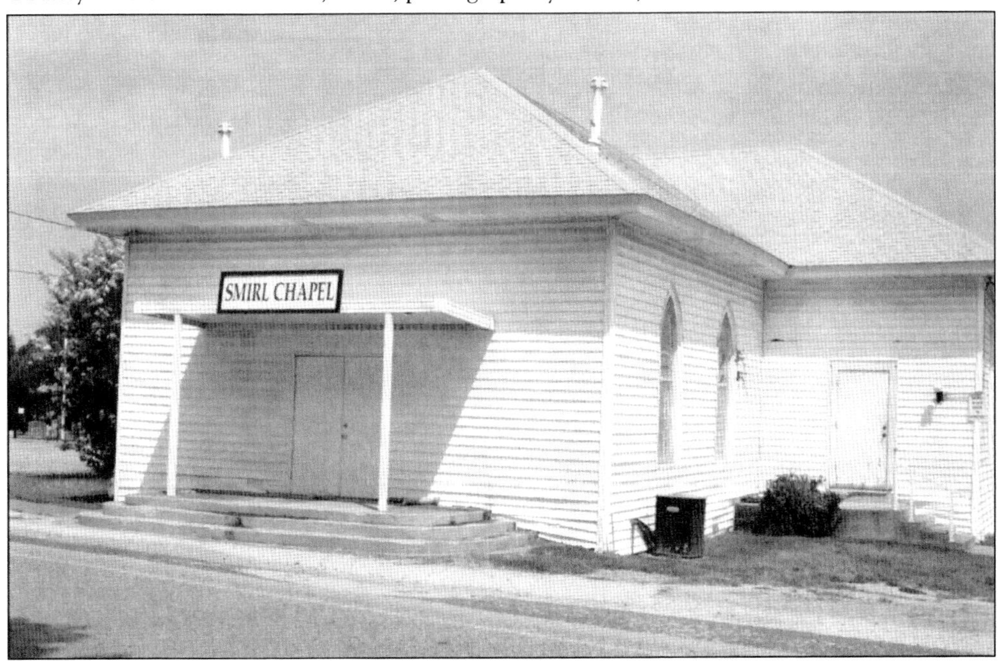

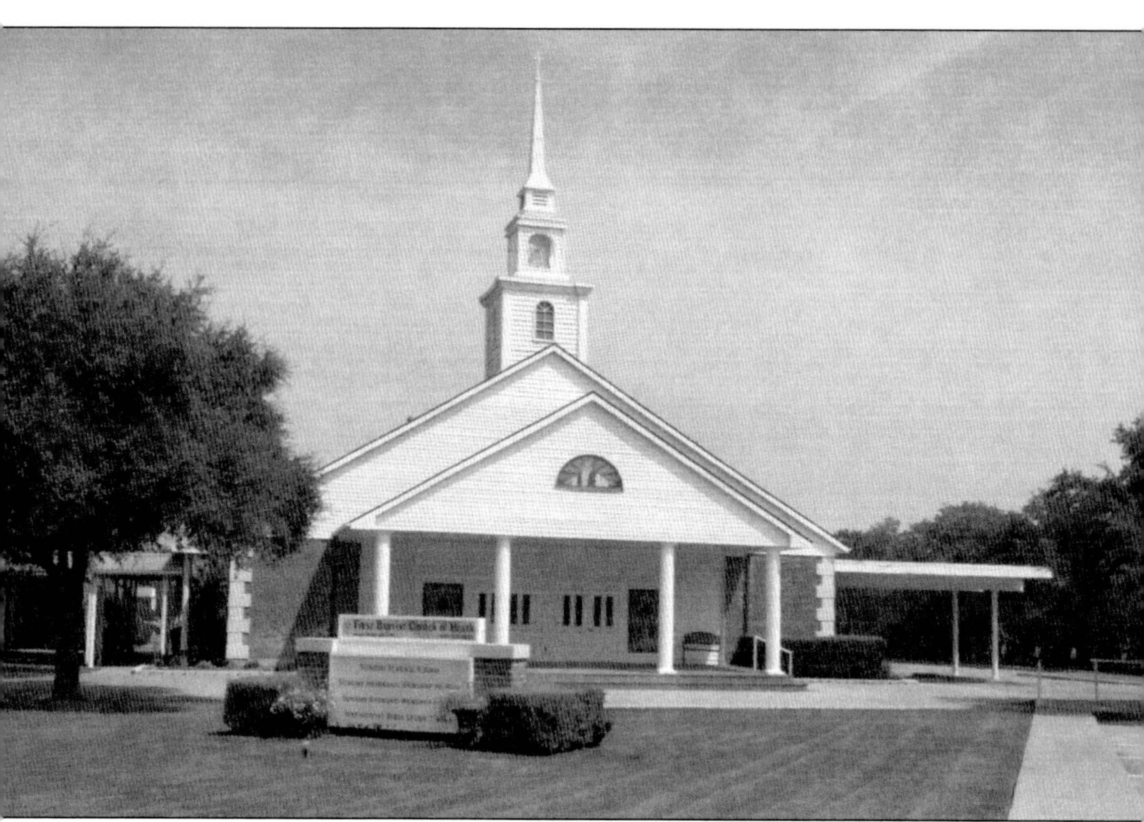

On September 26, 1874, these 11 people gathered at the Willow Springs School to form the Willow Springs Baptist Church of Christ: H.L. Darr; Angelina Darr; Elizabeth Darr (who later married J.T. Vance); Mrs. L.E. Holt (later Mrs. J.N. Mills); J.D.F. Holt; James A. Holt; D.C. Fondren and his wife, Lucy; A.L. Spence; J.T. Vance; and James Truss. The church was named for the numerous willow trees and a nearby natural spring. Later, in 1910, the name was changed to Heath Baptist Church because another church in the same association had the same name. The name changed again in 1971 to the First Baptist Church of Heath. Pictured above is the current home of the First Baptist Church in Heath, constructed in 1981.

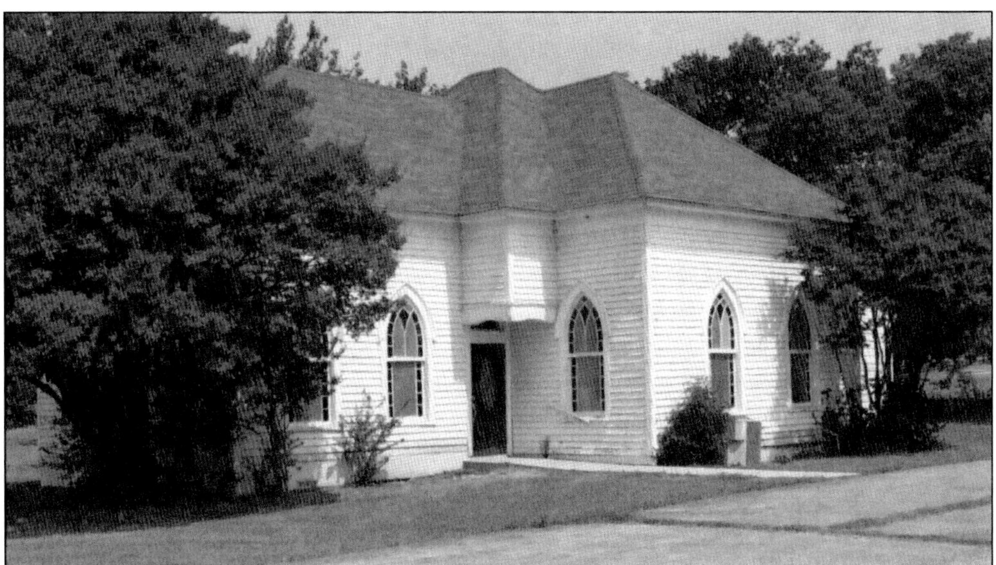

After its organization in 1909, the Heath Church of Christ met in the school building during days of good weather and under brush arbors until a church could be completed on two acres of land donated by William Henry Brooks. Some of the original founding families of the church include the McDonalds, Vinsons, Cullins, Dugans, and Willinghams. Today, members of the Heath Church of Christ still meet in that building, located next to Heath City Hall on FM 740.

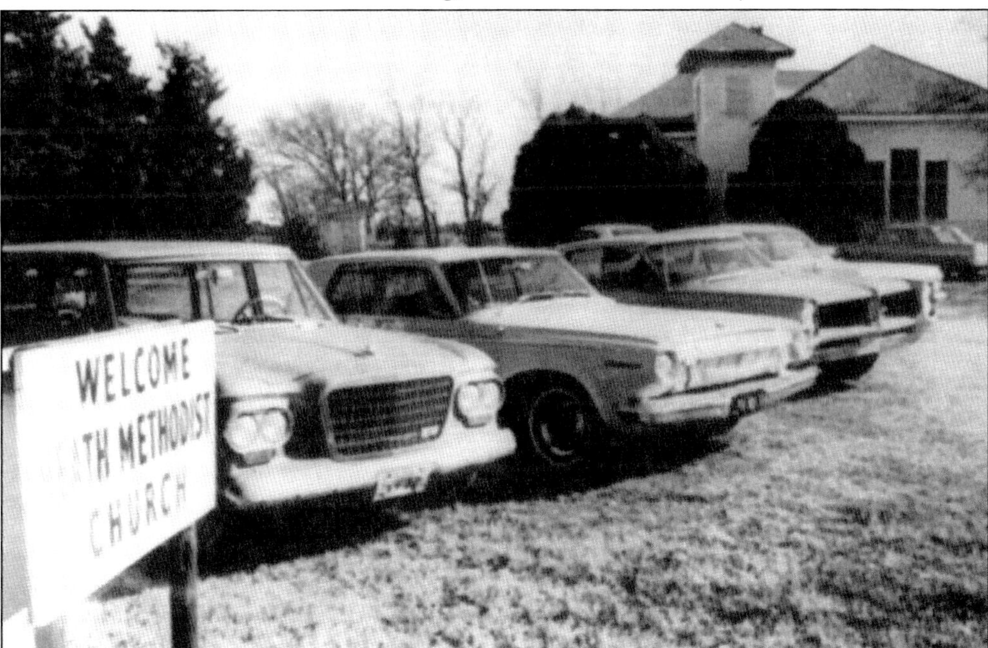

This image, originating from a 1960s issue of the *Dallas Times Herald* magazine, depicts the old Methodist church, which was born as the Bethel Episcopal Church on July 31, 1890. On that day, James Hardin sold a one-acre plot of land at the corner of FM 740 to the Methodist Episcopal Church South for $25. A small house was built as a place to worship, and the Reverend W.T. Jordan received the church's first members in 1894. (Courtesy of the First United Methodist Church of Heath.)

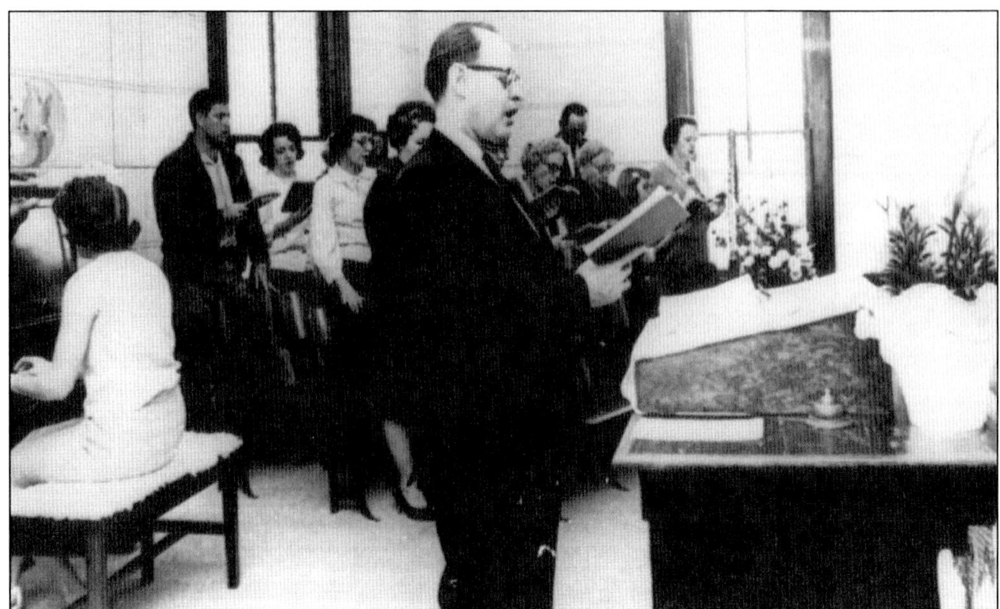

On November 29, 1909, the Methodist Episcopal Church South purchased a half-acre plot next door for $100, and the original property was sold. Between November 1909 and March 1910, the Bethel Episcopal Church was moved from the old plot to the new one, and the name was changed to Heath Methodist Episcopal Church. In 1916, members of the then Heath Methodist Episcopal Church came to worship in their newly constructed church house. The image here depicts a worship service held inside that church building. (Courtesy of the First United Methodist Church of Heath.)

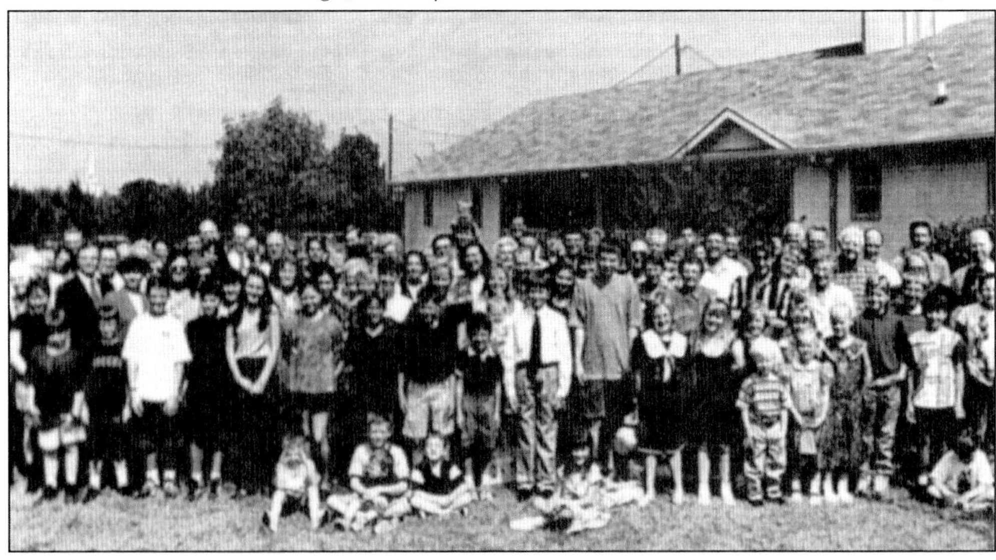

In 1974, when the Heath Methodist Church moved to its current location on a six-acre lot not far from the Heath Baptist Church, a temporary double wide house—shown above with members of the church congregation in the early 1990s—was brought in to be the church's new place of worship. Prior to its relocation to Heath, the building had been used by several other Methodist churches in the Dallas area—most recently the New World United Methodist Church in Garland. On Easter Sunday, April 14, 1974, Rev. Dan G. Smith led the congregation to worship in their new home. (Courtesy of the First United Methodist Church of Heath.)

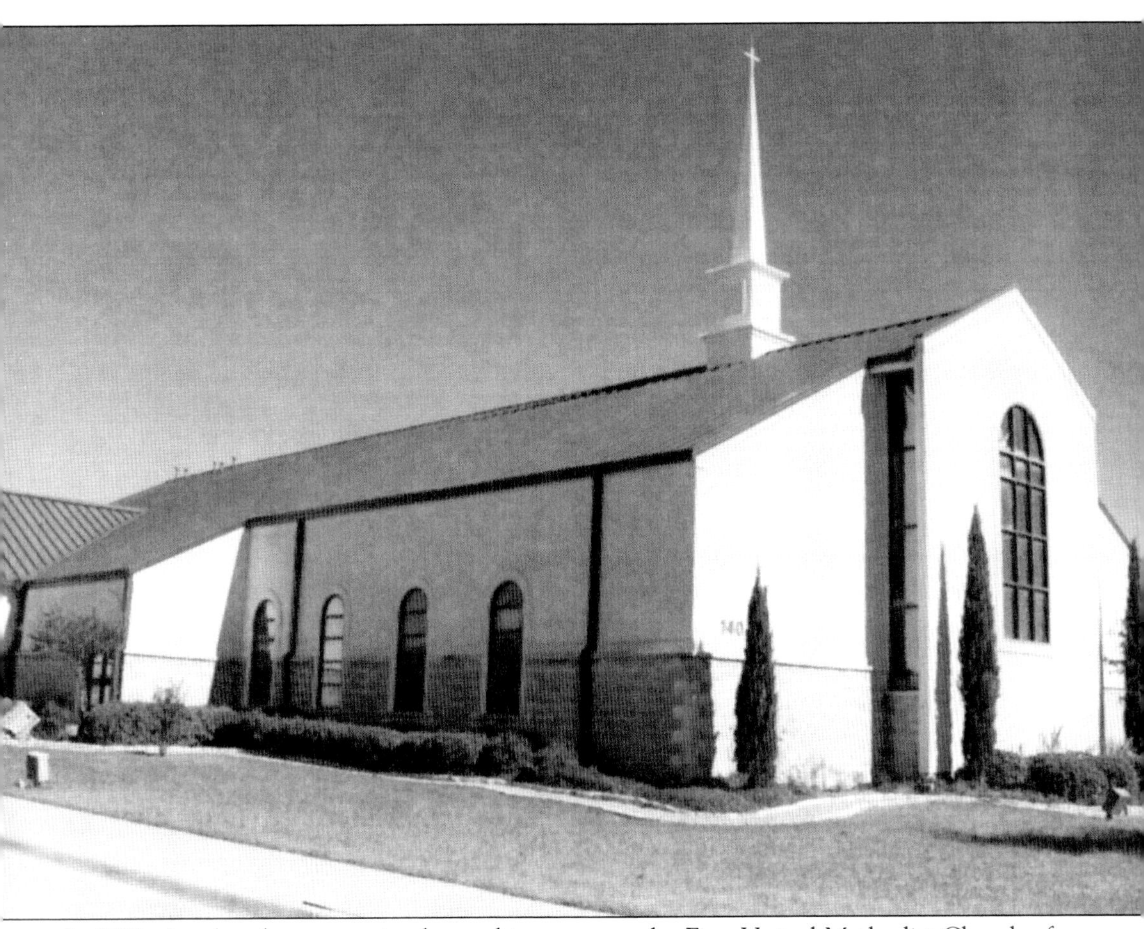

In 1979, the church once again changed its name to the First United Methodist Church of Heath, and in 1999, they broke ground on a new church building. On May 23 of that year, the new sanctuary, two offices, four Sunday school rooms, and a parlor were consecrated. In 2005, the sanctuary was expanded, and an office suite, more classrooms, a fellowship hall, and a youth loft were added. The church celebrated its 125-year anniversary on Sunday, April 19 with a special worship service and a church-wide potluck held afterwards in Fletcher Hall. During the service, longtime Heath resident and FUMC Heath member June Boyd rang the bell belonging to the old Methodist church building, and the congregation heard accounts of life in the old church from several longtime members. (Photograph by author.)

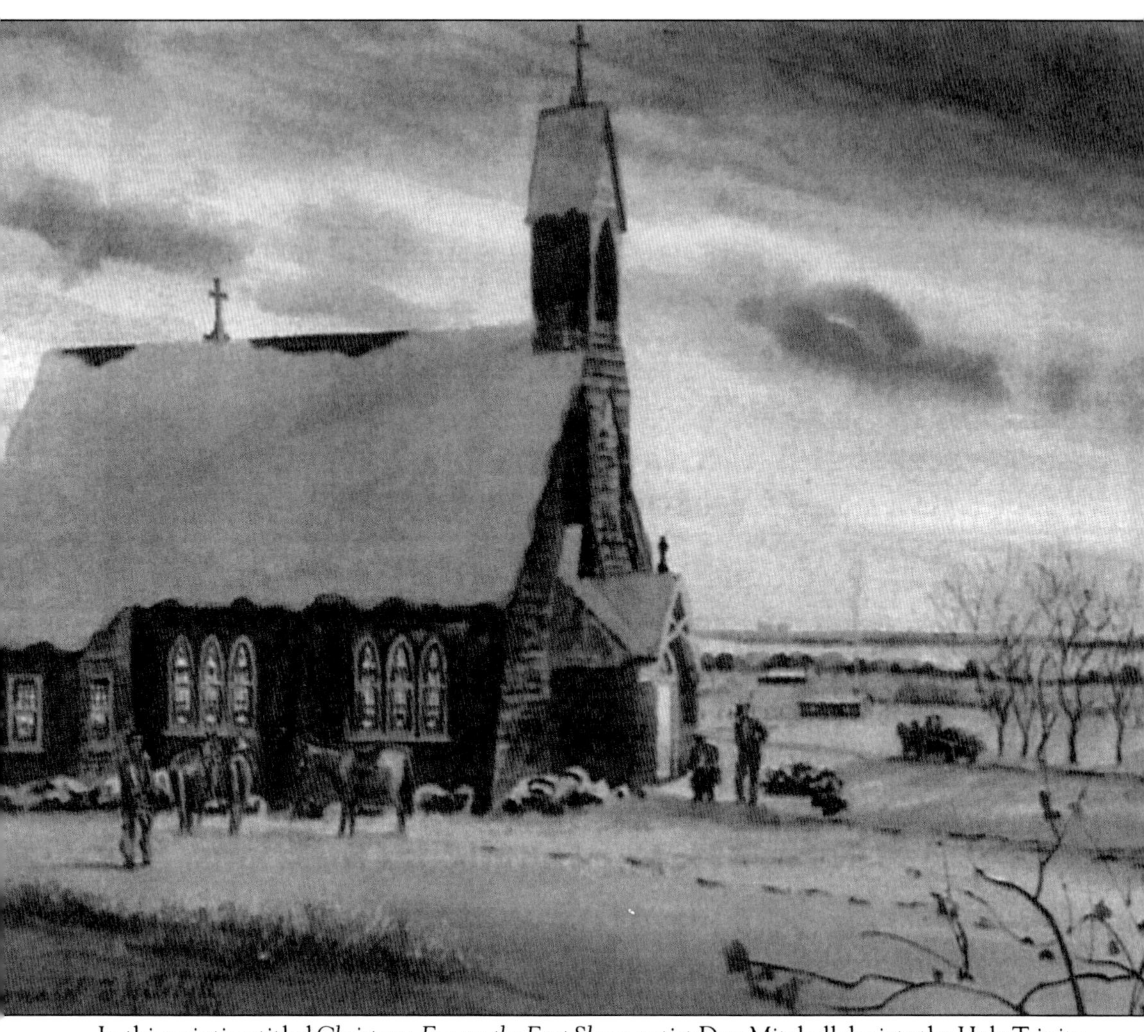

In this painting titled *Christmas Eve on the East Shore*, artist Don Mitchell depicts the Holy Trinity by the Lake Episcopal Church located off FM 740 in Heath. The church was founded in Forney in 1896 by the Venners and other families living in the area. The building, which was designed by a Massachusetts architect and constructed from lumber taken from the bottom of the East Fork of the Trinity River, was built at a cost of $2,800 and relocated to its current site on FM 1140 in August 1973. For its relocation, the steeple, bell, and both wings of the church building were removed. About 96 telephone lines and 110 high lines had to be taken down and replaced by the telephone and electric companies for transportation of the church building to its new home in Heath. A new educational building of nearly 8,000 square feet was completed in 2004 and now leases space to the Spanish school and the Fulton School and serves the Sunday school, as well as other mixed uses. (Courtesy of Heath City Hall.)

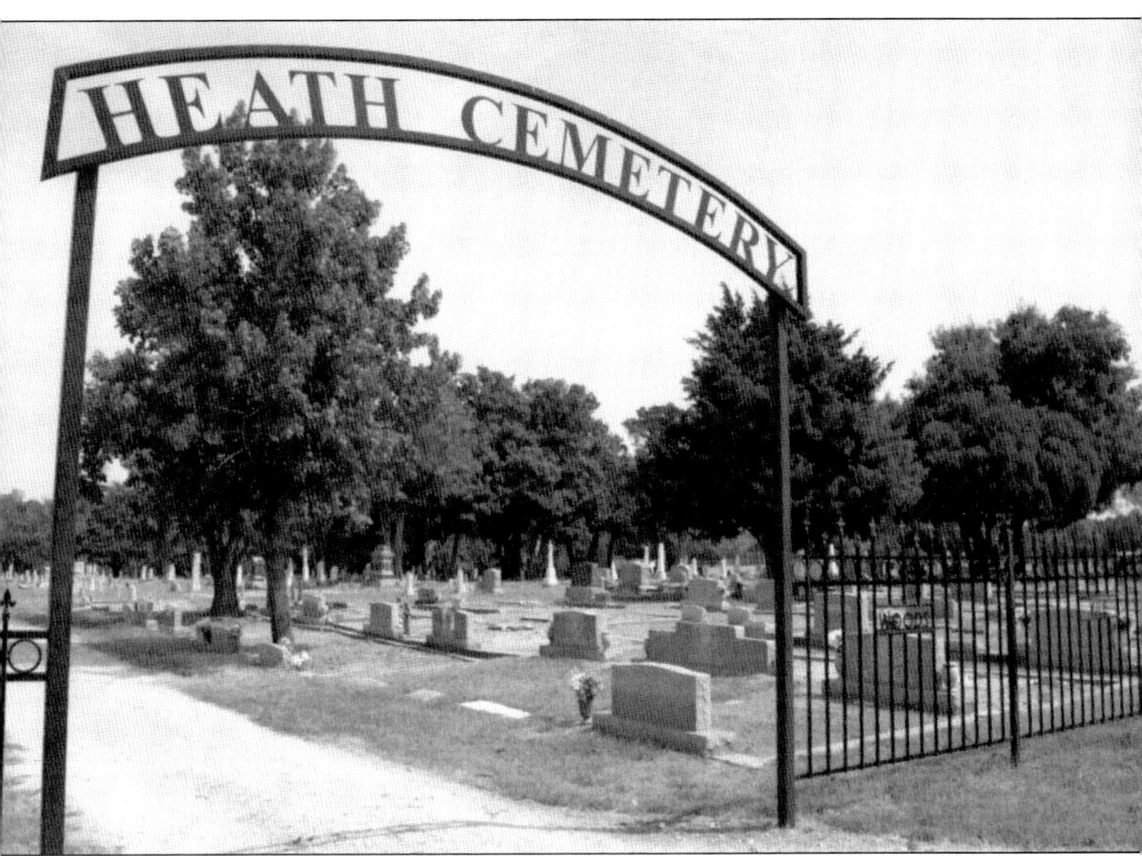

The Heath Cemetery is located behind the present-day site of the First Baptist Church of Heath. W.M. Burgett donated the original four acres of land, and the deed was signed in 1873, made out to M.C. Stephenson, J.L.N. Baker, C.W. Darr, John Howard, and George Barnes, who were all trustees or successors of the Willow Springs School property, where Willow Springs Baptist Church, later the First Baptist Church of Heath, was originally founded. Most of the pioneering settlers of the Heath community are buried in this cemetery. Although this is only a partial list, some of the families include: Barnes, Darr, Isbell, Vaughn, Gardenhire, Lofland, Hall, Roach, Lemley, Myers, Randles, Terry, Jones, Holt, Pinion, Denton, Lewis, Nash, Cullins, Vinson, Massey, Stovall, French, Piper, Evans, Vank, Seabolt, and Smirl. There have been over 900 burials in the cemetery.

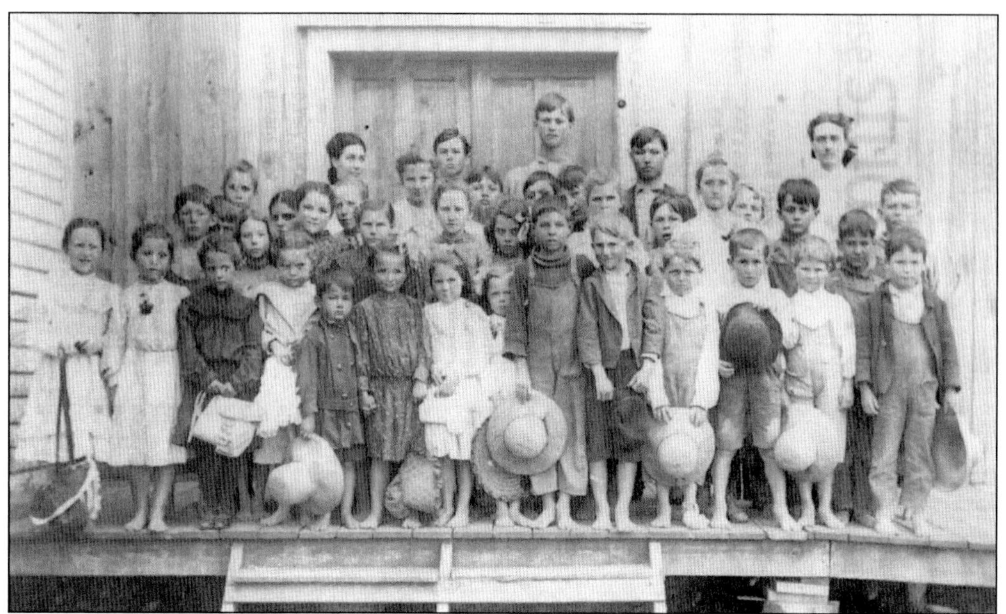

Heath saw its first school established in 1898, a one-room building that provided an education for 56 students. The image above shows boys and girls in front of that one-room public school in Heath in 1901. The business district and school system for Heath grew steadily, and eventually new schools were built in the area. Below is a class portrait. Coveralls were a very commonplace garment for Heath farmers and their children. Farming was how many families in the area earned their living, and many of the children would often have their own duties helping out on the farm. After the 1920s, the population of Heath declined, as farming revenue was no longer sufficient in supporting a family, unless the farm was quite large. (Above, courtesy of Fay Lofland; below, courtesy of Mark Poindexter.)

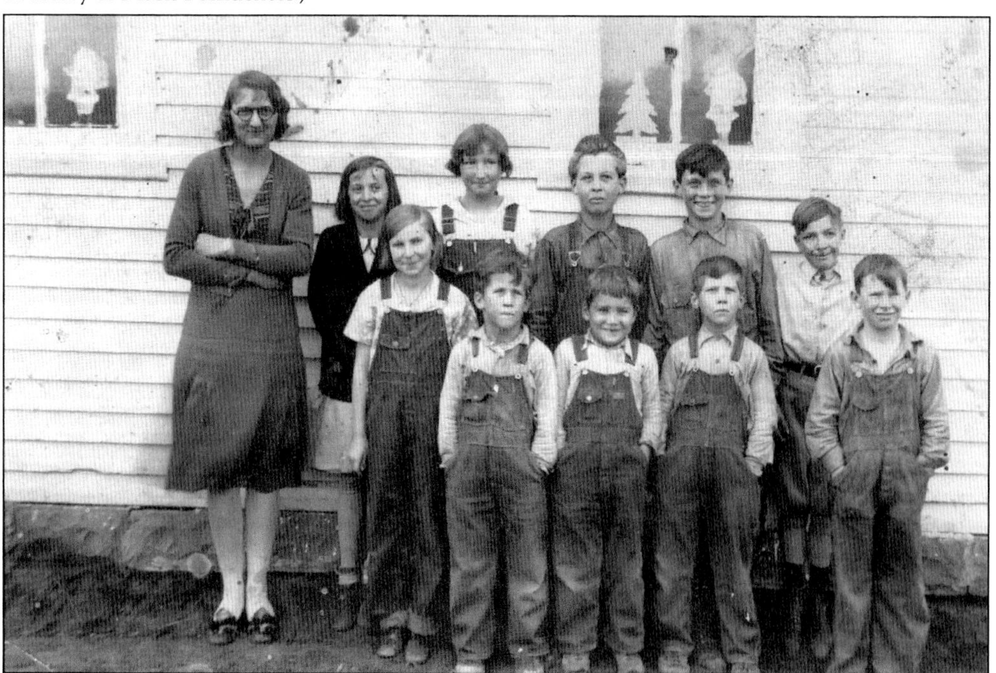

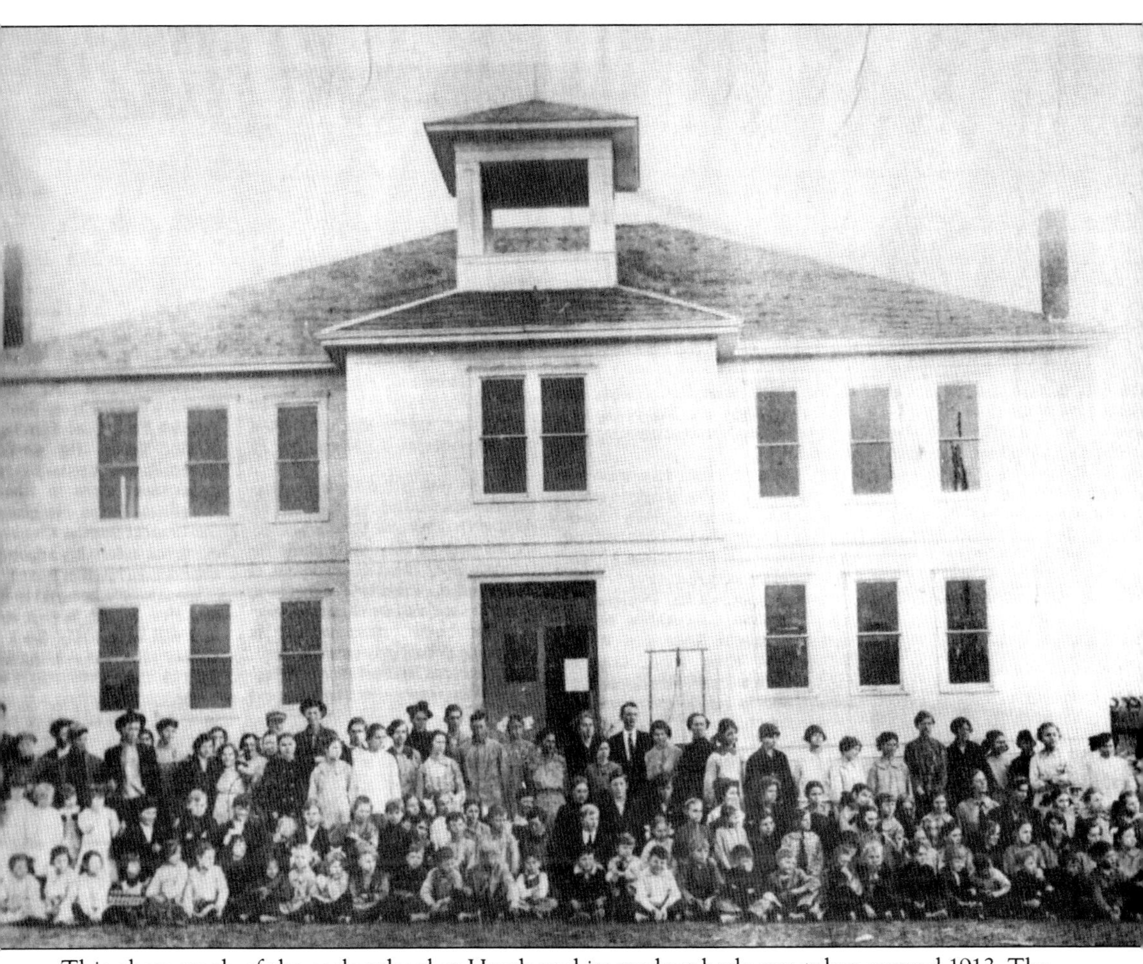

This photograph of the early school at Heath and its student body was taken around 1913. The school was established in 1902 and offered classes from first through 10th grade. The building—located west of the present-day site of Heath City Hall—consisted of six large classrooms, with an auditorium and stage covering half of the second floor. This second floor was torn down in later years, and the bottom floor served as a community center. The number of grades per classroom was determined by the number of students in the various grades, with the higher grades usually having the least number of students due to frequent dropouts. The teachers also served as coaches during athletic activities, and students assisted teachers in janitorial duties. Everyone pitched in during the wintertime to keep the coal-burning stoves going. Those wanting a drink of water had to draw it out of the well in front of the building and use their own fold-up cups. (Courtesy of Heath City Hall.)

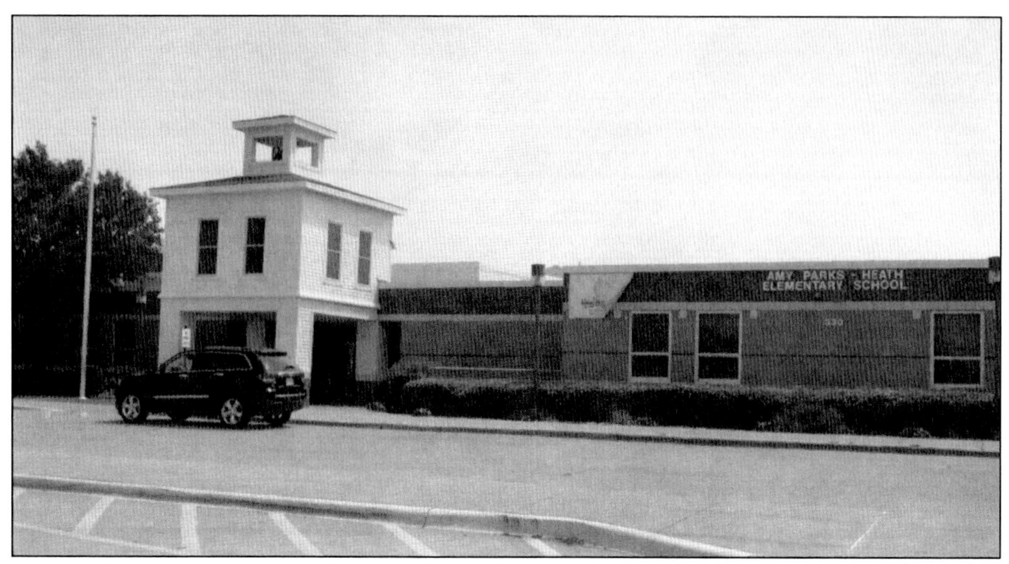

Amy Parks Heath Elementary School is located near the site of the old two-story Heath School, and its bell tower was inspired by photographs of the old schoolhouse. In fact, the bell in the bell tower belongs to the old Heath School and was donated by Jack and May Barnes Townsend. Designed to house 650 students from kindergarten through the sixth grade, the 60,300-square-foot structure cost $4.5 million to construct and was a part of an $8 million bond package promoted by a citizens group called Building Better Beginnings in February 1994. (Photograph by author.)

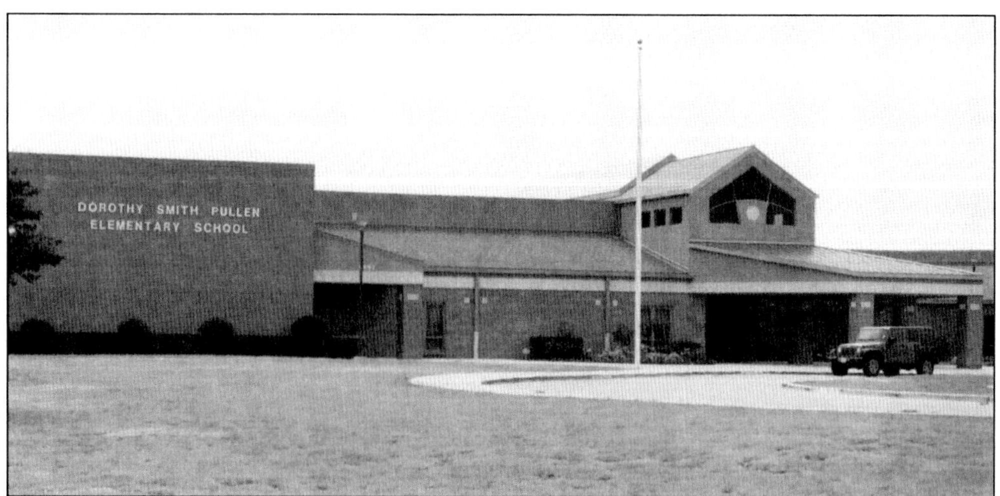

Dorothy Smith Pullen Elementary School—part of the Rockwall Independent School District—opened its doors to students in the fall of 1999. The 65,504-square-foot building cost $8.58 million to construct and houses 650 students from kindergarten through the sixth grade. The school was built as a result of the efforts of a citizens group called 2000 and Beyond . . . Together Bond Committee to successfully promote the passing of a $48.67 million bond package, which also resulted in the construction of Maurine Cain Middle School, located next door to Pullen Elementary. (Photograph by author.)

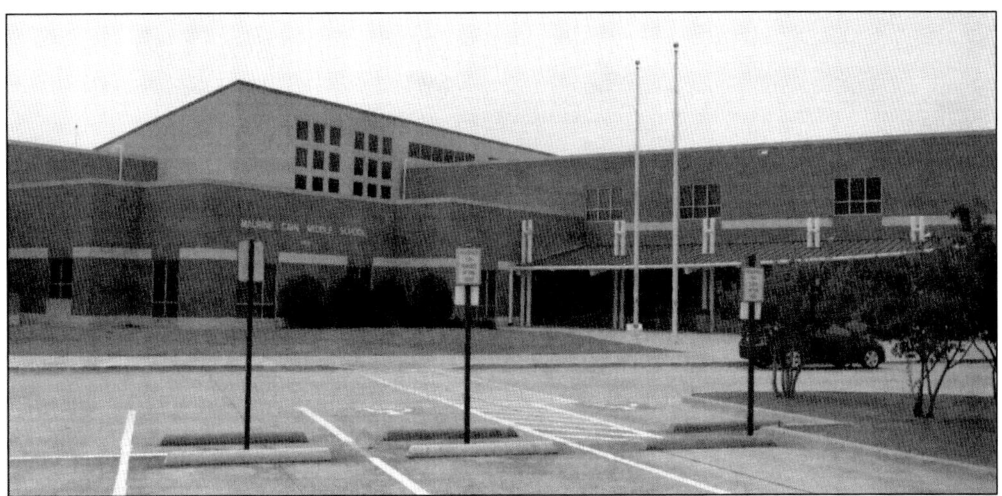

Maurine Cain Middle School in Heath, part of the Rockwall Independent School District, was built at a cost of $18 million and houses 1,000 seventh and eighth grade students inside its 148,400-square-foot structure. In February 1998, a committee called Rockwall Citizens for Good Schools helped pass a bond package totaling $48.67 million to build Pullen Elementary and Cain Middle School, expand Rockwall High School, and fund capital improvement projects in five older schools. (Photograph by author.)

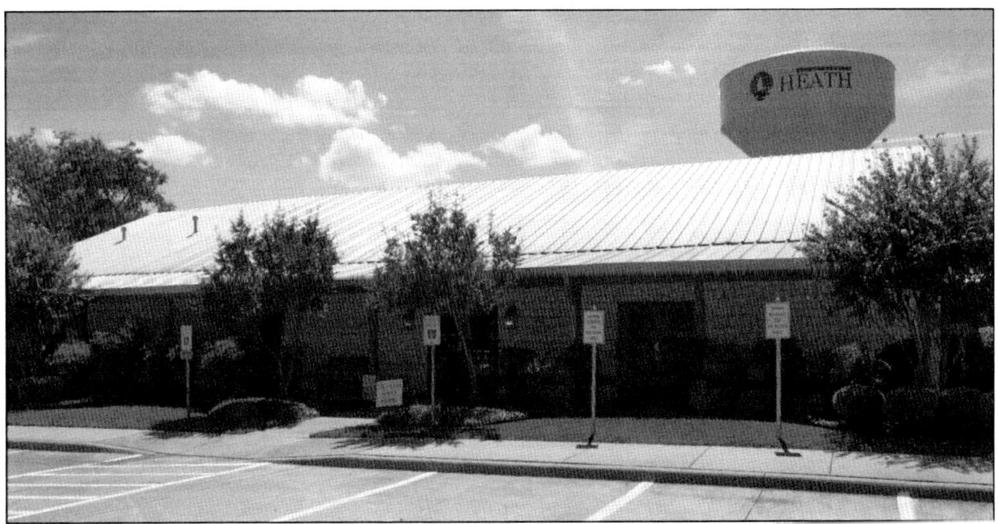

In 1987, Suzanne Nash and Norma Morris founded the Fulton School in Heath, selecting Dr. Bernard Fulton (1910–2009) as the school's namesake. The Fulton School operates as an independent coeducational college-preparatory school on a 16-acre campus next to the Holy Trinity by the Lake Episcopal Church. Its student body consists of over 180 students from preschool through 12th grade. In the background at the top right is one of the two water towers located in Heath. (Photograph by author.)

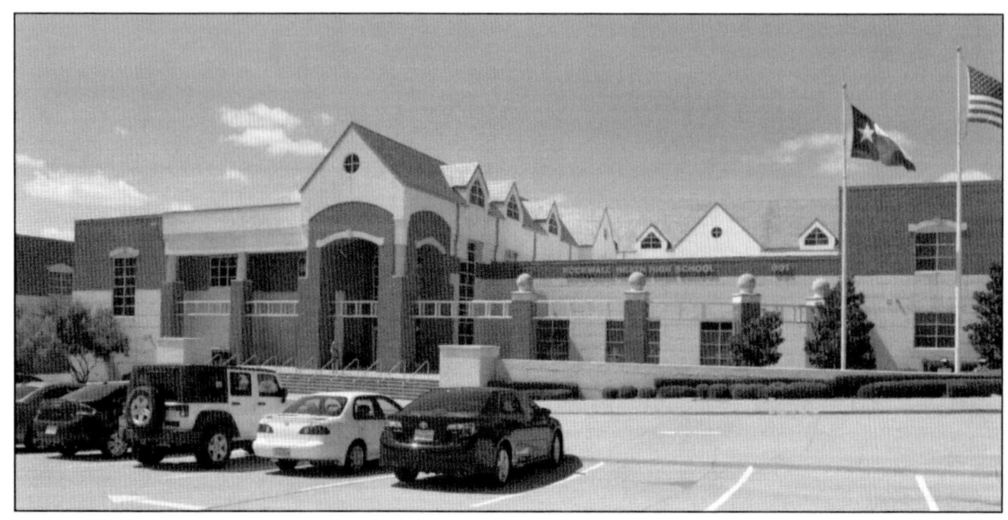
Rockwall-Heath High School officially opened its doors to students in 2005, with the first graduating class being the class of 2008. The second phase of construction was completed in 2010 and added a new fine arts wing, a band hall, and a 1,500-seat auditorium. Approved and signed during the Rockwall Independent School District election bond in 2007, the bond is the most expensive in RISD history at $198 million and included the construction of Celia Hays Elementary and Sharon Shannon Elementary Schools, plans for a third high school, and the conversion of Utley Freshmen Center into a middle school. The school colors are red, black, and white, with a hawk as the mascot. (Photograph by author.)

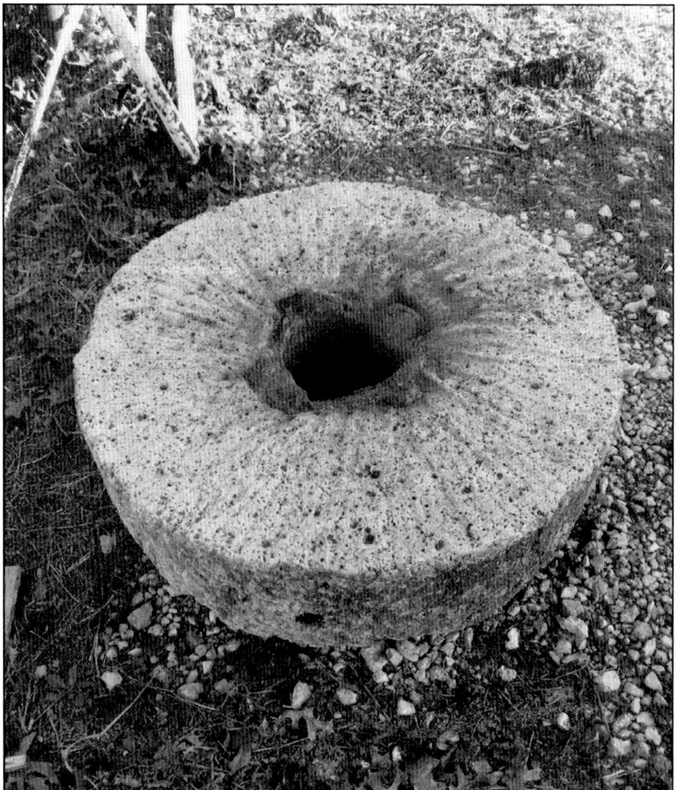
During recent construction of the land located several feet behind the location of the old Brady's Country Store at the intersection of Laurence Drive and FM 740, construction crews unearthed an old gristmill stone about two and a half feet in diameter, shown here. According to local history, one of the earliest families to settle near the Heath family homestead was the Kyser family. When he moved his family to Heath, James Kyser brought with him a small, hand-driven gristmill, which he shared with fellow settlers who had traveled many miles to ground corn and other grain into flour. (Courtesy of David Herbert, City of Heath Public Works Director.)

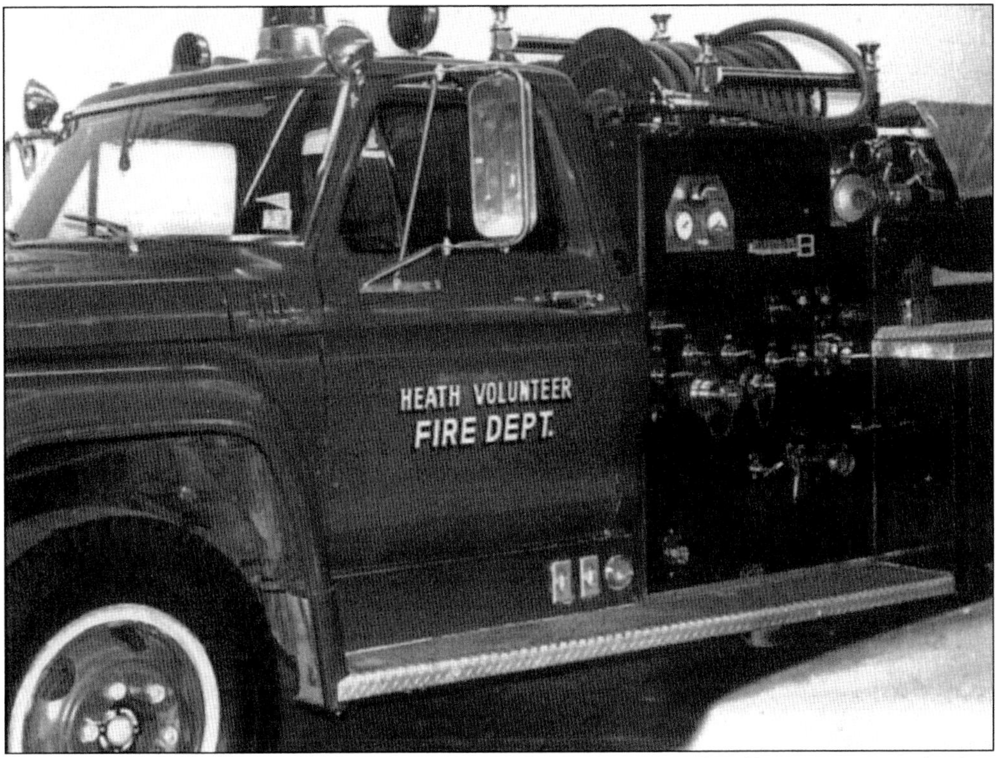

The City of Heath Volunteer Fire Department first began in 1971, with Bill Way serving as the first fire chief. Five years later, in May 1976, an ordinance was passed to officially form the department. Pictured here is one of the old fire engines of the department. (Courtesy of the Way family.)

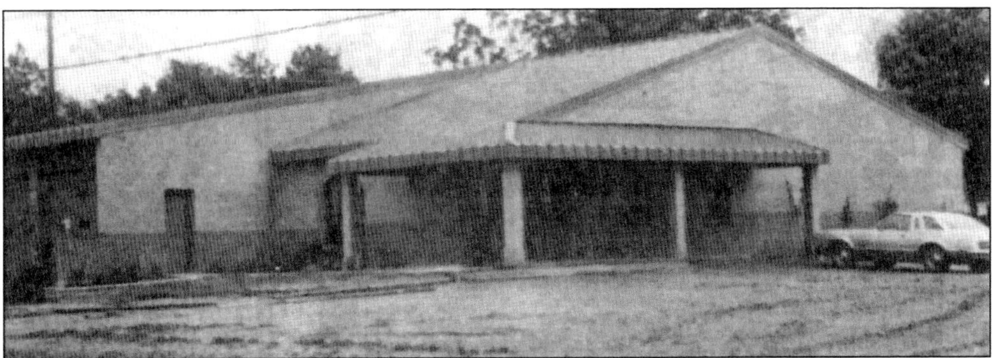

In 1982, voters approved Proposition No. 3 in the April 3 municipal election for the issuance of $100,000 for the construction of a new city hall building, fire station, and civic center. The new building was constructed by the City of Heath in conjunction with Heath resident Joe Frasier and was designed by John R. Lindsey of Rockwall. Today, the 4,200-square-foot complex houses offices for the city, a community room, and a department of public safety that integrates police, fire, and first-responder emergency medical services. The above photograph, by Mack Fleming, was taken in 1983 after the building's initial construction was complete. (Courtesy of Heath City Hall.)

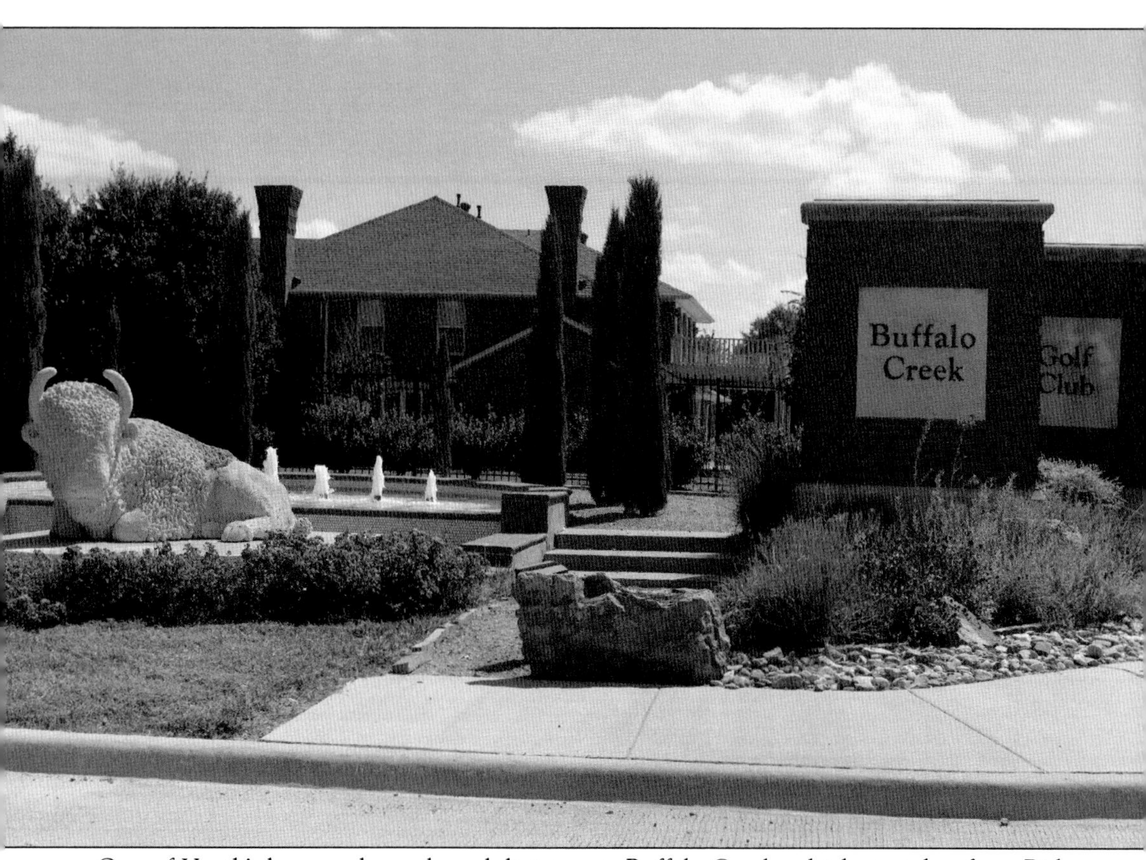

One of Heath's large and popular subdivisions is Buffalo Creek, which stretches from Ridge Road to Horizon Road with another entrance off FM 549. The community of approximately 700 homesites, ranging in price from around $300,000 to $1.5 million, is also home to one of the premier 18-hole championship golf courses in Texas. Designed by PGA legend Tom Weiskopf and Jay Morrish, the course has hosted a number of prestigious tournaments, including the US Open as the final qualification site. The community also features a private tennis facility with five lighted courts used by professional leagues and summer day camps. A community swimming pool, nature preserve, children's playground, and fishing ponds round out the amenities offered at Buffalo Creek in Heath. (Photograph by author.)

Two

Ancestries of Heath

Looking back on the longtime families in Heath, one would almost certainly expect to see familiar faces reappear in article after article, photograph after photograph. That is because many of the families who came to settle in the area would often live, work, and play together like one giant family. It was not too rare in those days for neighbors to marry into each other's families, to hold huge family gatherings on their local farms, or to get together for some exciting games of 42 (dominoes). Throughout its history, Heath has been called home by many large families who came to settle in the area, and many of these families still dwell there today. In fact, the city itself was named after the Heaths, the first pioneering family to settle its land. Heath was first known as Black Hills after John O. Heath established a post office with that name. Later, the area became known as Willow Springs and remained that until 1886, when it became Heath.

Heath experienced significant growth in its early years as folks came to settle the area from surrounding states. By 1892, Heath had a population of 75, and that eventually grew to 225 by 1904. However, three fires and the Great Depression cut back the growth of the town, and in 1936, the population was 150, with only five businesses in operation. The heavy rains that filled up Lake Ray Hubbard helped stem a large growth for the community of Heath as the population reached 449 in 1970 and tripled in size over the next decade, reaching 1,459 by 1980. New schools and developments were added over the ensuing years, and today, Heath continues to steadily grow with a population estimated at 6,921.

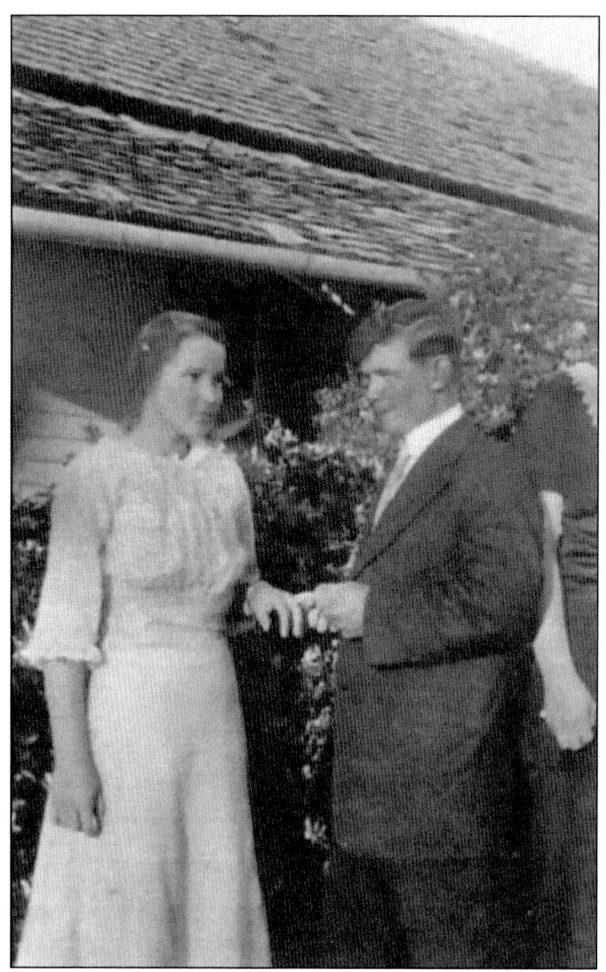

Pictured at right are William Thomas Seabolt and wife Rosa Lee Darr—the founders of Darr Estates located off Smirl Drive in Heath— on their wedding day in 1916. Will and Rosa began their married life on a farm located on a dirt road called Darr Road in 1916 and had three sons (Willie Lee, William Maon, and Michael Gene) and two daughters (Rosemary and Sorita Lou). They farmed cotton and corn while raising cattle, pigs and turkeys. In the image below are, from left to right, Rosemary Seabolt in the arms of her mother, Rosa Lee Seabolt; Rosa's mother, Mary Jane Adams Darr; an unidentified child; and an unidentified woman. (Both, courtesy of Rosemary Seabolt Klutts.)

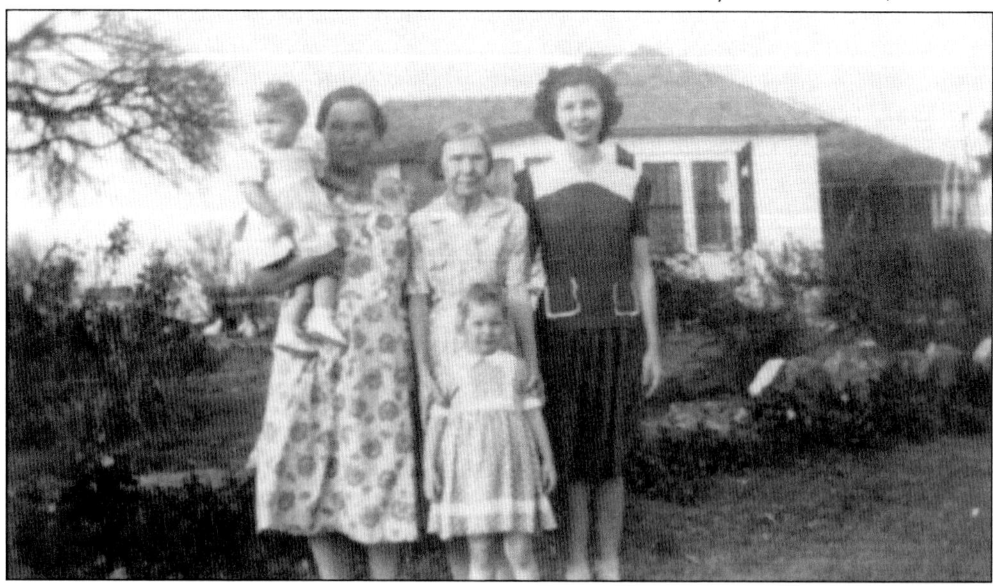

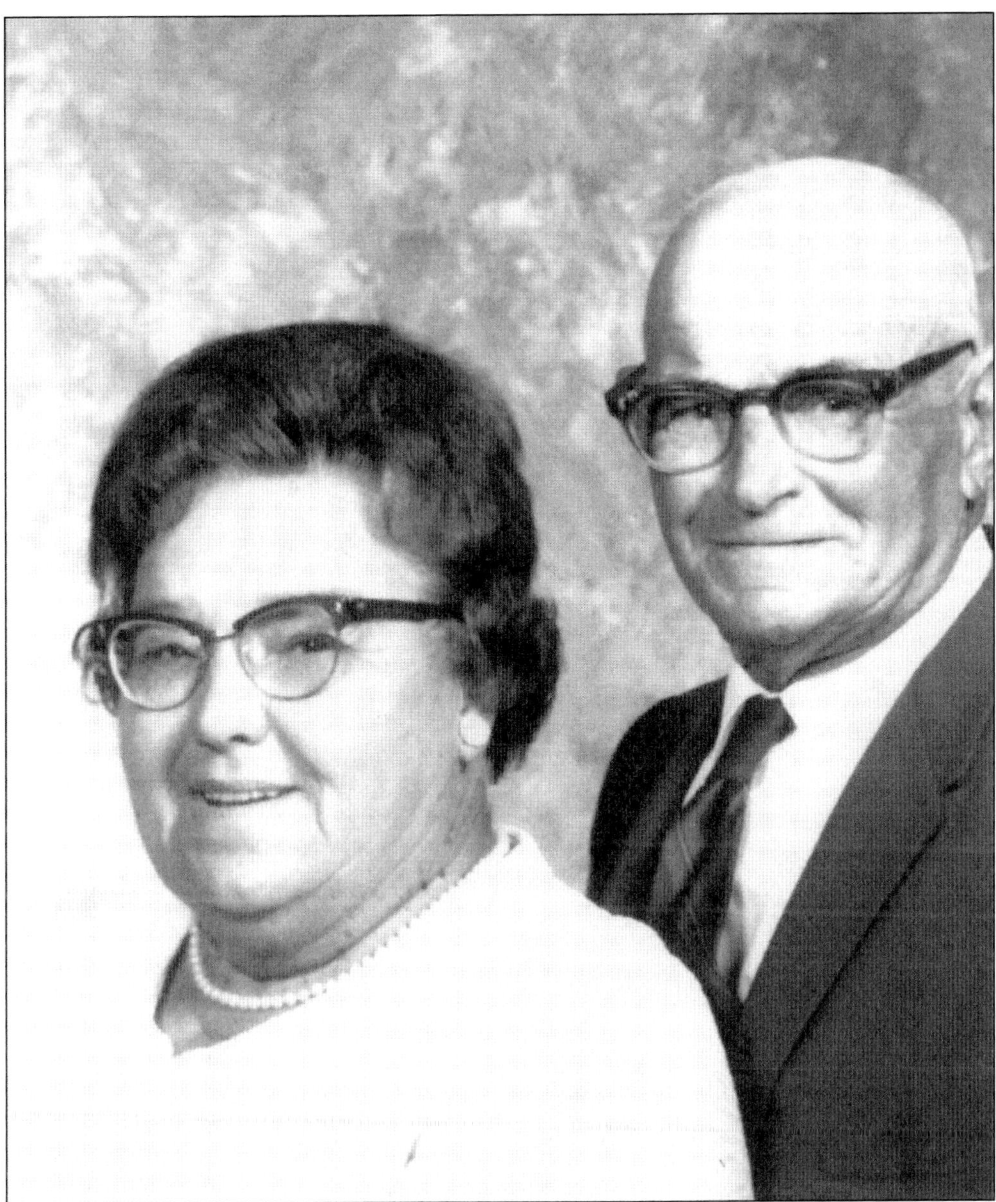

During the development of Darr Estates, William Thomas Seabolt and his wife, Rosa Lee Darr, could often be seen in the area checking up on its progress. As he was not allowed to drive Rosa Lee's car, Will would often drive down to the development area via FM 740 on his red Farmall tractor, while his wife would drive her "big red car," as daughter Rosemary Klutts described it, carrying a hoe to clean the areas around the trees and street curbs. According to Rosemary, the Seabolt children were very thankful that their parents were able to see Darr Estates completed and two of their children build homes there during their lifetime. (Courtesy of Rosemary Seabolt Klutts.)

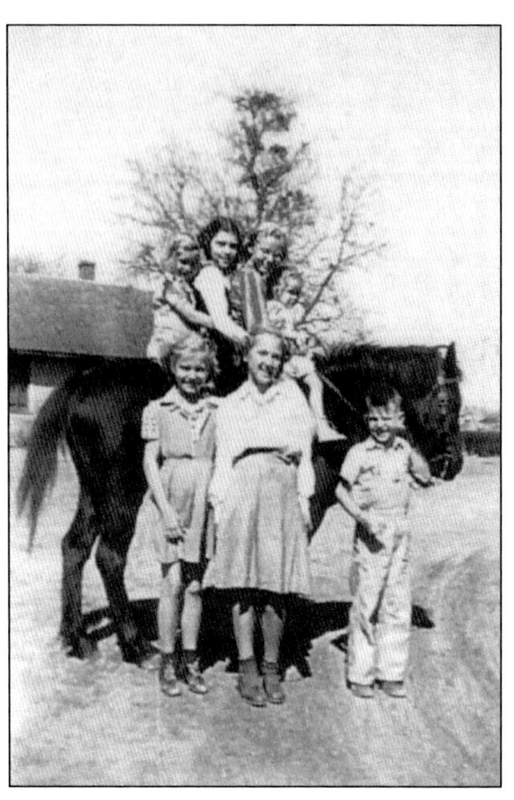

Pictured are, from left to right, (standing) Tommie Sue Hall, B. Terry, and Sherman Parker; (on horseback) Rosemary Seabolt, Marian Parker, Patsy Hall, and Sorita Seabolt. Many of the streets in Darr Estates today are named for the Seabolt children, such as Sorita Circle and Rosemary Drive. (Courtesy of Rosemary Seabolt Klutts.)

Nodie Curtis Darr, son of Earlie Vernon and Eva Darr, was presented with this certificate of appreciation for his service to the country as a sergeant in the Army during World War II. His brother Lewis Lee "Pete" Darr and Heath Gin owner John Vaughan were cosigners of the document, presented to Nodie by the Woodmen of the World Life Insurance Society. Woodmen of the World was founded in 1890 and has close to 1,000 local chapters throughout the United States dedicated to improving lives nationwide through community projects. (Courtesy of Rosemary Seabolt Klutts.)

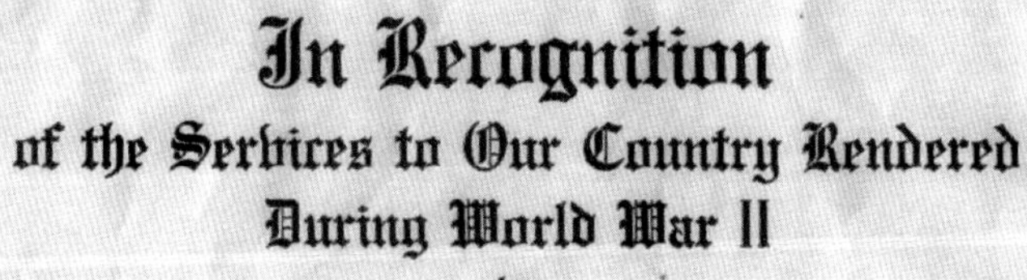

In Recognition
of the Services to Our Country Rendered
During World War II
by
Sovereign

Nodie C. Darr

Woodmen of the World Life Insurance Society
Presents With Pleasure This
Appreciation Certificate

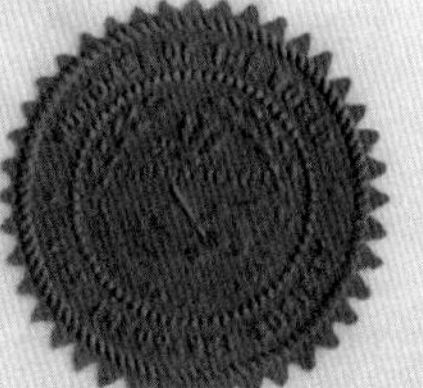

Farrar Newberry
President

W. McBradu
Secretary

Lewis L. Darr
Consul Commander

John W. Vaughan
Financial Secretary

One of the earliest residents of Heath was William Flemming Lemley (pictured) and his wife, Nancy Elizabeth Stiles, who moved to the area between the years of 1870 and 1875. Lemley bought land, acquiring several hundred acres of land in Heath; built a house; and was a farmer. He was born on April 24 between 1836 and 1843 in Madison County, Alabama, the son of John Lemley Jr. Lemley died on March 18, 1931, and was buried in Heath Cemetery. (Courtesy of Ada Lou Myers Abernathy.)

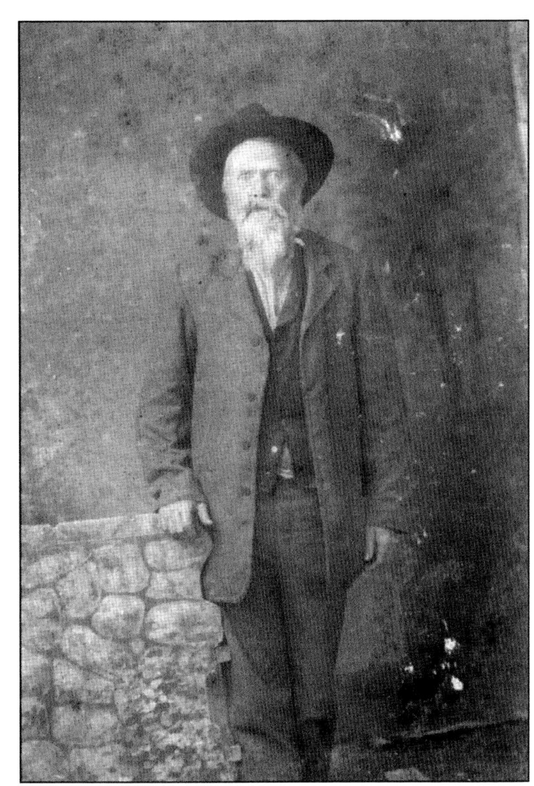

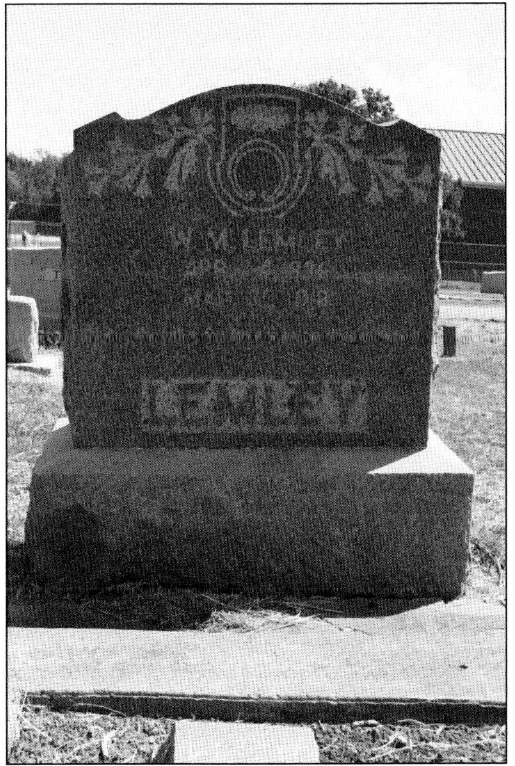

The Lemleys had 12 children, 10 of which grew to adulthood. They are Mary Ledocia (1892–1914), William Louis (January 1871–February 1871), Eliza Elizabeth (1872–1942), John Elisia (1874–1943), Biddie Ann (1876–1958), Minnie Lee (1879–1943), George Elisas (1882–1925), Bessie Emley Belle (1885–1937), Bertha Pearl (1887–1952), Nancy Chilnussia (1889–1966), Fannie May (1891–1964), and David Briten (January 1894–October 1894). Names and dates were provided by Reba Jett. (Photograph by author.)

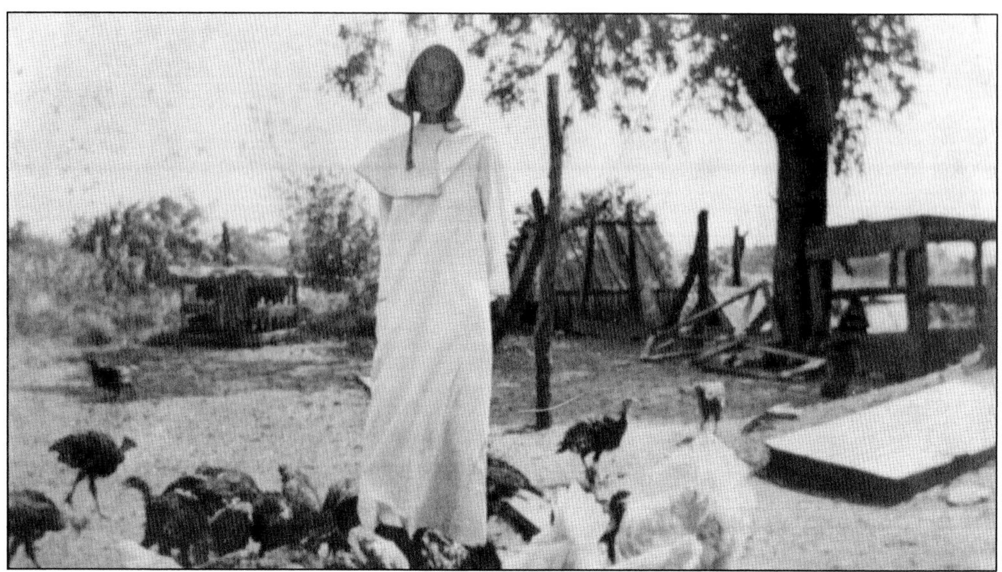

Nancy Elizabeth Stiles married William Flemming Lemley on April 15, 1867, when she was but 14 years old. The couple moved to Heath with her mother and several other family members, and she bore 12 children, 10 of which grew to adulthood. Many made their homes in Rockwall County. After Lemley's death, Nancy continued to manage the farm and grew mostly cotton and wheat. She died in her home on August 18, 1932, having lived in the same house for 57 years. Although she is dressed in white in the above image, she is remembered by one of her granddaughters as always being dressed in black. William (first row, second from right) and Nancy (second row, second from right) Lemley are pictured below along with other Lemley family members. (Both, courtesy of Ada Lou Myers Abernathy.)

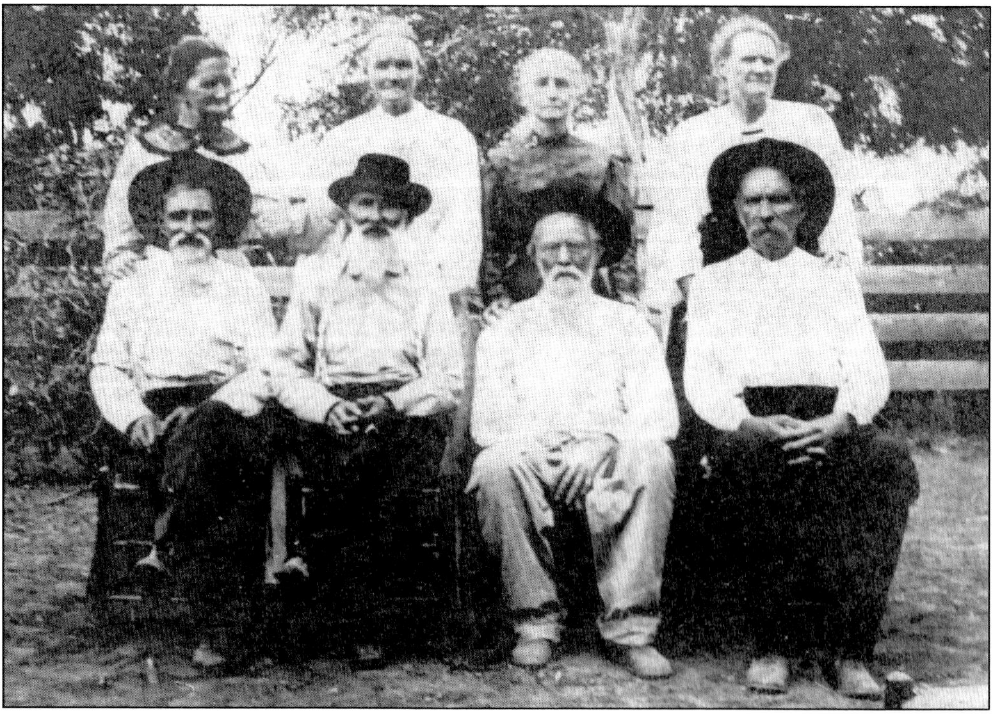

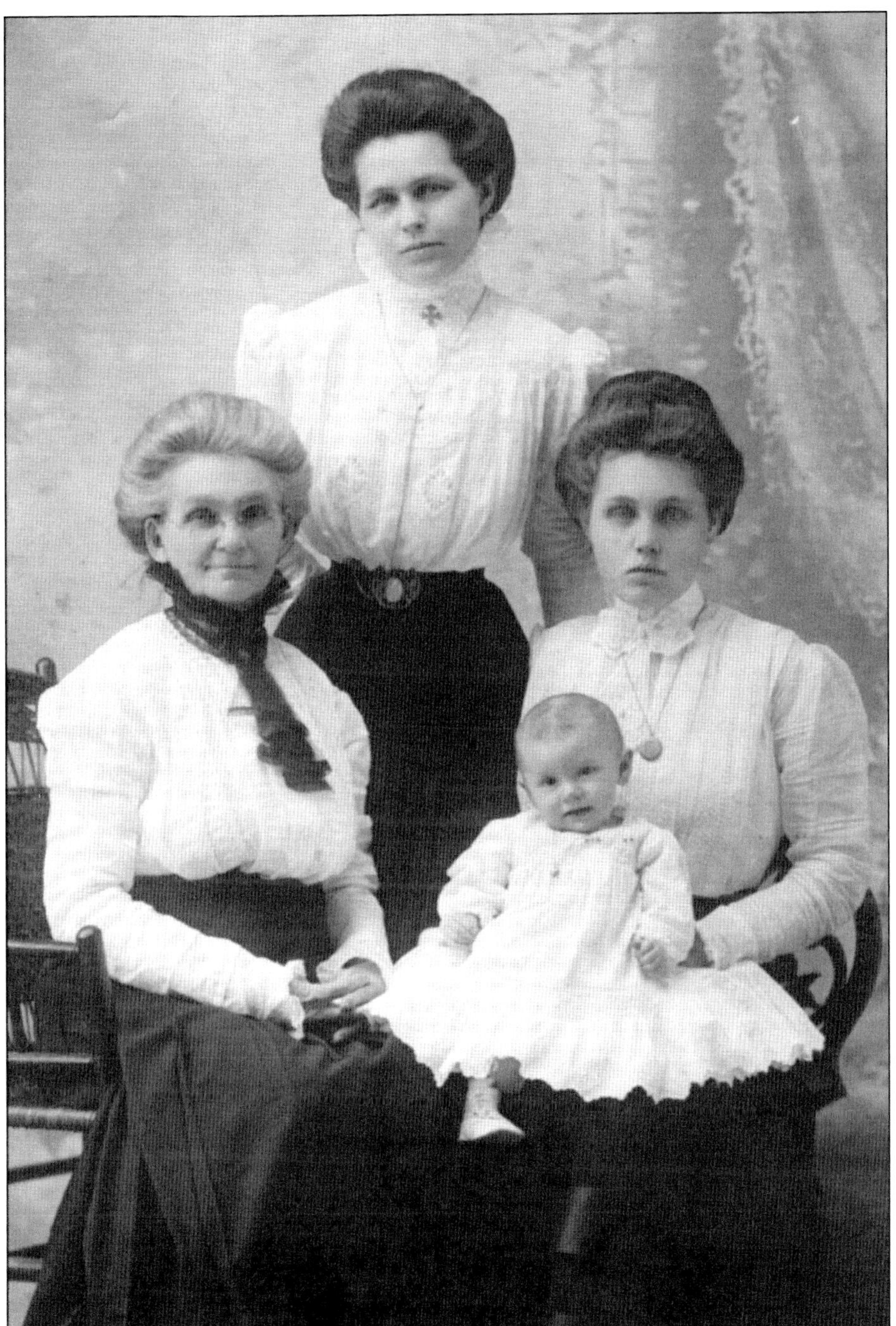

This image shows four generations of the McLendon-Isbell family. Anna Louise Burch McLendon and her husband, Preston Alexander, came from North Carolina to Texas in 1869 and established a farm in an area that later became known as McLendon. Anna Louise's daughter Emma Lena McLendon Isbell was born on February 1, 1872. She came to Rockwall County at an early age and married M.K. Isbell on October 27, 1887. They made their home in Heath. She died on March 26, 1946. Pictured here are, from left to right, Anna Louise Burch McLendon Austin, Emma Lena McLendon Isbell, and Grace Isbell Vaughn with baby daughter Lena. (Courtesy of Fay Lofland.)

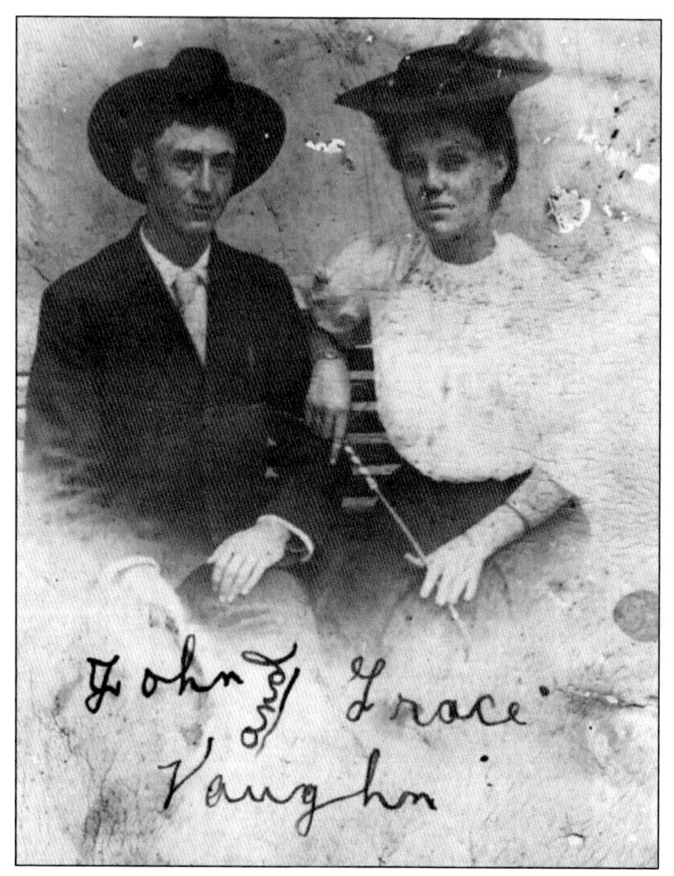

This rare photograph depicts longtime Heath residents John and Grace Vaughn in their younger days. The Vaughns owned a cotton farm and ran the Heath Gin Company for over 40 years. Grace Vaughn is the daughter of M.K. Isbell and Emma Lena McLendon Isbell. Her father ran the general merchandise store in Heath for many years. Below are, from left to right, twins Mary and Martha Vaughn, daughters of John and Grace. (Both, courtesy of Fay Lofland.)

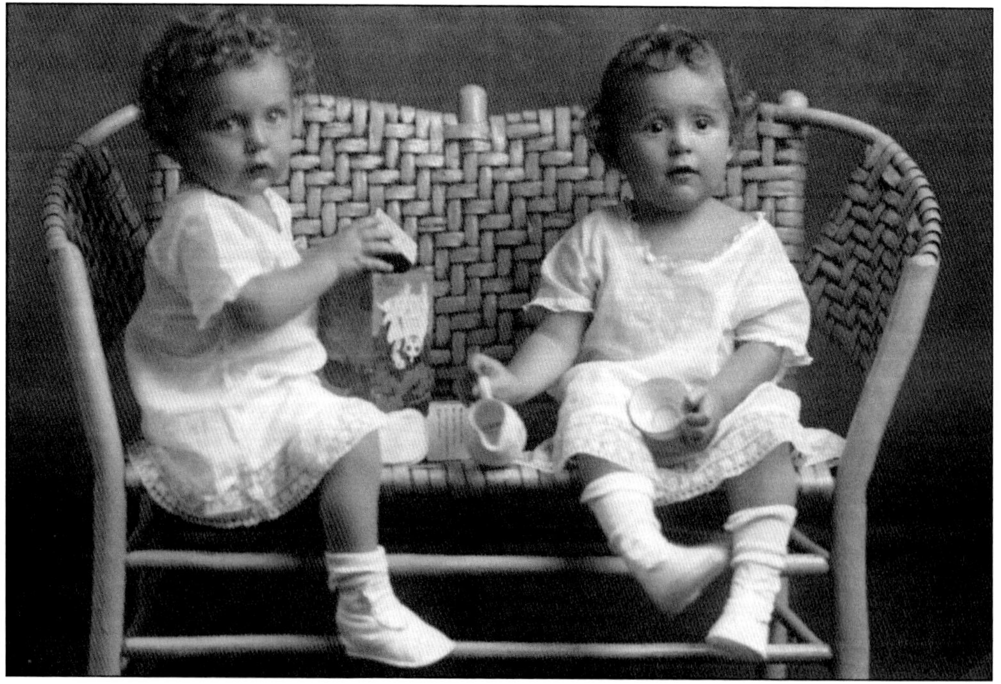

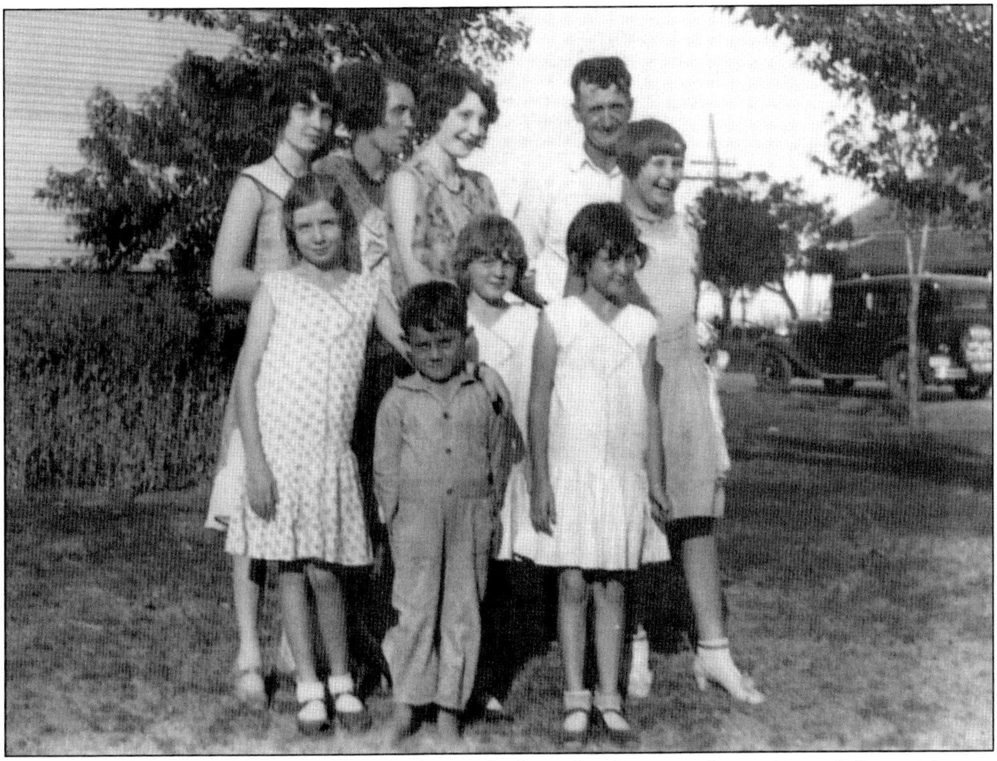

Pictured here are John and Grace Vaughn with their daughters and son. From left to right are (first row) daughter Isabell, son John Henry, twins Mary and Martha, and daughter Johnnie Mae; (second row) daughter Addie Faye, mother Grace, daughter Lena, and father John. (Courtesy of Fay Lofland.)

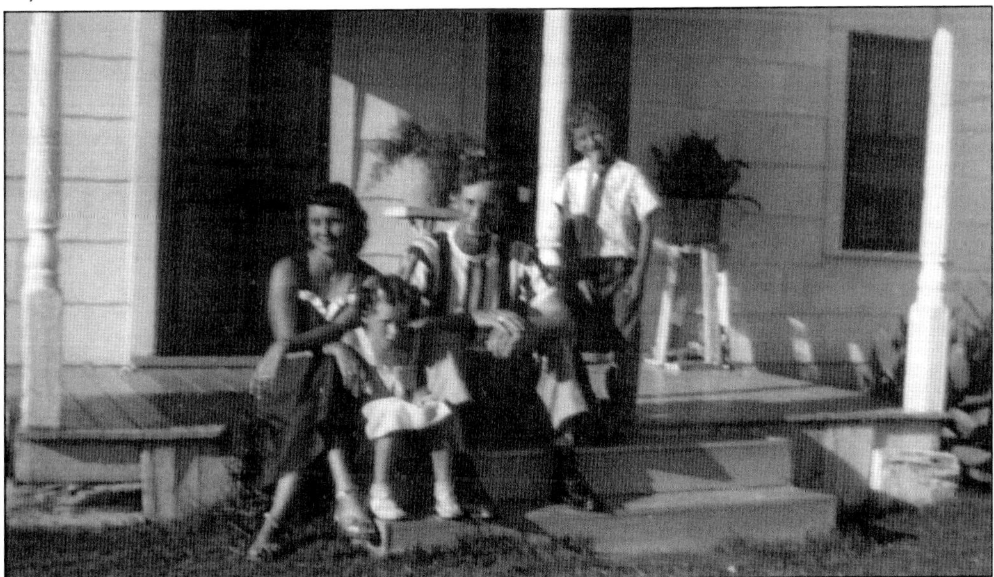

From left to right are Martha Vaughn Gray; daughter Jenny Ann Gray; her husband, Woodrow Gray; and son Leslie Vaughn Gray at their home in Heath in September 1949. Their home was located on what is now FM 740. (Courtesy of Maxine and Leslie Gray.)

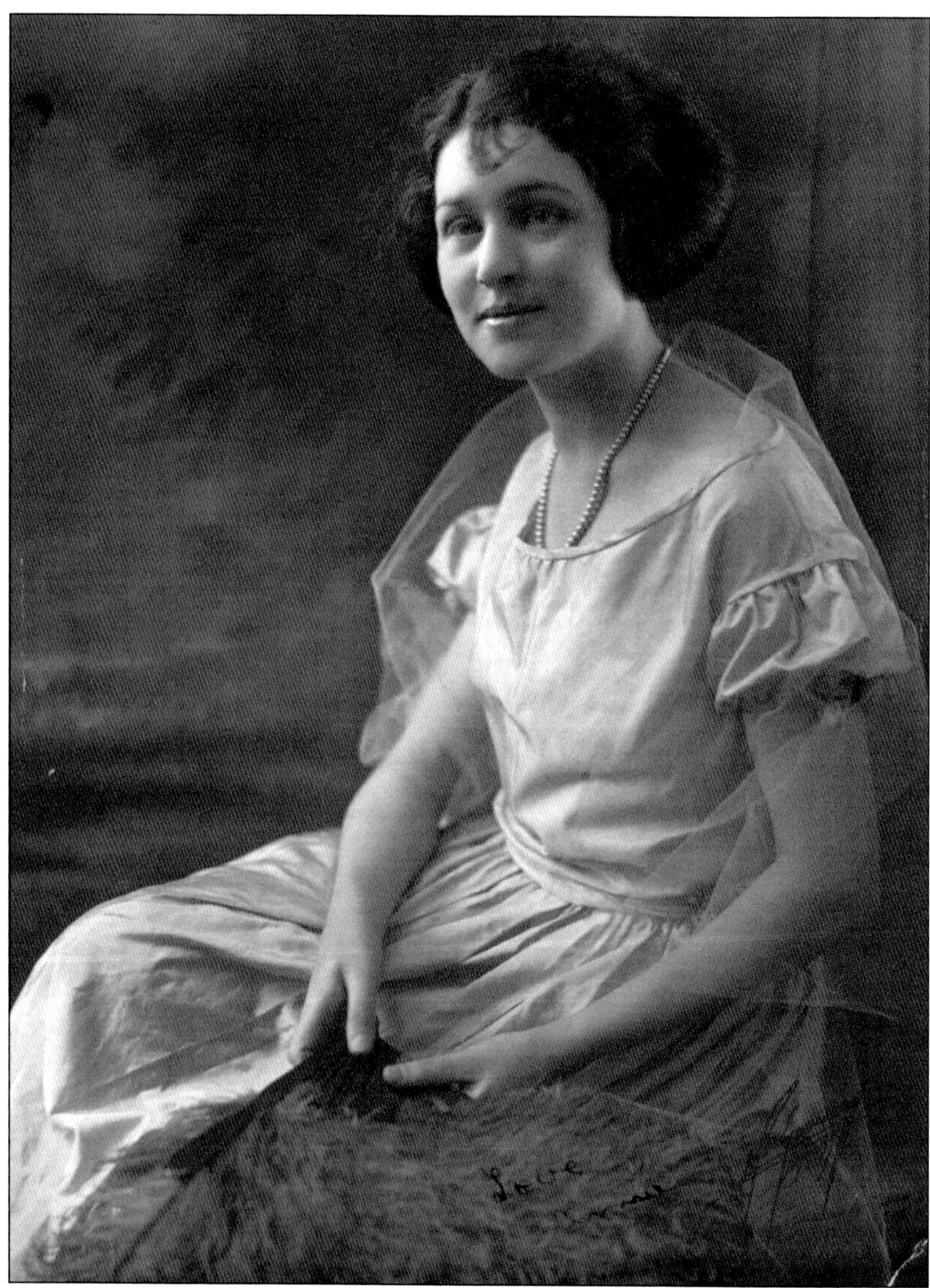

Anna Rebecca Isbell was born October 16, 1900, and lived all her life in Heath. Her parents were M.K. Isbell and Emma Lena McLendon Isbell and her siblings were Grace Isbell Vaughn, Grady Isbell, Fay Isbell Lofland, Frank "Abe" Isbell, and Mary Isbell Musgrave. She married John Fred "Ted" Gardenhire, and they ran a general merchandise store that once belonged to Anna's father, M.K. Isbell. Ted and Anna had one child, Anna Fred. Anna Rebecca died on October 11, 1996, and was buried in the Heath Cemetery. (Courtesy of Fay Lofland.)

Both the Lofland and Crawley families lived in Gravelly, Arkansas. Three of the Lofland brothers married sisters of the Crawley family. They moved to Texas and bought large areas of land in Rockwall County. Pictured here is Thomas David Lofland holding his son James Thomas "Jim" Lofland with his wife, Martha Lou Crawley Lofland. They made their home in Heath and farmed land, as well as owned interest in a store and a gin. They had three children: James Thomas, Claudia Lou, and Charles Joseph. Thomas David died of pneumonia on January 3, 1898, when his oldest son, James Thomas, was only four years old. About eight years later, Martha Lou married Robert Alfred Raburn—the president of the Farmers Guaranty State Bank of Heath—and they had two children, Robert Beverly and Mary Thelma Raburn. (Courtesy of Fay Lofland.)

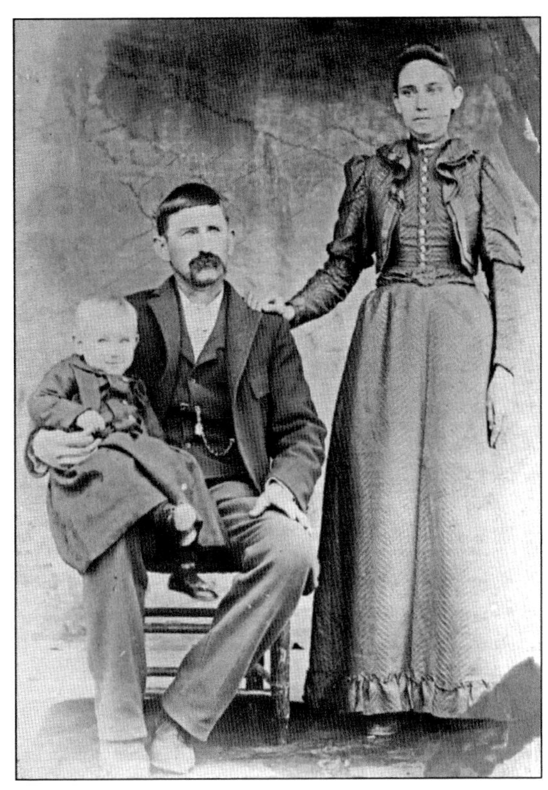

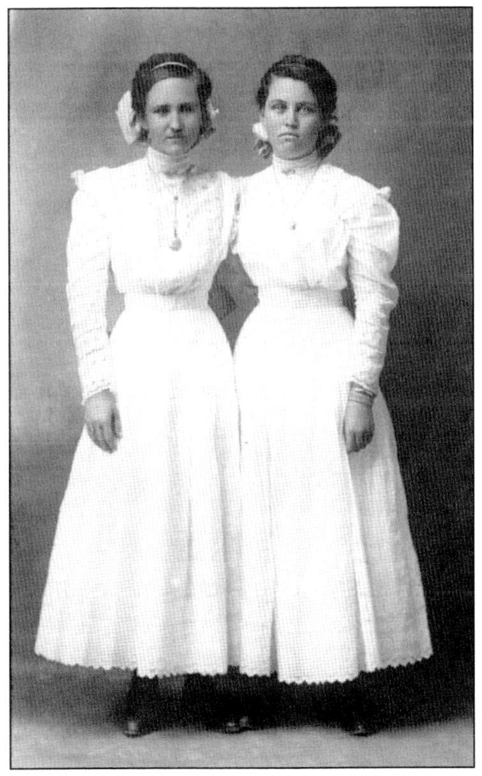

Pictured are Claudia Lou Lofland (left) and Fay Isbell (right). They were best friends and often wore matching dresses. While growing up, Claudia's older brother, Jim, would get upset whenever she and Fay would ride his horse without his permission. His attitude towards Fay later changed, however, and after finishing Wesley College in Terrell where he played on the football and baseball teams, he and Fay began dating and later married. Claudia and Fay continued to be best friends their entire lives. (Courtesy of Fay Lofland.)

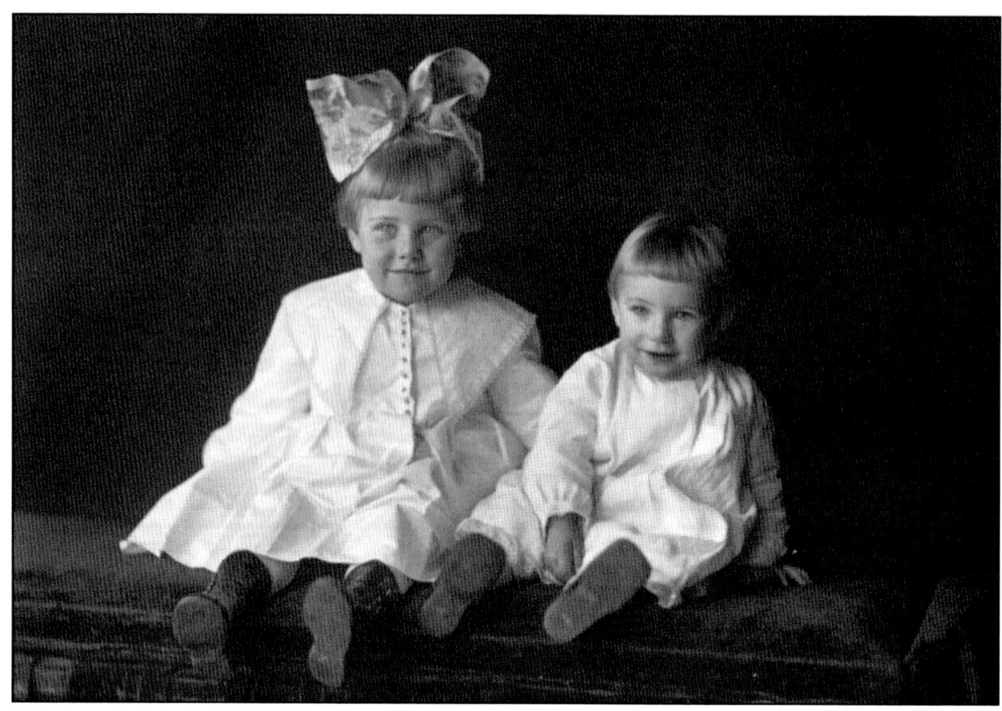

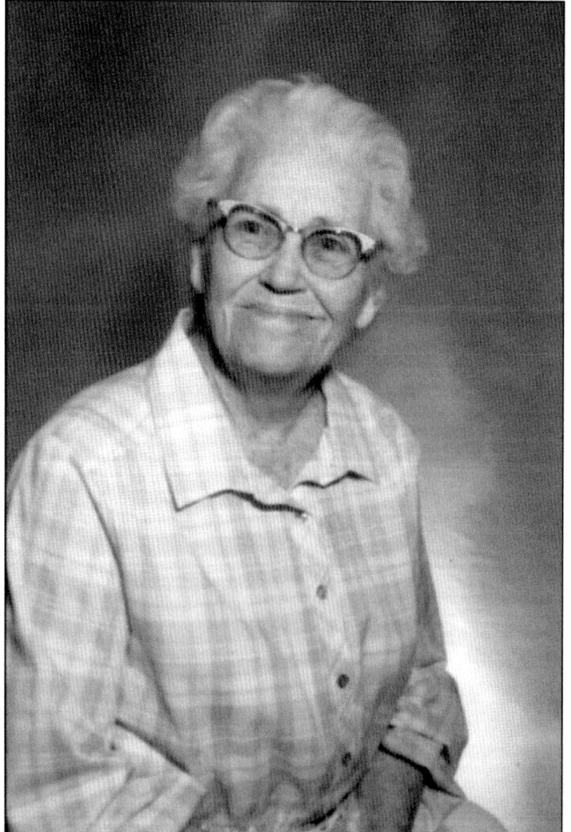

Pictured here are Lofland sisters Emma Lou (left) and Gena Lucille "Jackie" (right), daughters of Fay and Jim Lofland, as toddlers. Emma Lou was born on November 16, 1914, and Jackie was born on November 14, 1916. (Courtesy of Fay Lofland.)

Fay Lofland married J.T. Lofland on June 29, 1913, when she was 18 and he was 20. Fay never worked outside the home, and she always had a knack for making family and friends feel welcome in her house. She was never too busy to listen to others and help with their problems. Fay learned to cook at the young age of eight from her bedridden mother, who showed her how to make homemade biscuits for the family. She was also talented with handiwork and made beautiful tatting, clothing, quilts, pillowcases, and aprons, which she gave to everyone in Heath at Christmas. She was the oldest member of the First Baptist Church for many years. (Courtesy of Patsy Stodghill.)

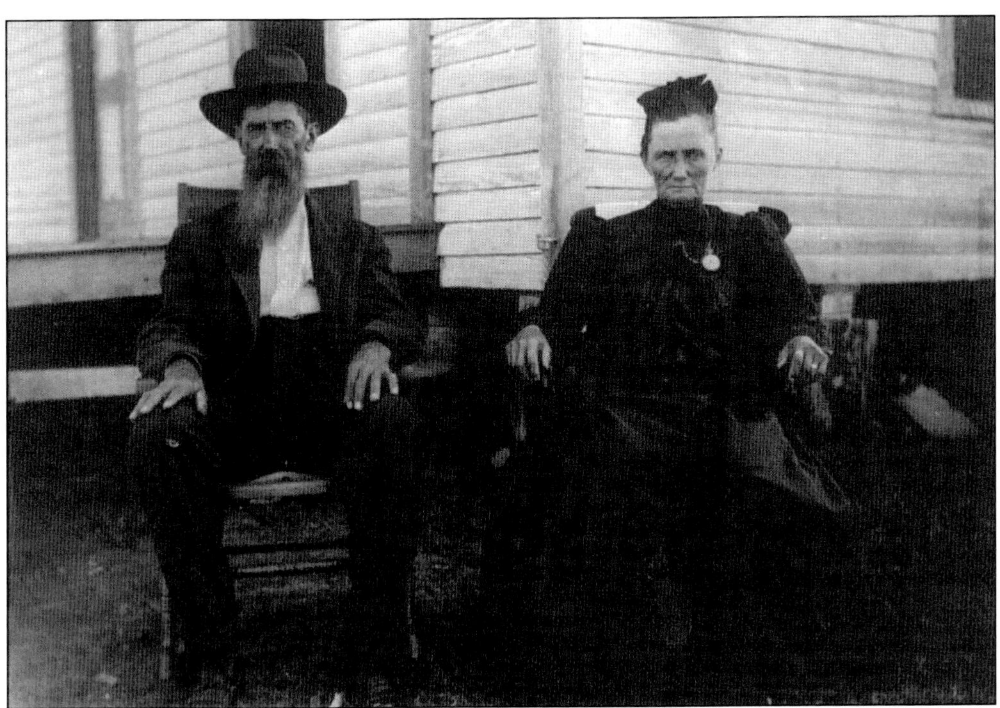

The Hall family settled in the Heath area in 1886 when John H. Hall and his wife, Mary Jane Seay (pictured above), moved to Texas on a wagon train from Bartow County, Georgia. They bought large portions of land that became known as the Hall Lease and later as Rabbit Ridge, three miles northeast of Heath. They lived in a huge white two-story house on a hill. (Courtesy of Patsy Stodghill.)

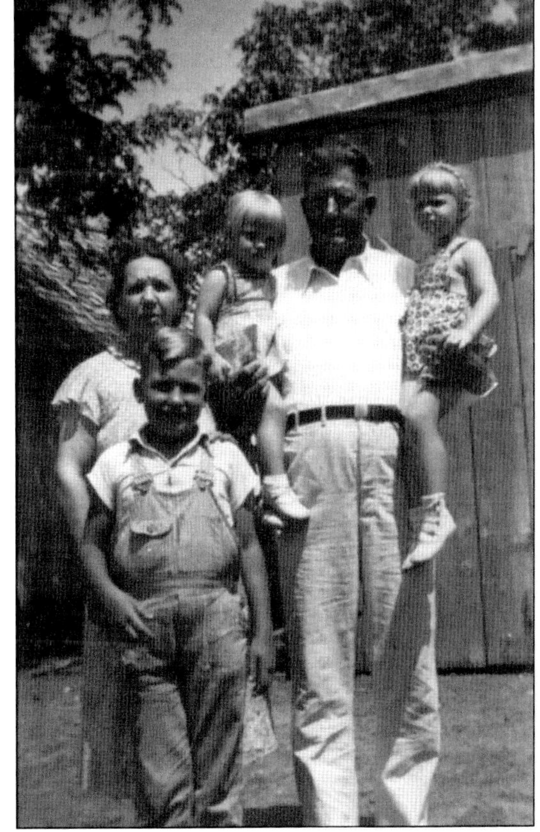

John Thomas "Tom" Hall married Clara Estella "Stella" McFarland on January 12, 1902, and the two settled about half a mile from Tom's parents' house in the Rabbit Ridge area. Tom was a big man, standing at six feet, six inches and weighing 250 pounds. He owned land and farmed while his wife, Stella, was known as an excellent seamstress. They had six children: Allene, Lela, William Curtis, John Thomas Jr., and twins Clayton and Clifford. Tom and Stella are pictured here with their grandchildren, from left to right, Thomas Dowell, Tommie, and Patsy Hall. (Courtesy of Patsy Stodghill.)

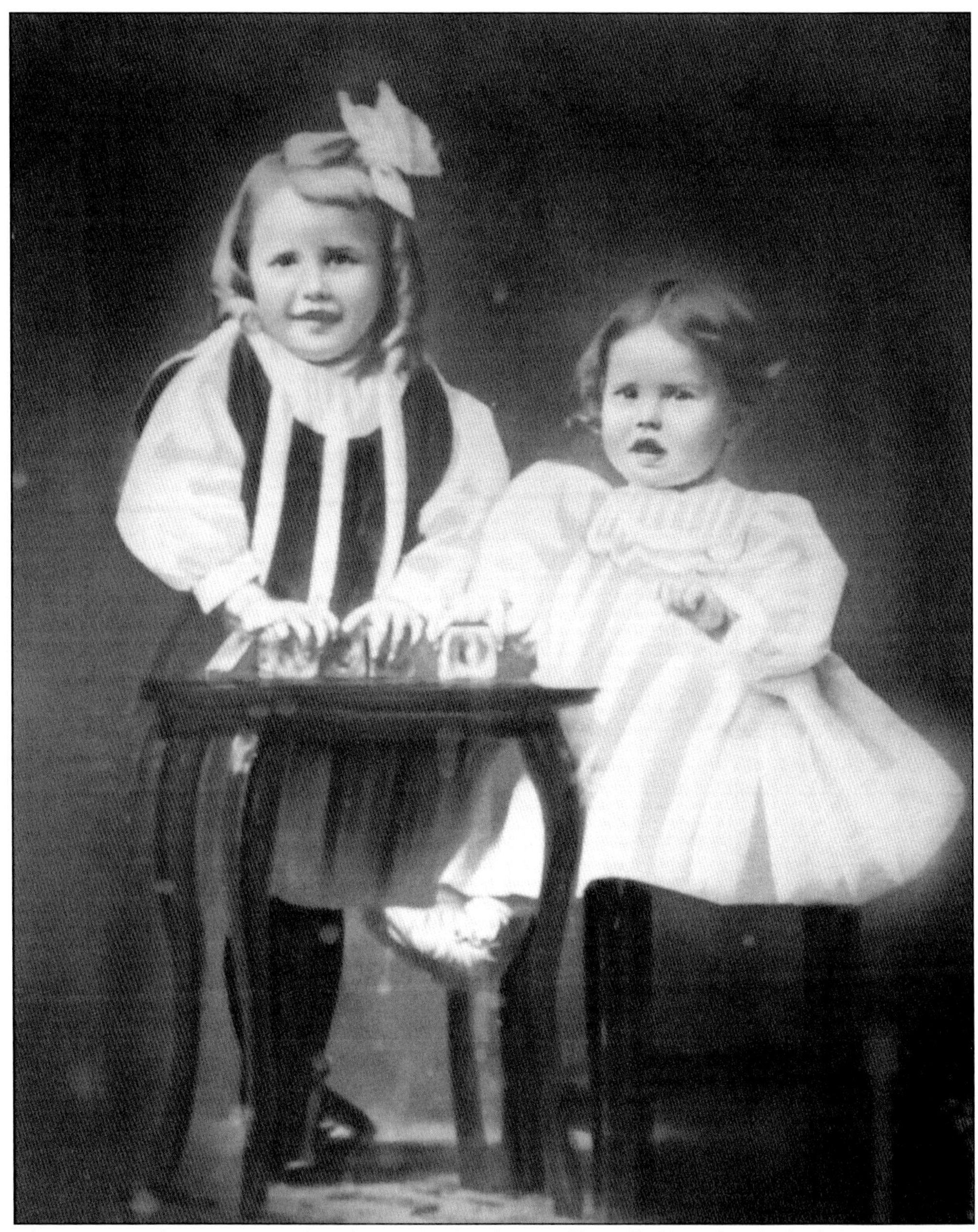

This portrait shows Tom and Stella Hall's daughters Allene (left) and Lela (right) as children. They had a couple of very large portraits like this one made by Gentry of Dallas. (Courtesy of Patsy Stodghill.)

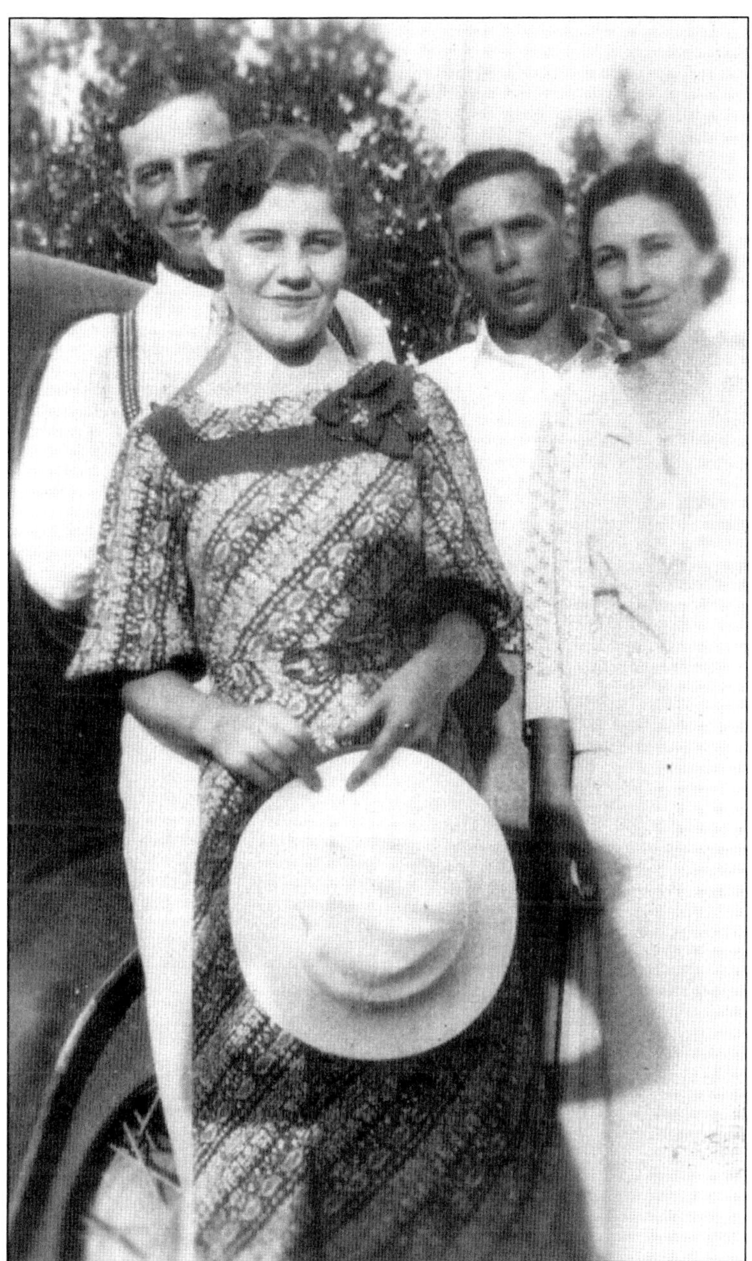

The Lofland sisters married Hall brothers. Emma Lou Lofland married William Curtis Hall on July 28, 1934, when she was 19 and he was 23. Jackie and John Thomas "Jake" Hall, Jr. were married eight years later on October 9, 1942, at the ages of 26 and 29, respectively. Jackie worked as an accounting clerk for the US Department of Agriculture until her retirement in 1966. Although she had no children, she was very caring toward her family. Jake was a war hero who served in World War II. Curtis worked at the Heath Gin after he married Emma and drove large trucks hauling bales of cotton and cottonseed to Dallas. He became a carpenter, as did Jake, and they worked on some of the largest building projects in Dallas. Emma was an excellent housekeeper, homemaker, mother, and wife who excelled in handiwork, including embroidery, crochet, crewel, and needlepoint. (Courtesy of Patsy Stodghill.)

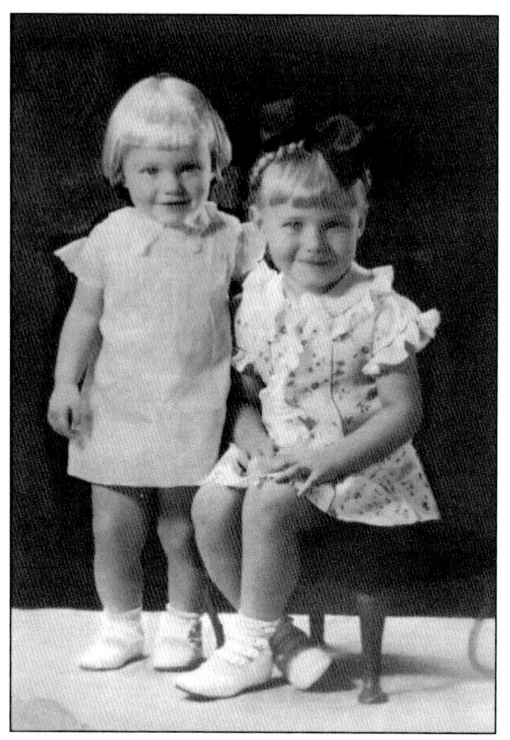

At left are Tommie and Patsy Hall, daughters of Emma Lou and Curtis Hall. The family took part in all the activities in the community. Emma Lou was an excellent housekeeper and was also actively involved in the Eastern Star. She cofounded the Camp Fire Girls chapter in Heath and was a room mother every year, as well as a chaperone on school trips. Curtis was a carpenter. He was friendly and had a good sense of humor. He died of a heart attack at 49 years of age in 1960. His funeral was held at the First Baptist Church in Heath, and it could not hold all of the people who attended. Patsy married Donald Stodghill, and their children are Steven Hall Stodghill and Sheri Sue Stodghill Fowler Parks. Tommie married Bob Fomby of Magnolia, Arkansas, and their children are Susie Yasger, Patti Ruhland, and Bobbie Fomby. Below is a family portrait made in 1954. From left to right are Tommie and Patsy with their mother Emma Lou and father Curtis. (Both, courtesy of Patsy Stodghill.)

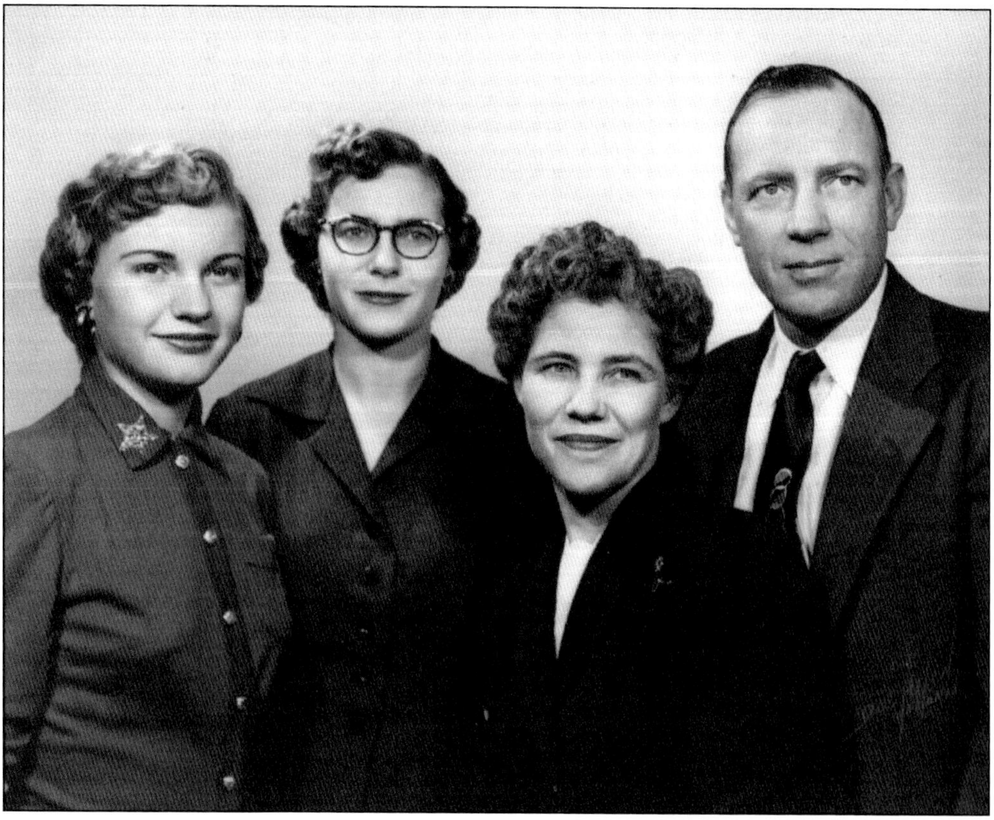

Dr. Francis Marion McChristy (pictured at right) and his wife, Mary Elizabeth Harter McChristy, came to Heath about 1887 by train from Palmyra, Missouri. Their first home was located near the present-day site of the First Baptist Church of Heath, where they lived for 18 years before moving to the McChristy farm one mile south of Heath. F.M. McChristy was a medical doctor who practiced many years in Rockwall County. He helped establish the Heath Drug Store in 1900 and was manager and part owner, with his doctor's office located inside the store. He traveled countless miles on horseback (often at night) in all types of weather to see his patients. Around 1900, he delivered a baby weighing less than three pounds, and with vigilance and loving care, the baby girl grew well and strong. (Both, courtesy of Gale Terry.)

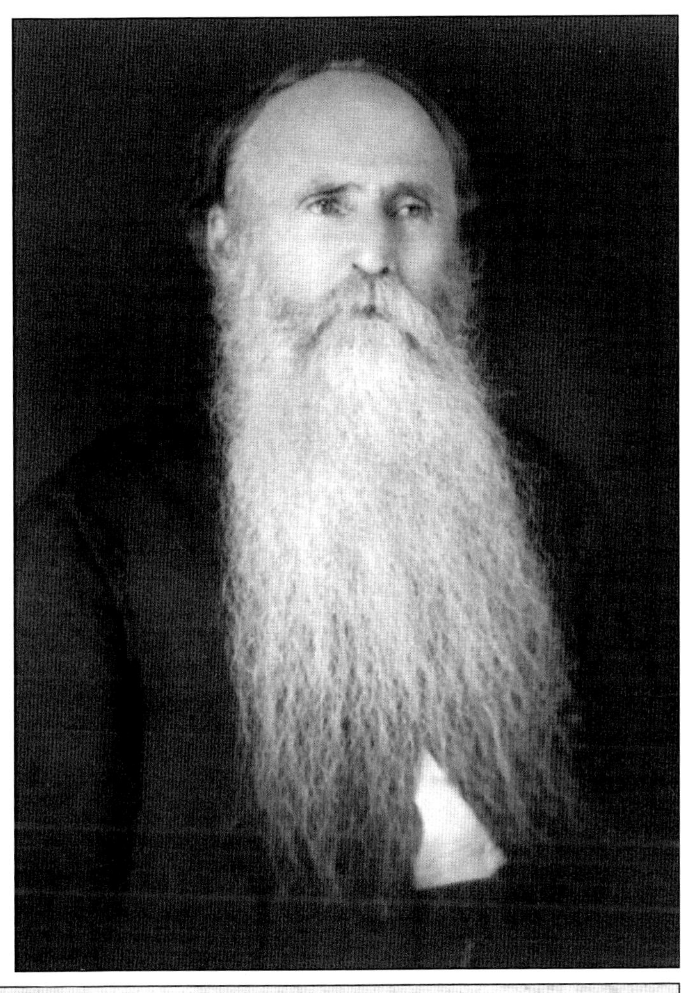

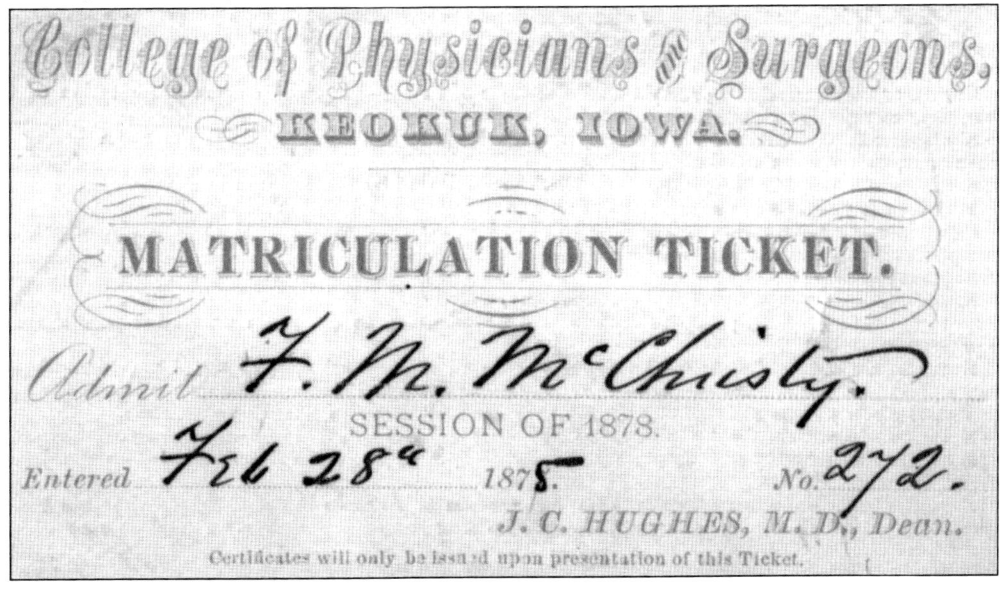

College of Physicians & Surgeons,

KEOKUK, IOWA.

MATRICULATION TICKET.

Admit F. M. McChristy.

SESSION OF 1878.

Entered Feb 28th 1875. No. 272.

J. C. HUGHES, M. D., Dean.

Certificates will only be issued upon presentation of this Ticket.

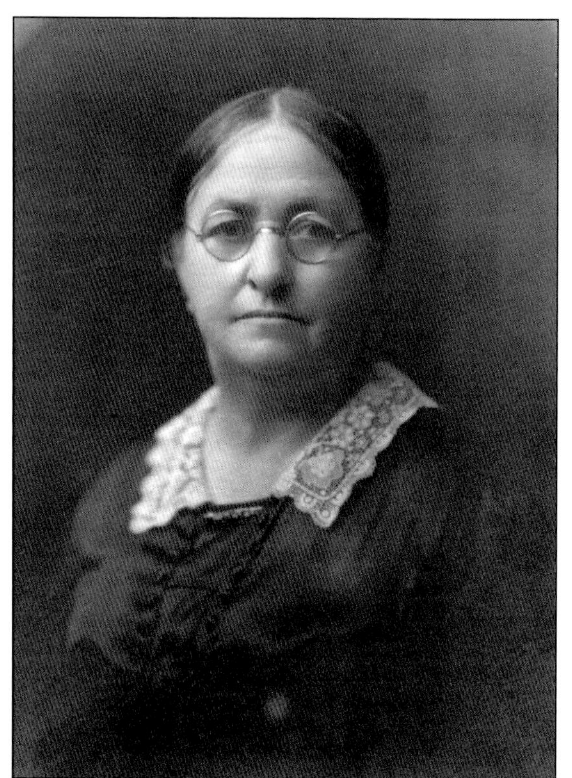

Mary Elizabeth Harter married Dr. F.M. McChristy on October 7, 1875, and they had 10 children—three boys and seven girls. Five were born in Heath and all 10 grew to adulthood there. Daughters Minnie and Laura were the only ones who lived in Heath their entire lives. Music was an important element in the McChristy household. Dr. McChristy served as deacon of the Willow Springs Baptist Church and led the singing. He also played the violin. The family had an organ in their home and all of the girls played it, except Minnie, who played the accordion. Sons Joe and Caleb each played a type of horn. (Courtesy of Gale Terry.)

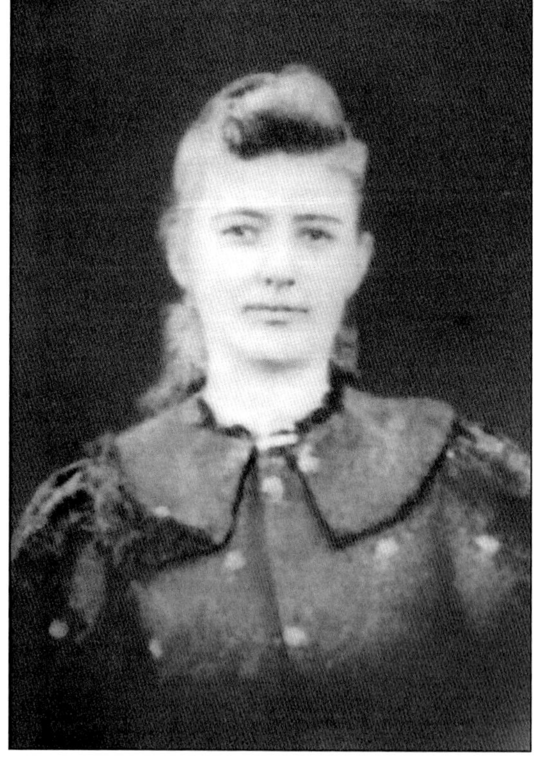

Laura McChristy was born March 27, 1880. She married Nathaniel Futrell in 1898, and they had two children, Leah Della and Frank Futrell. Laura was known as a faithful Christian, obedient daughter, true wife, and precious mother throughout the community. She was stricken with a fatal disease and died on October 13, 1904, at the young age of 24. Just before she died she sang every word to *The Sweet By and By*. She was laid to rest in Willow Springs Cemetery, now known as Heath Cemetery. (Courtesy of Gale Terry.)

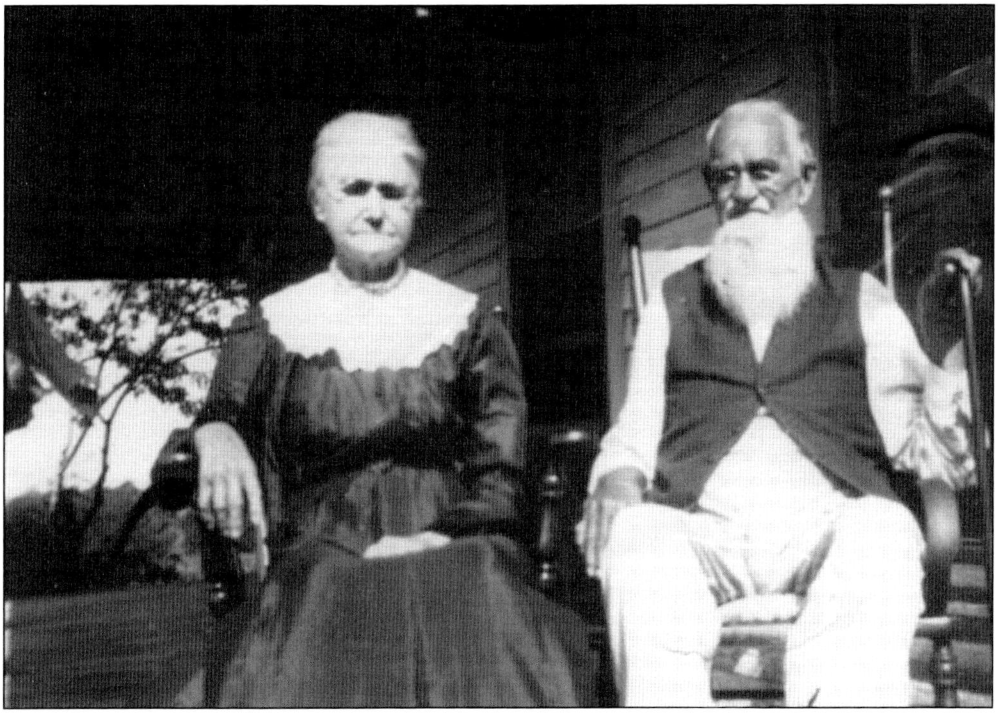

Nathaniel Futrell was one of four children of Dora and Wiley Futrell, pictured here at their homestead. Dora was born on April 1, 1844, and died on December 16, 1925. Wiley was born on October 29, 1827, and died on December 20, 1918. Their other three children were Lowe, Tissi, and Sarah Futrell. The Futrell farm in Heath was located in the area of the present-day site of Rush Creek Yacht Club. The farm was self-sufficient, and the family ate everything they grew. (Courtesy of Gale Terry.)

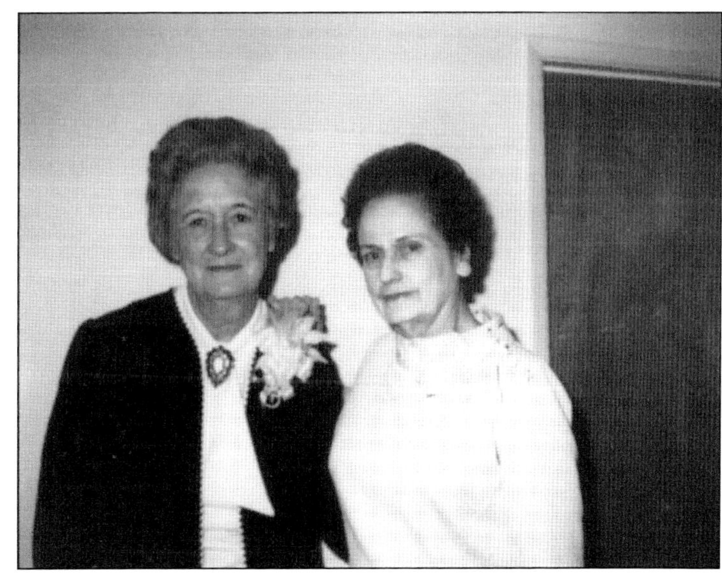

Shown here are first cousins Laura Frank Lofland (left) and Elizabeth Cullins Pinion (right). Elizabeth's parents were Minnie and Charlie Cullins, who lived in Heath all their lives. Elizabeth married John Pinion, and they also lived in Heath all their lives. Elizabeth played the piano and organ at the First Baptist Church of Heath, as well as at Pinion Hall. (Courtesy of Gale Terry.)

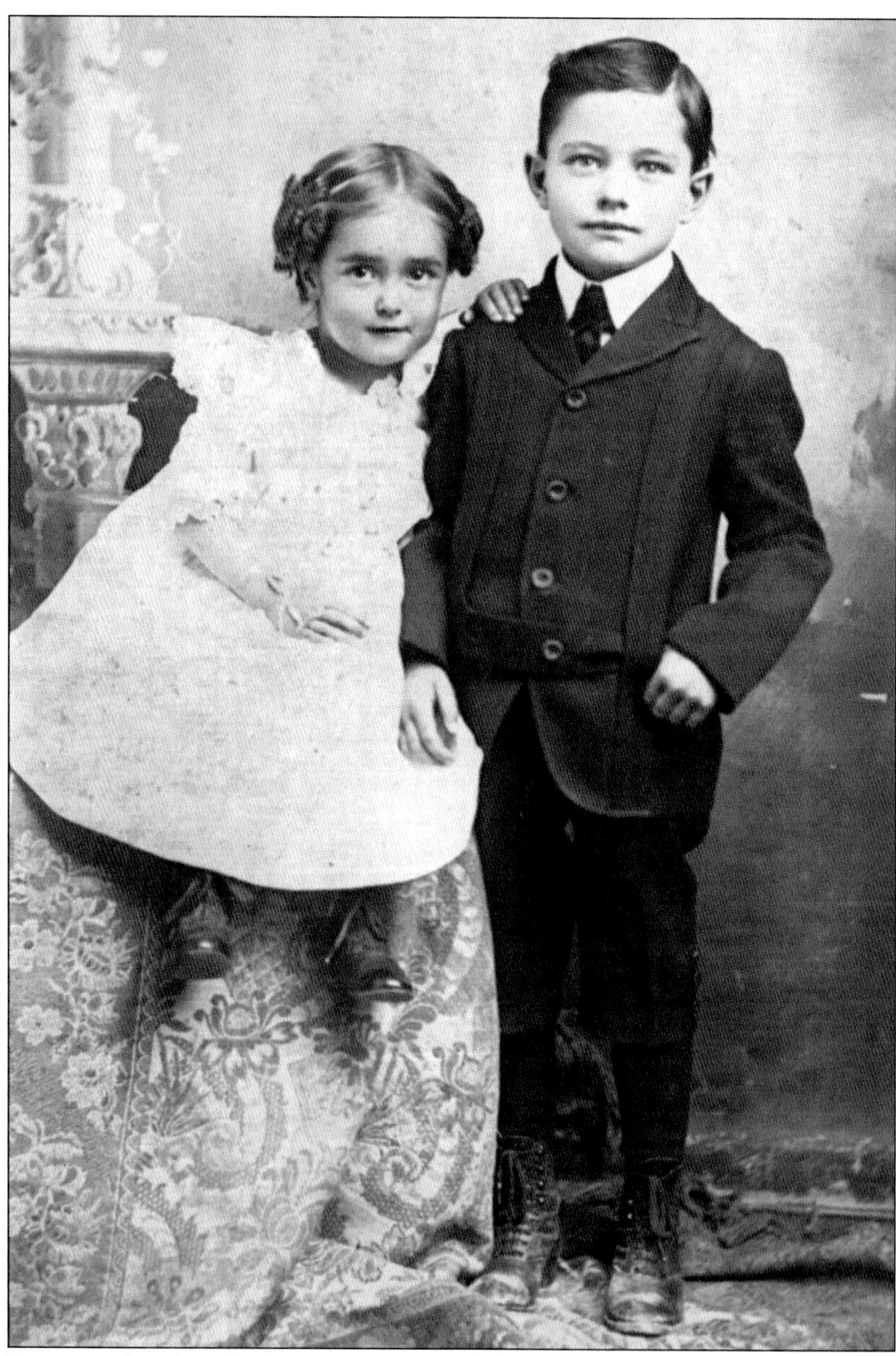

Here are Leah and Frank Futrell, children of Nathaniel and Laura. Leah married O.D. Lofland, and their three children were Laura Frank, Wilson Leon, and O.D. Jr. (Courtesy of Gale Terry.)

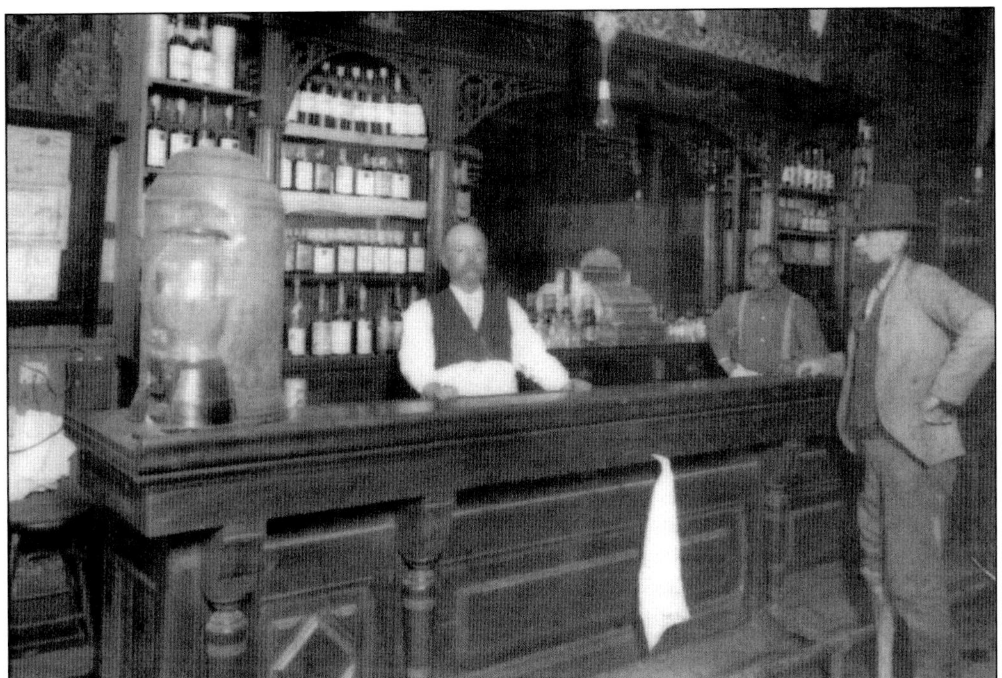

The Myers family first settled in Heath in 1903, making their home on Barnes Bridge Road. They came from Wythe County, Virginia, and they changed their name from Moyer to Myers before settling in Texas. Daniel Webster "Dan" Myers married Nancy Chilnussia "Chill" Lemley, daughter of William Flemming Lemley and Nancy Elizabeth Stiles, on November 13, 1906. Dan and Chill were blessed with nine children: Melvin, Opal, Manon "Dood," Travis, Verdah, Daniel Webster, Roy Hugh, and twins Ina Sue and Ada Lou. The above photograph shows John Myers (with the peg leg to the right), father of Daniel Webster Myers, at a bar in Dallas. Below is a postcard dated 1909 addressed to John as Peg Leg Myers. (Both, courtesy of Ada Lou Myers Abernathy.)

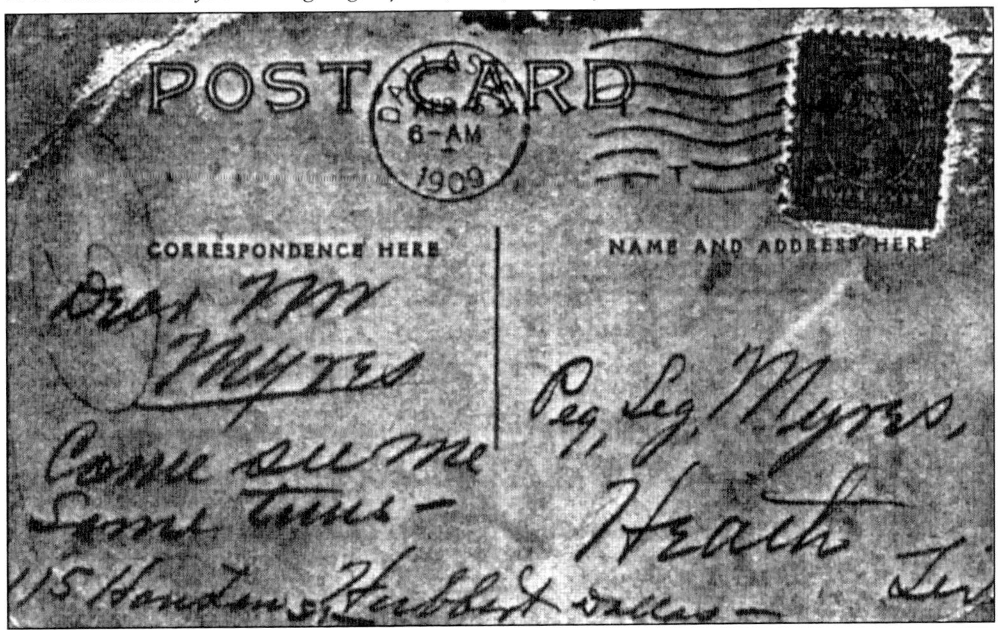

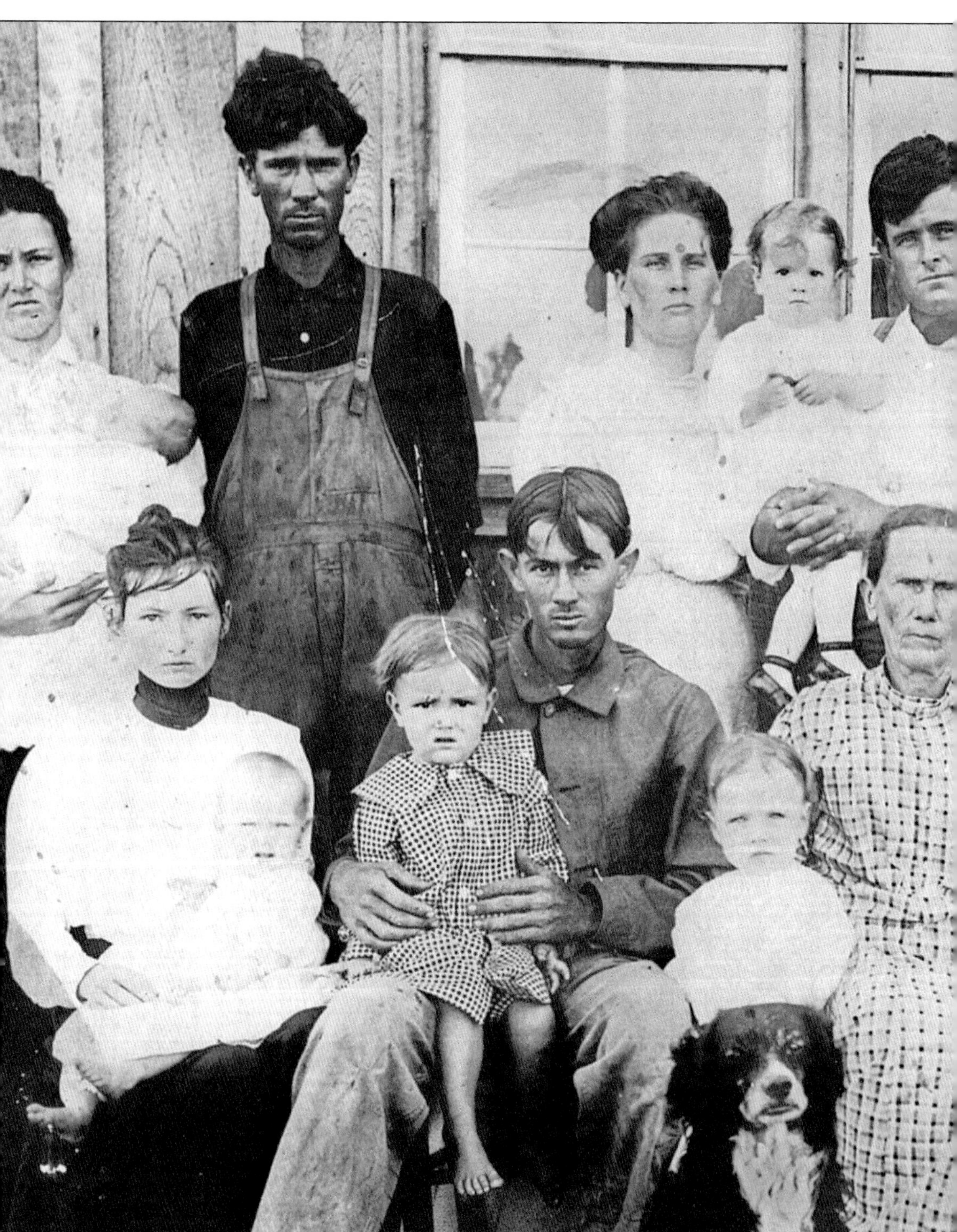

Pictured here in July 1910 is the Myers family. From left to right are (first row) Chilnussia Lemley Myers holding Opal, Daniel Webster Myers holding Melvin, Bamy Ward Myers holding Viola Myers and Vera Cheek, John Myers, Lou Myers Cheek, and Robert Cheek; (second row) is Alice

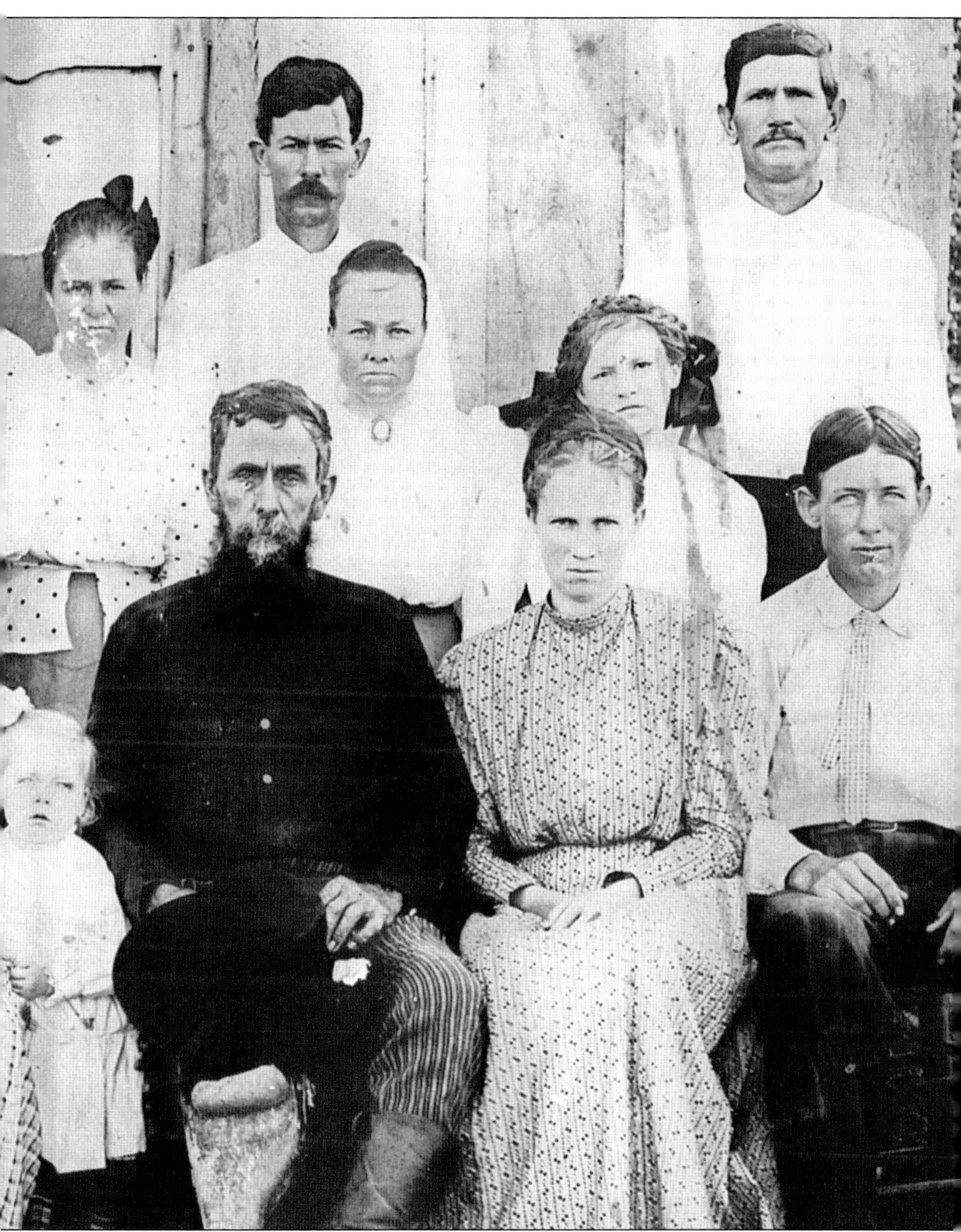

Neoma Weeks Myers holding Raymond Rovonie Myers Sr., Joseph Samuel Myers, Elda Myers Moran, Chan Moran holding Marie, Lizzie Myers (wife of George), George Myers, Mandy Cissell, Madie Cissell, and Jim Cissell. (Courtesy of Ada Lou Myers Abernathy.)

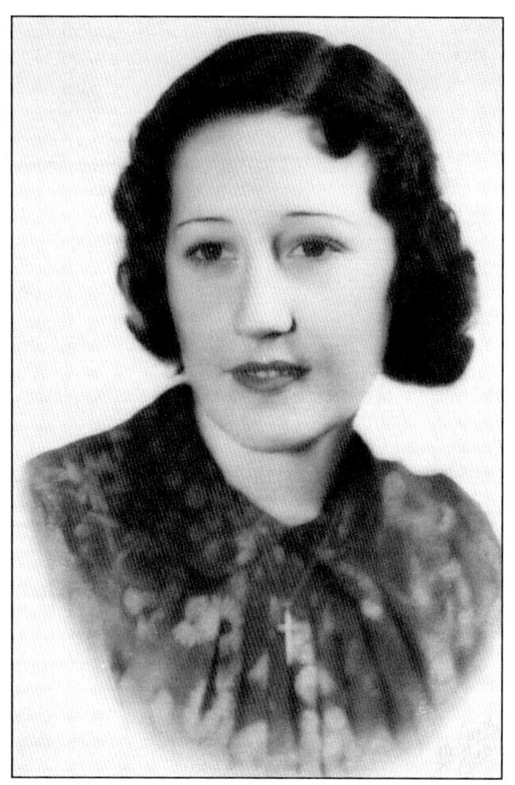

The Terrys were one of the earliest families to settle in Heath, coming to the area in the early 1900s. Many large pecan trees grew around their farm located near Barnes Bridge. Elijah "Lige" Washington Terry came from Tennessee to Texas with his first wife, Alaska Masonhammer (who later died from pneumonia), and their three children, Elmer, Faye and Mable. Following Alaska's death, Lige married Ina Nancy Robertson Lemmons, and they raised an additional eight children, including twins Waymond and Raymond: Austin, Lorene, Mildred, Clyde, Mary Jo, and James Leon. Pictured here is Aileen Evans, who later married Waymond. (Courtesy of Gale Terry.)

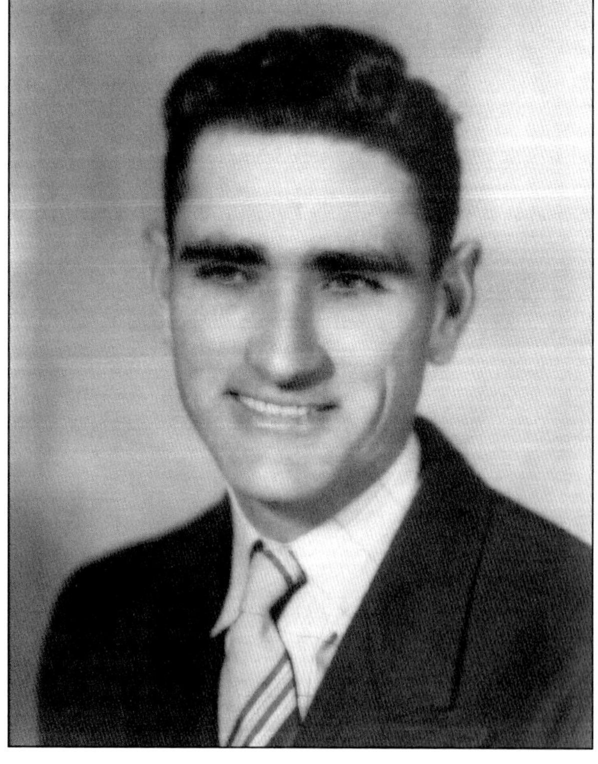

Waymond Terry (pictured here) married Louella Lincoln after the passing of his first wife. Their three daughters were Barbara, Betty, and Charlotte. Louella died giving birth to Charlotte, and Waymond later married Aileen Evans. They had two children, Ronnie and Kennedy. Raymond, Waymond's twin, adopted Charlotte at birth, and he and his wife raised her as their own child. (Courtesy of Gale Terry.)

In this image, the children of twin brothers Waymond and Raymond Terry stand outside the home of Waymond and Aileen Terry in Heath. From left to right are (first row) Charlotte, Ronnie, and Betty; (second row) Barbara, Charles, and Joy. (Courtesy of Betty Terry Lofland.)

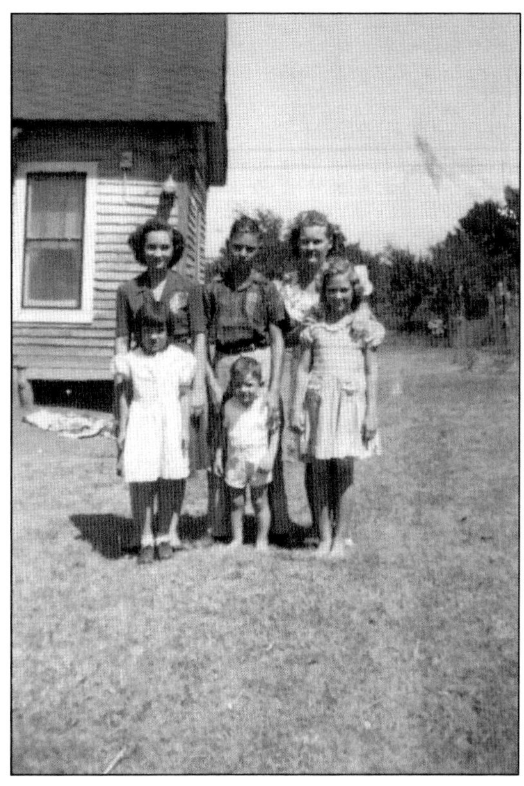

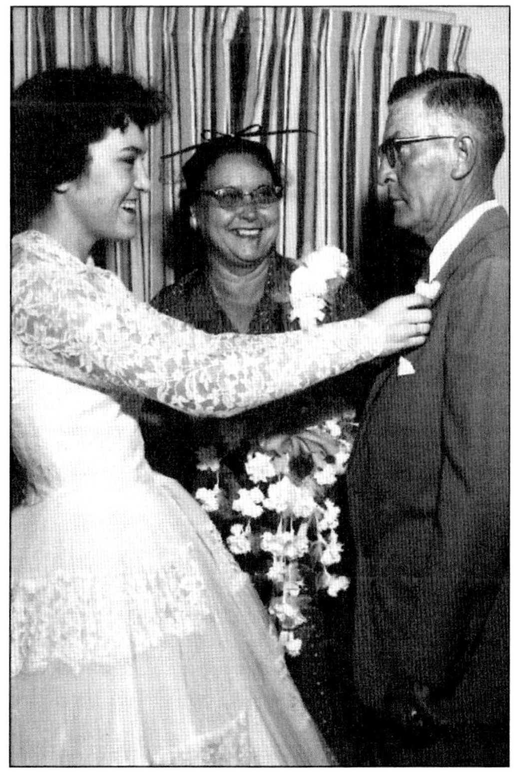

Raymond and Leona Terry adopted Waymond's daughter Charlotte when his wife, Louella Lincoln, passed away. Raymond, also known as "Cotton," was born in Archer City, Texas, on March 17, 1910. He and Leona were married and had twins Charles Ray and Joy Faye. Cotton was a farmer and served as Rockwall County commissioner for 22 years. He and Leona were both active parishioners at the First Baptist Church of Heath. Raymond became a deacon in 1940 and served in that capacity until his death in 1978. This photograph was taken at Charlotte's wedding to Kenneth Garrett. They had one child, Terry Garrett, who is the current director of the Heath Department of Public Safety. (Courtesy of the Terry family.)

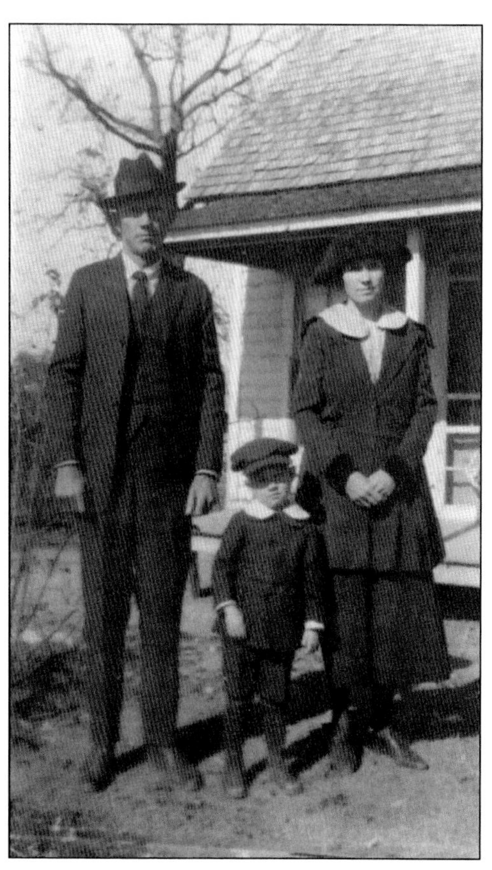

Dr. John J. Lasater came to Heath from Marshall County, Alabama, in 1905. He married Mary Ledocia Lemley, and they had six children. Dr. Lasater died an accidental death from in-law Tom Roach in 1905. Hester Ettie Lasater married Robert Randles, and the two had one son, Robert Lasater. Shown are Robert and Hester Lasater with their son Robert outside their home in Heath in 1920. Hester was born June 8, 1888, in Rockwall and was the daughter of Dr. John and Mary Lasater. Hester taught Sunday school at the First Baptist Church of Heath for many years. Below is Oliver Dawson, husband of Rosmyn Randles, who was the daughter of Oscar and Marye Randles. (Both, courtesy of Reba Jett.)

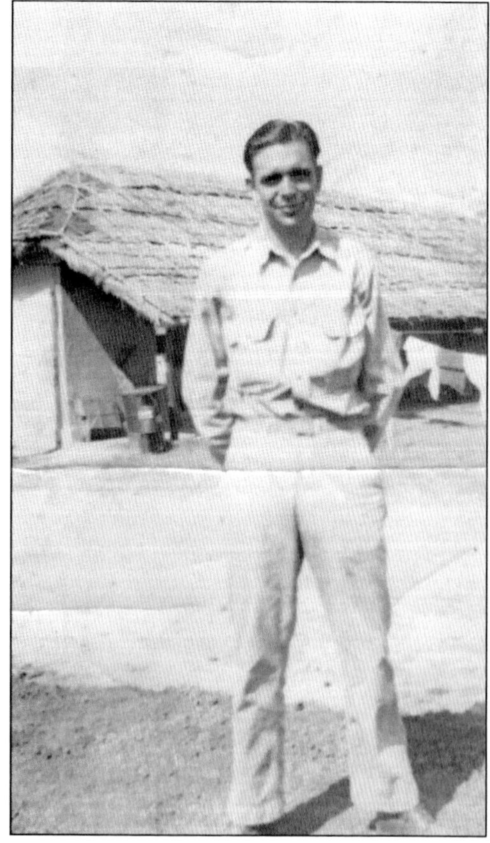

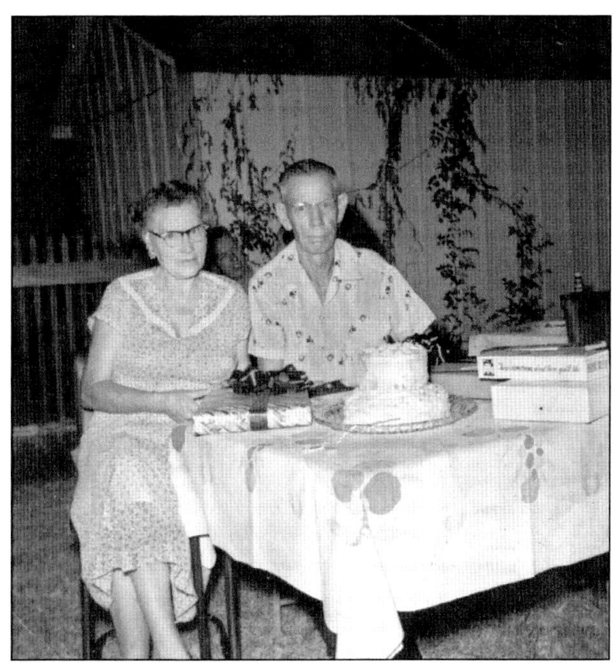

Shown at right are Robert G. Campbell and his wife, Nancy E. Lasater. Nancy's father was Dr. John J. Lasater, and her siblings were Hester (Lasater), Marye (Randles), Viola (Woods), John Moffett, and Lee (who died young). The image below depicts five generations of the Randles-Lasater families. Included in the photograph are Hester Randles, Gladys King Randles, Reba Randles Jett, Bobbie Jett Holland, Bridget Holland Butler, and Sam Jett. (Both, courtesy of Reba Jett.)

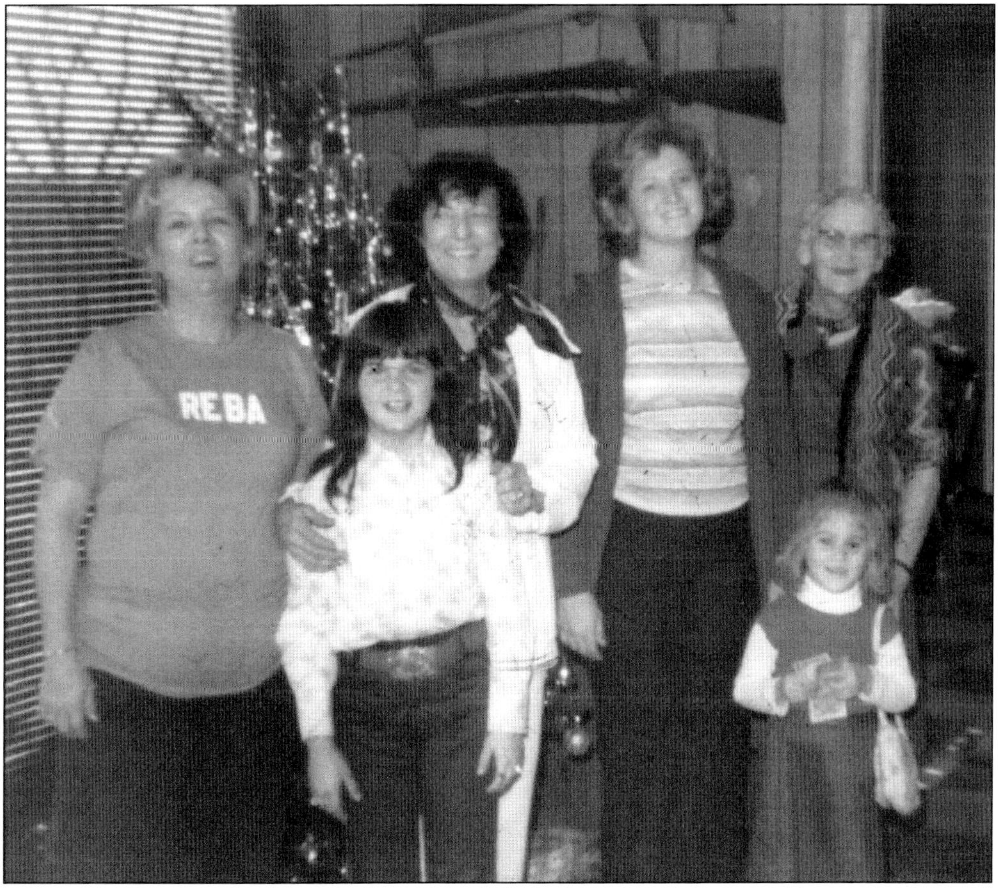

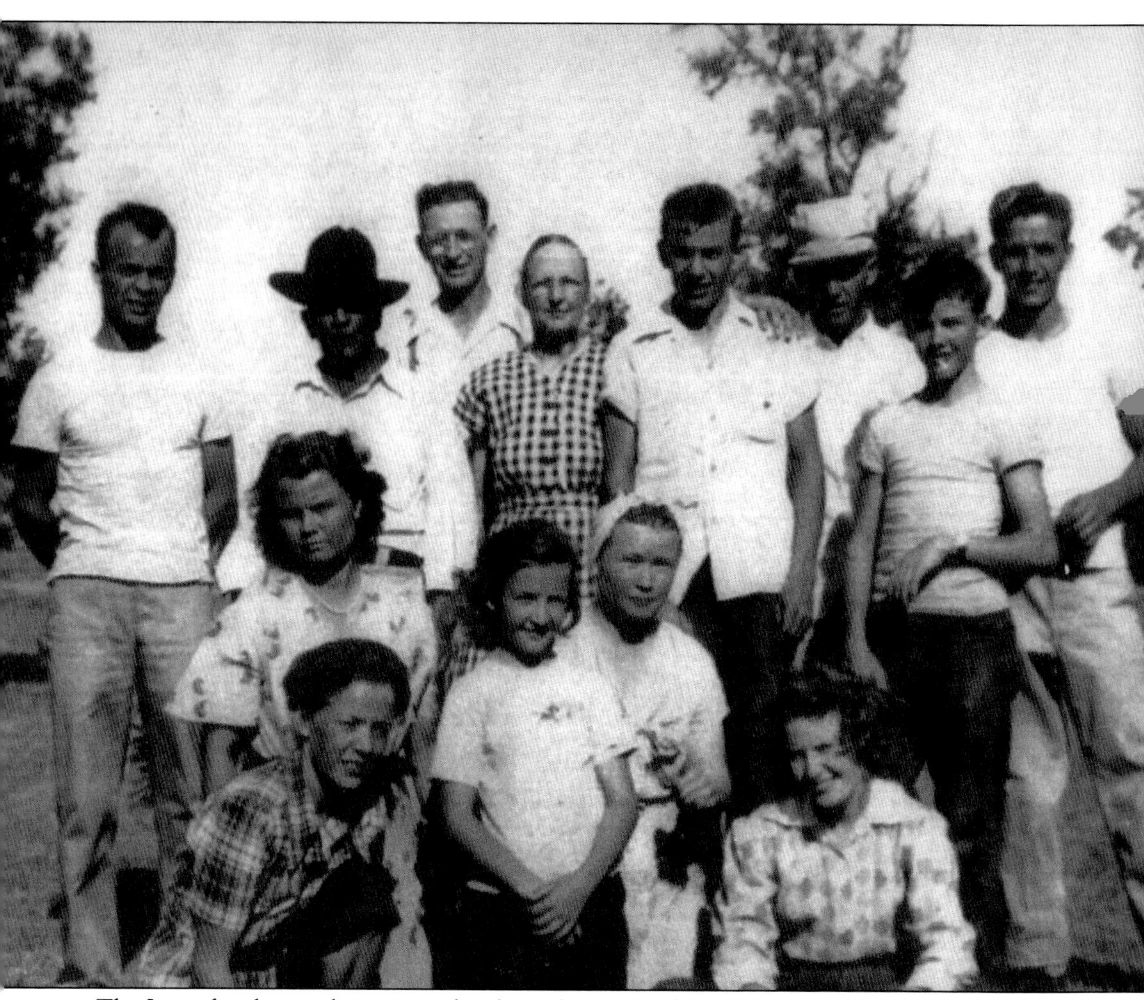

The Jones family, another group of early settlers, came from Tennessee. This image dated 1948 shows the Jones family: J.C., Everett (father, also known as E.C.), Earnest (McClay), Lois (mother), Wayne, Troy, Leon, Billy Gene, Marie (Lindsey), Inez (Massey), Evelyn (Costa), Louise (Moore), and Ima Jo (Boss). Fayne—Wayne's twin—was killed in 1946. (Courtesy of Runell White.)

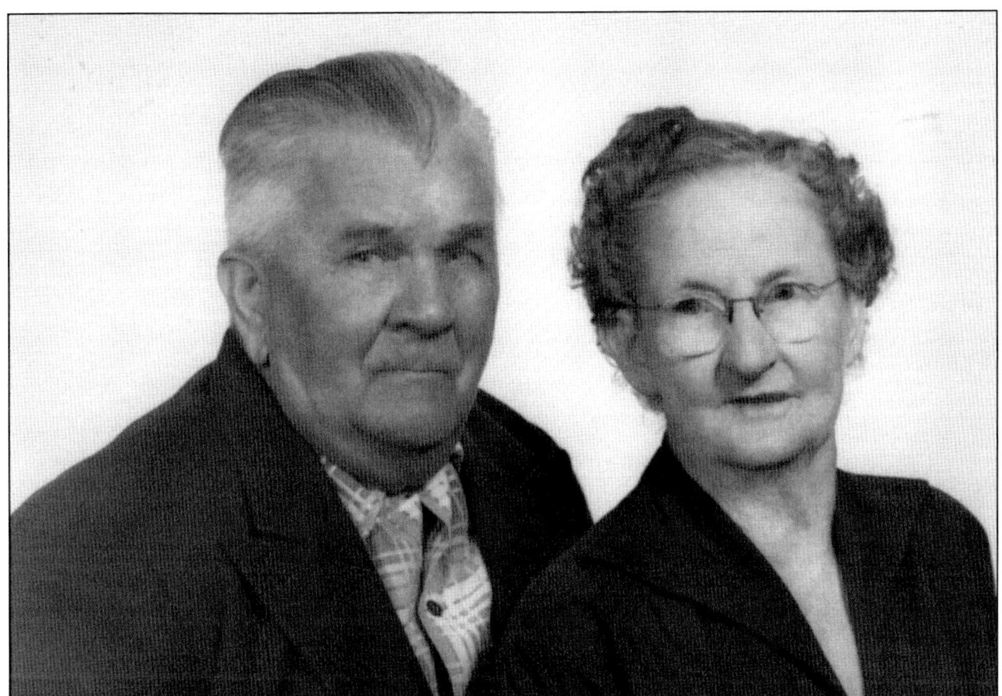

Above are E.L. "Everett" Jones and his wife, Lois. They raised 12 children (listed on the previous page). The image below shows, from left to right, Opal Lindsey with her brother Clarence Lindsey and Inez Jones in Heath. Later, Clarence married Marie Jones, who was Inez's sister. (Above, courtesy of Wayne Jones; below, courtesy of Runell White.)

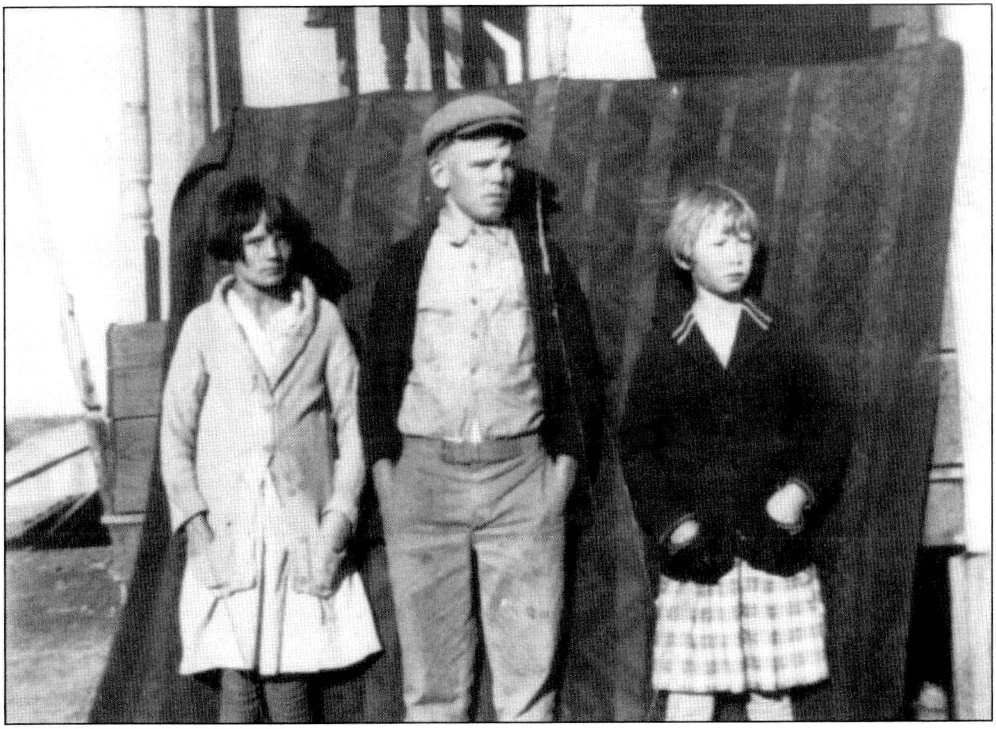

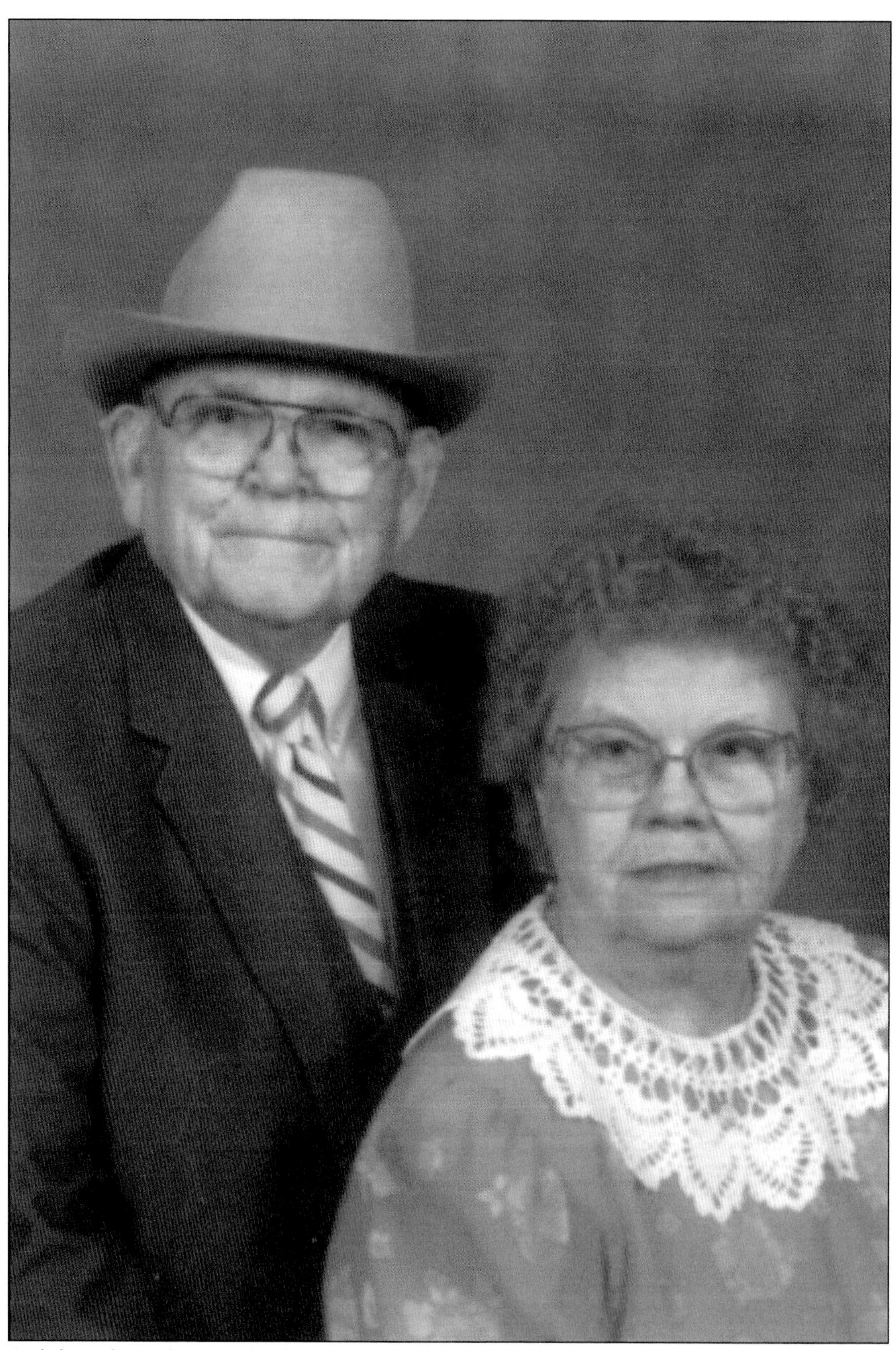

At left is a later photograph of Clarence and Marie Lindsey. (Courtesy of Syble Bolding.)

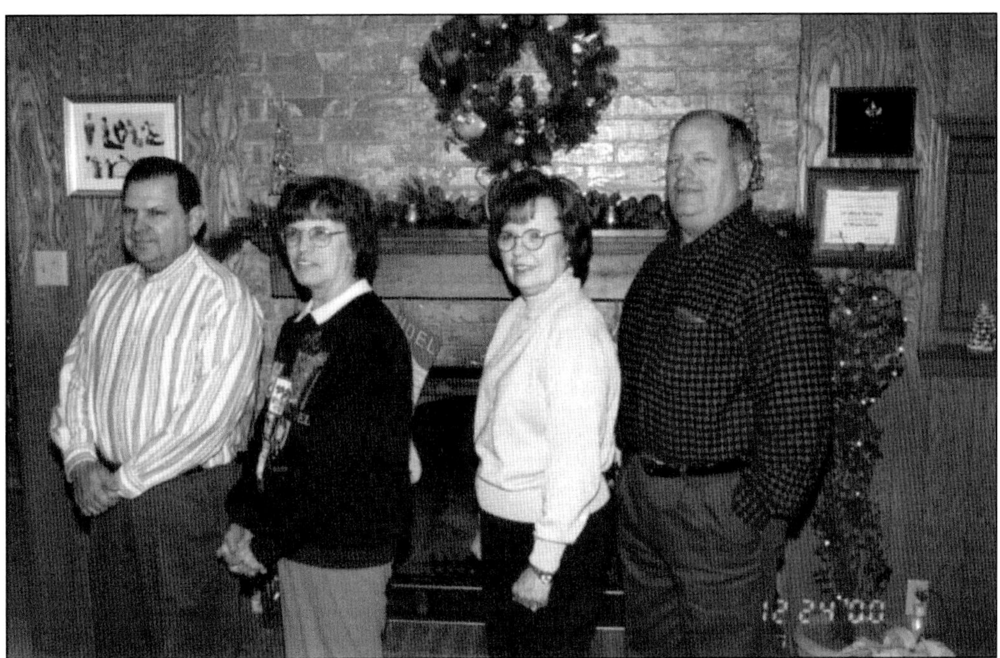

The Lindsey children are pictured above. From left to right are David Lindsey, Freda Lindsey Myers, Syble Lindsey Bolding, and Douglas Lindsey. (Courtesy of Syble Bolding.)

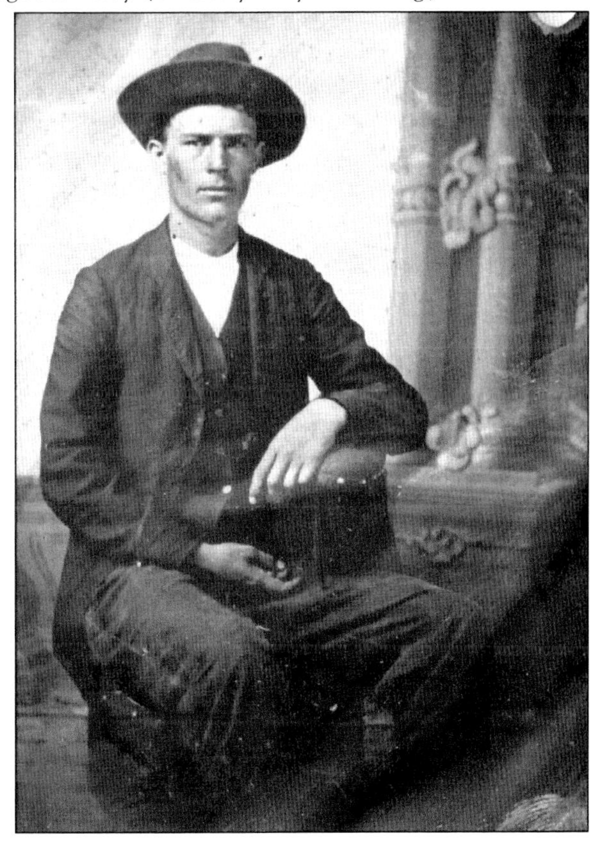

In 1869, Isaac Jefferson Holt moved his family of seven from their farm in Iuka, Mississippi, to Willow Springs, Texas. The journey took the family seven weeks by oxcart. Isaac and Laura Elizabeth "Bettie" McDaniel, born in 1829, married in 1849 in Montgomery County, North Carolina. Their five children were John "Doc" Franklin, James Allen, George Savanah, Isaac Jefferson Jr., and Elizabeth. Isaac was born in 1816 in Gold Hill, South Carolina, a carpenter by trade. He was almost 50 at the start of the Civil War and volunteered to serve with Company F, of the 45th Regiment of the North Carolina Troops. He surrendered at Appomattox Court House in Virginia, on April 9, 1865, with General Lee. Isaac died in 1870 from injuries and exposure during the war, shortly after arriving in Willow Springs. He is buried in what is now the Heath Cemetery. (Courtesy of Carolyn Holt.)

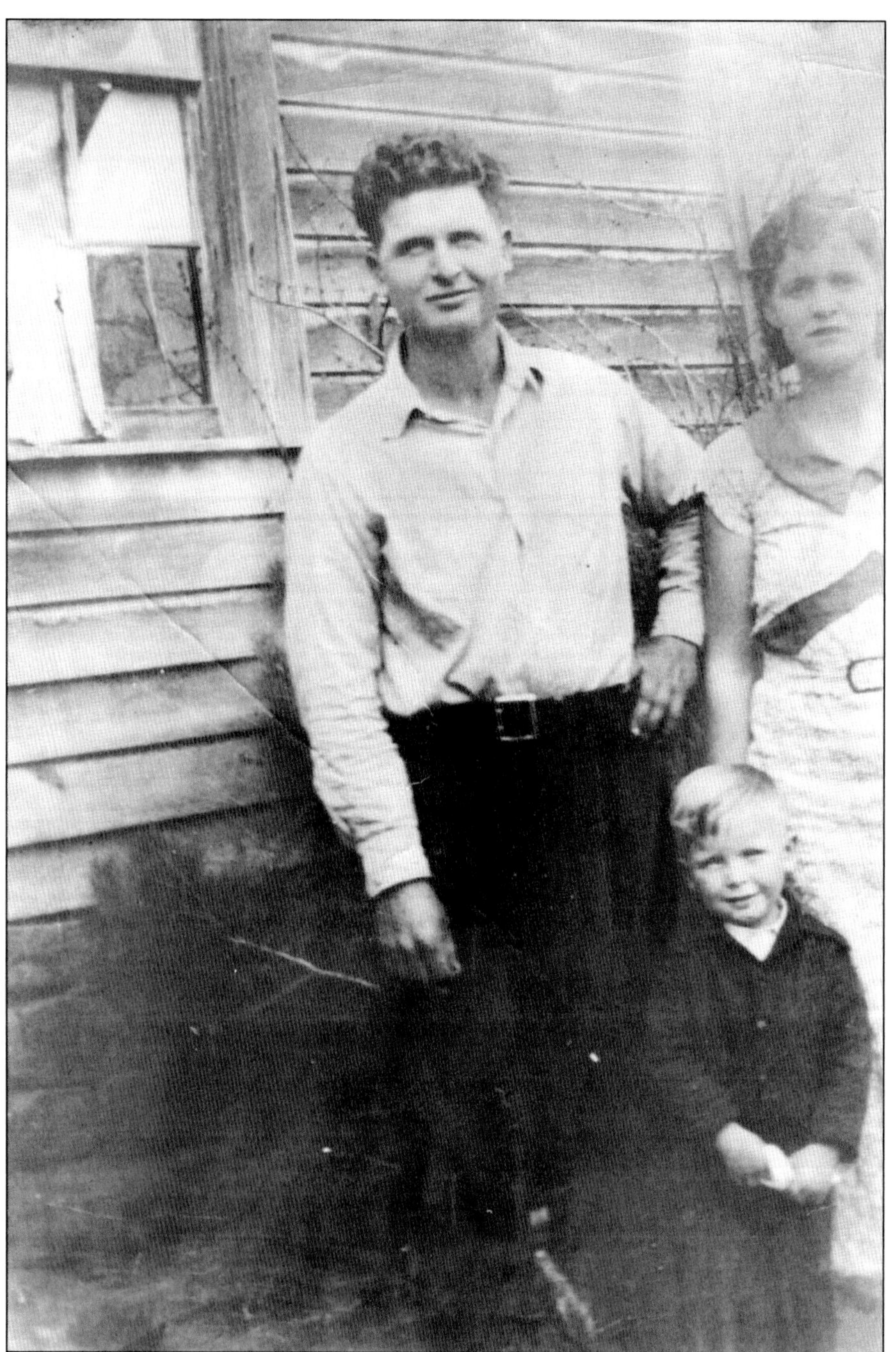

The Poindexters settled in Heath in 1930. Tilmon Ernest Poindexter, Vina Poindexter, and their son Tilmon Eugene "Gene" Poindexter stand outside their newly purchased farmhouse on 120 acres on Rabbit Ridge (named for the population of jackrabbits found in the area). Over the years, the Poindexter family maintained the farm and canned nearly all of the food grown on it. They raised cows and chickens, sold chicken eggs, and made mustang grape jelly from the mustang grape vines growing in the nearby woods. The farm was sold for $120,000 in 1975 and later burned in a fire. (Courtesy of Mark Poindexter.)

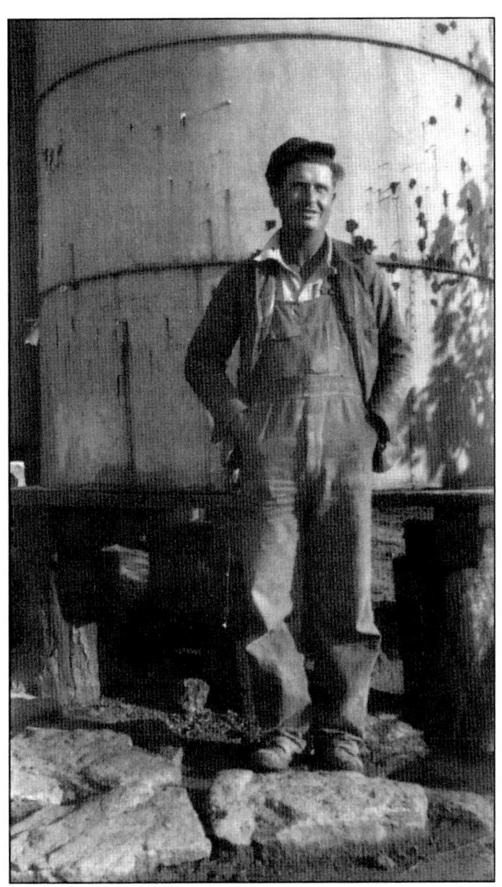

In the image at right, Tilmon Earnest Poindexter stands next to the water tank on the farm, which served as the main water supply during long periods without rain. Below is Tilmon's wife, Vina Poindexter, holding her grandson Mark Poindexter out on the family farm around 1960. Mark would go on to serve as a volunteer firefighter for Rockwall before assuming full-time duties as the fire chief in October 2000. (Both, courtesy of Mark Poindexter.)

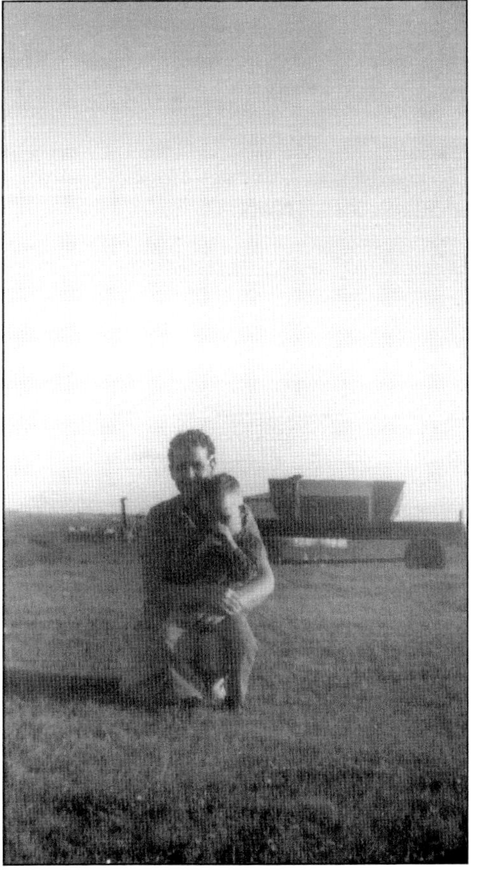

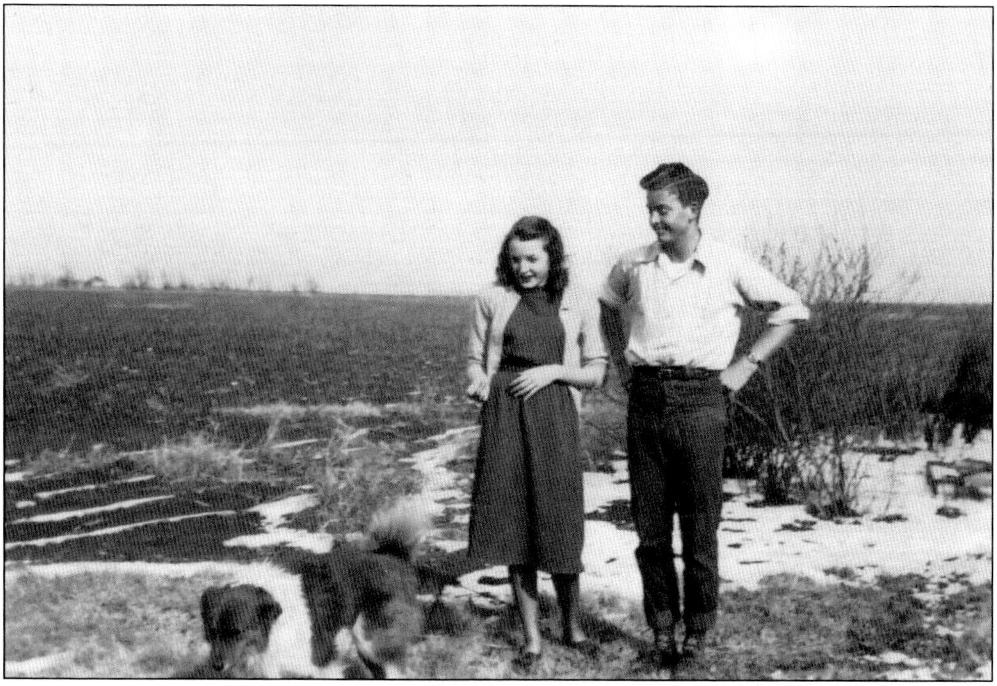

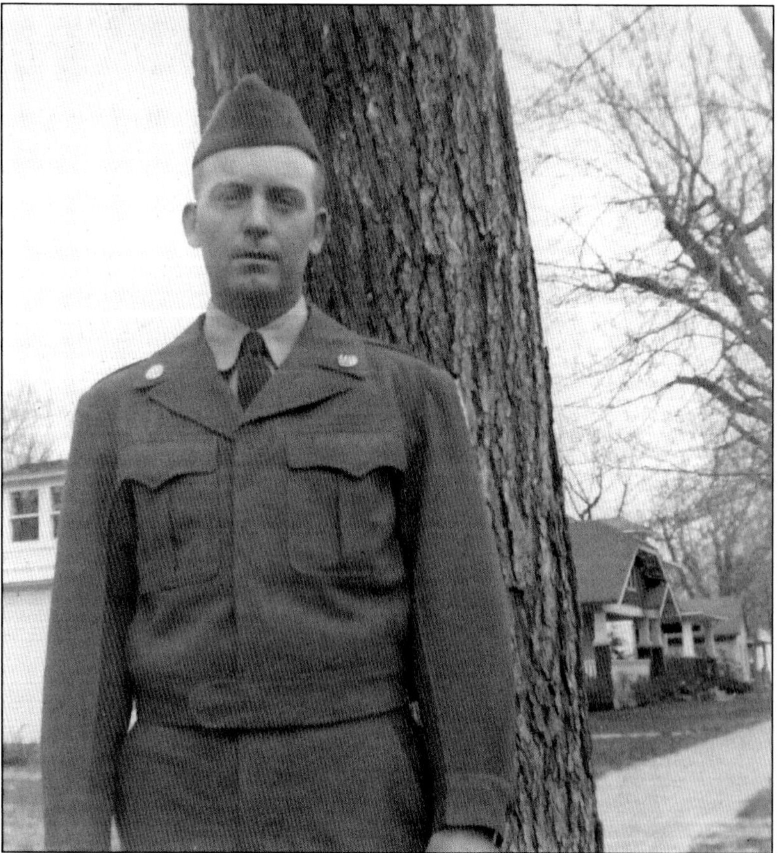

Above, Mark Poindexter's father and mother, Gene and Ida McIntire Poindexter, take their dog for a stroll on the 120 acres of the Poindexter farm after a snowfall in the 1950s. Gene was the only son of Tilmon Poindexter and a graduate of Rockwall High School, and he also served in the military during the Korean War. At left is Gene in full military uniform. (Both, courtesy of Mark Poindexter.)

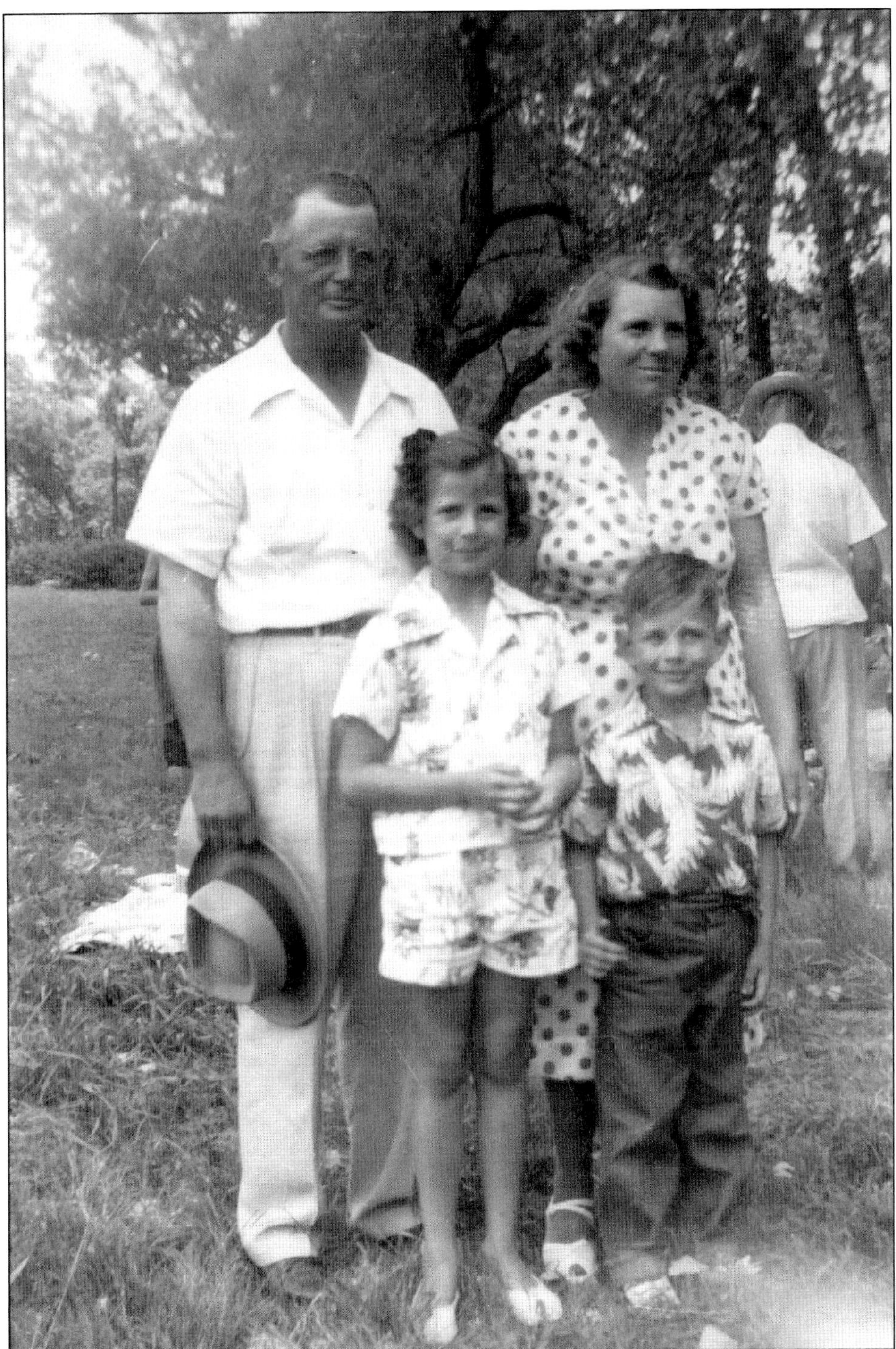

The Hunnicutts were another longtime family of Heath and close friends with the Poindexters. They lived out near where the gas station is currently located at the intersection of 550 and Laurence Drive. Pictured here are, from left to right, (first row) Mary and Randy; (second row) Opal and Eunice. (Courtesy of Mark Poindexter.)

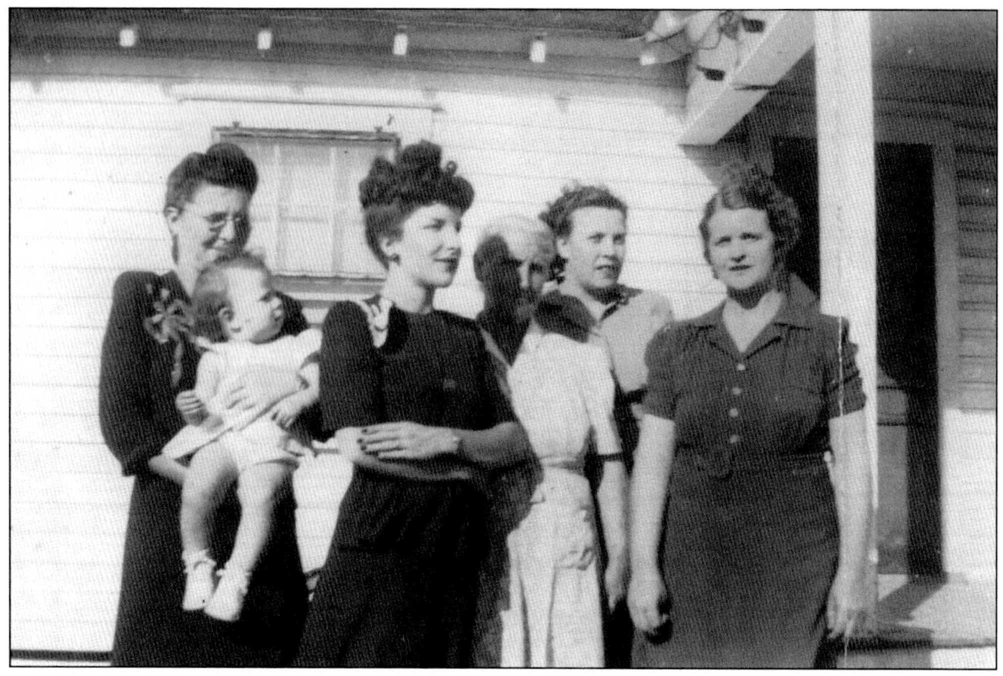

Pictured above are some of the women in the Hunnicutt and Poindexter families during a get-together in 1946 in front of the Poindexter farmhouse. Pictured are, from left to right, Melura Poindexter holding baby Mary Hunnicutt, Melura's daughter Bobbie Jean, India Hunnicutt, Leon Poindexter (back), and Vina Poindexter. Below is an image depicting the husbands and wives of the Hunnicutt and Poindexter families. From left to right are Tim and Vina Poindexter, Boice and Melura Poindexter, Orb and Leon Poindexter, and Opal and Eunice Hunnicutt. (Both, courtesy of Mark Poindexter.)

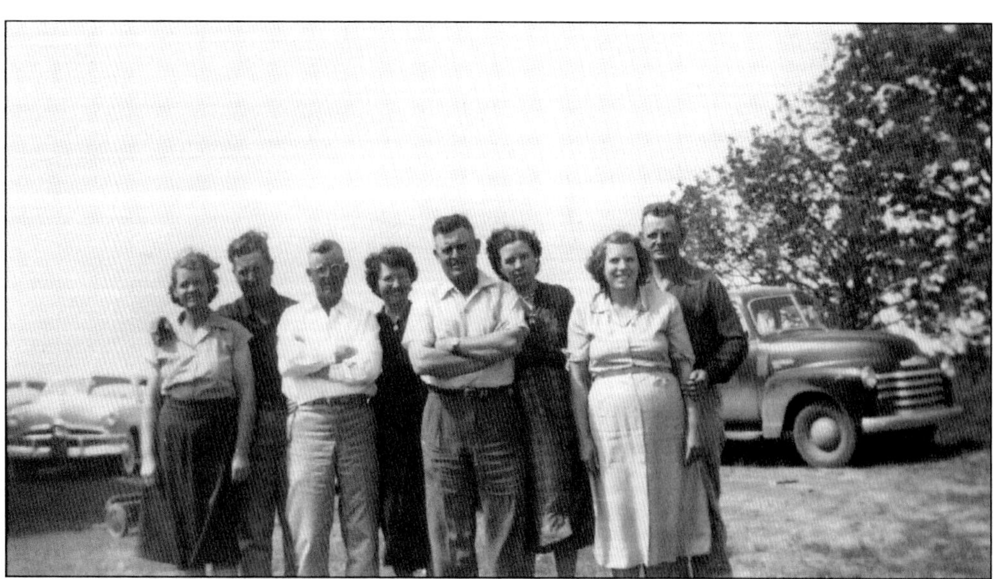

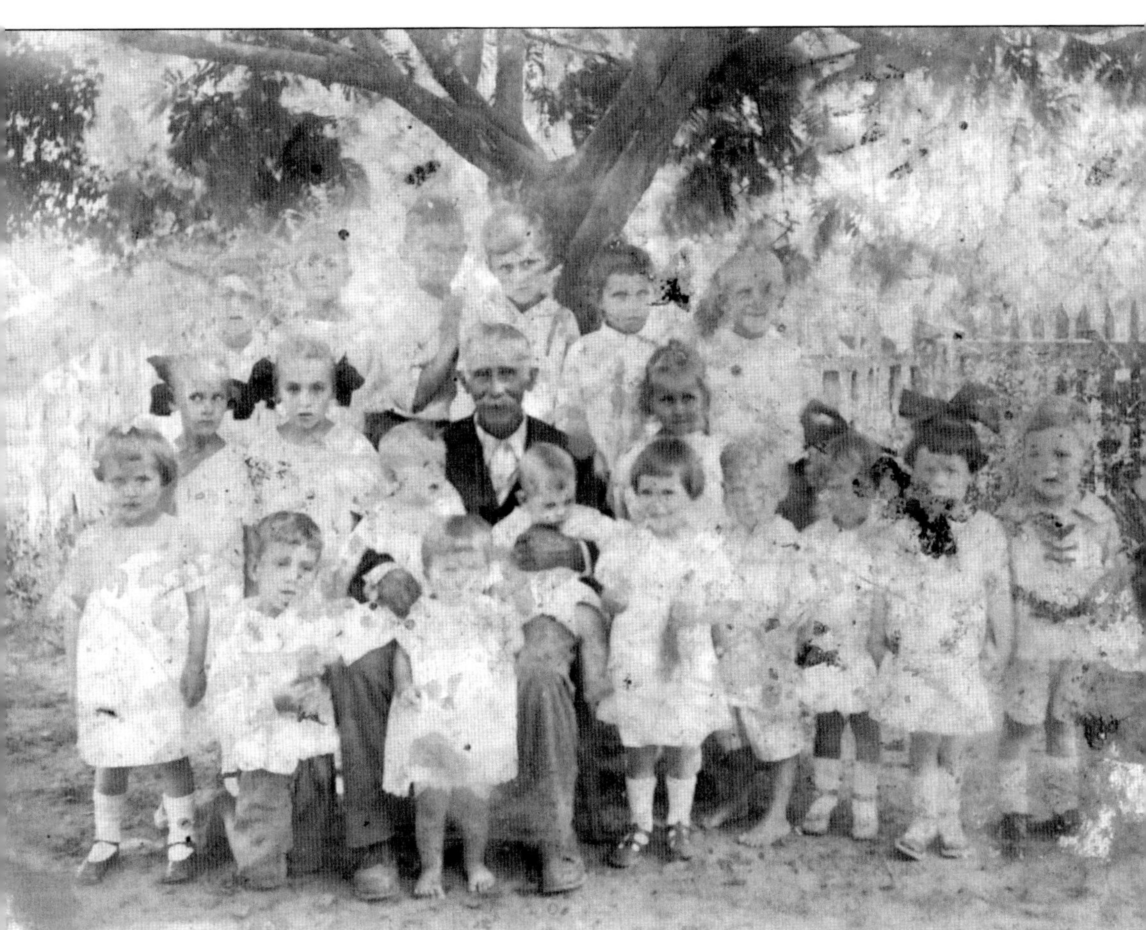

This incredibly rare image dated 1920 depicts many members of the Poindexter and Hunnicutt families as children, along with some kids belonging to other prominent families of Heath. Pictured here are, from left to right, (first row) Amy Poindexter, J.T. Lofland, Odas Hunnicutt, Gene Poindexter, Walter Poindexter, Gladys Lofland, Oral Hunnicutt, Helen Ryals, Alma Ryals and unidentified; (second row) Thelma Poindexter, Velma Poindexter, Grandpa T.E. Poindexter, and Clarice Poindexter; (third row) Dick Lofland, Beulah Hunnicutt, Opal Hunnicutt, Raymond Lofland, Noble Poindexter, and Lyle Poindexter. (Courtesy of Mark Poindexter.)

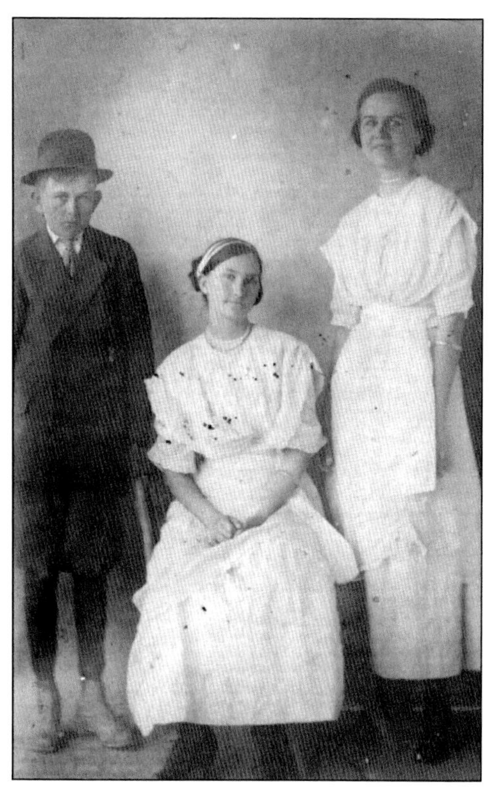

The Pinions were one of the later families to settle in Heath. The image at left depicts members of the Pinion family. From left to right are John Pinion, Clora Pinion, and Bertha Pinion Darr. Below, Ella Cora Pinion sits with her grandchildren on the Pinion farm in Heath. Cora came from Tennessee in a covered wagon and settled in Heath. From left to right are (first row) James Denton, Ella Pinion holding a doll, and Lloyde Marie Pinion; (second row) Charlotte Pinion and John Denton. (Both, courtesy of Charlotte Pinion Krider.)

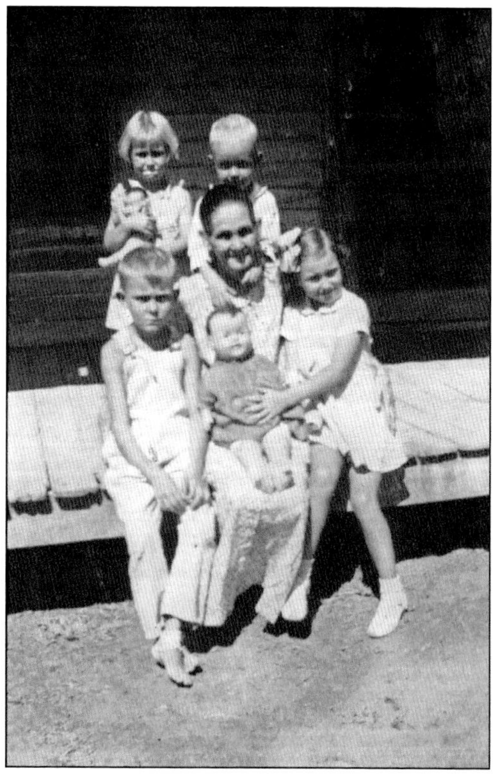

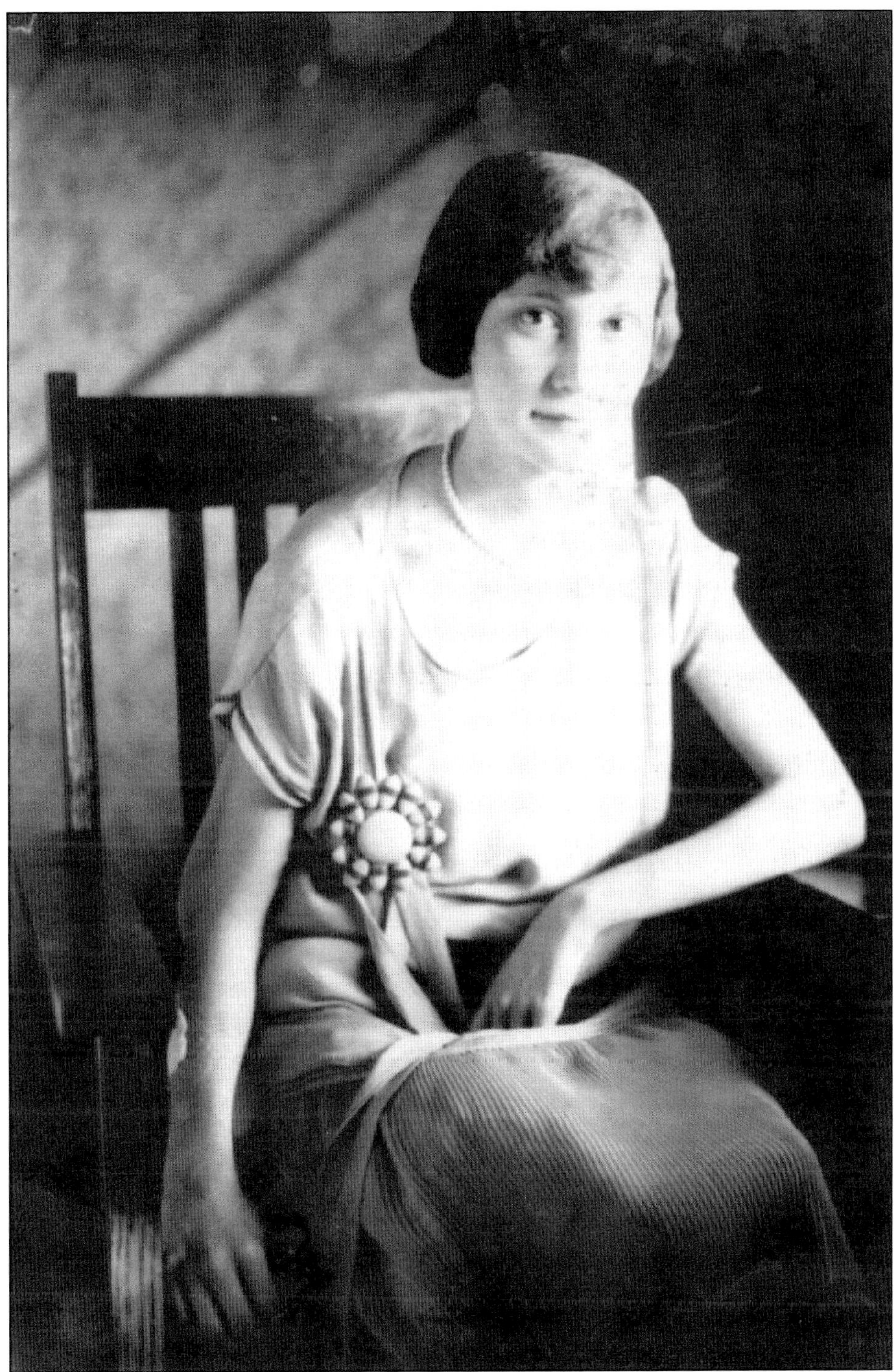

Verna Pinion lived all her life in Heath. She was born July 9, 1909, to Thomas J. Pinion and Ella Cora Pinion. She married Lonnie Lee Denton on December 19, 1926, in Terrell, Texas, and was a lifetime member of Heath Baptist Church. She died on March 30, 2004. (Courtesy of Charlotte Pinion Krider.)

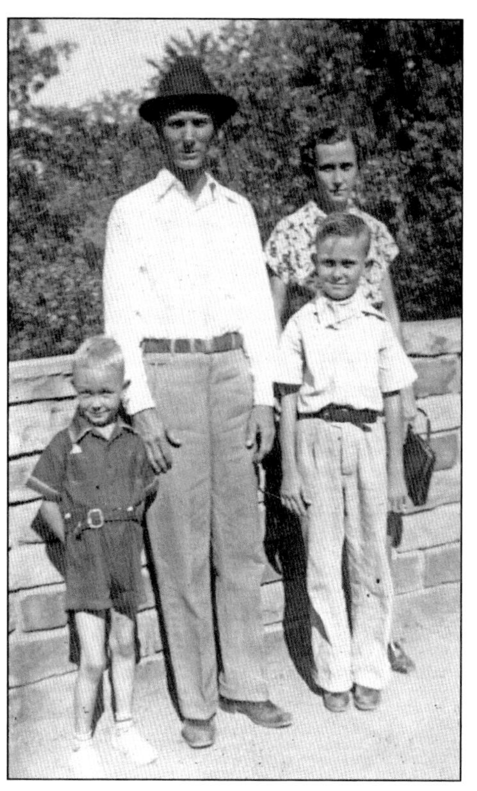

At left are Lonnie and Verna (Pinion) Denton and their sons John Austin and James Lonnie on a trip to the Dallas Zoo. They lived near the First Baptist Church of Heath and had a formal croquet court installed in their front yard, which they generously allowed folks from the community to come play. Lonnie is the son of John M. Denton and Martha Ellen "Ella" Denton. His siblings are Edith M. Denton Cook and William Mack Denton. Lonnie also had a brother who died at birth on July 13, 1912. (Courtesy of Patsy Stodghill.)

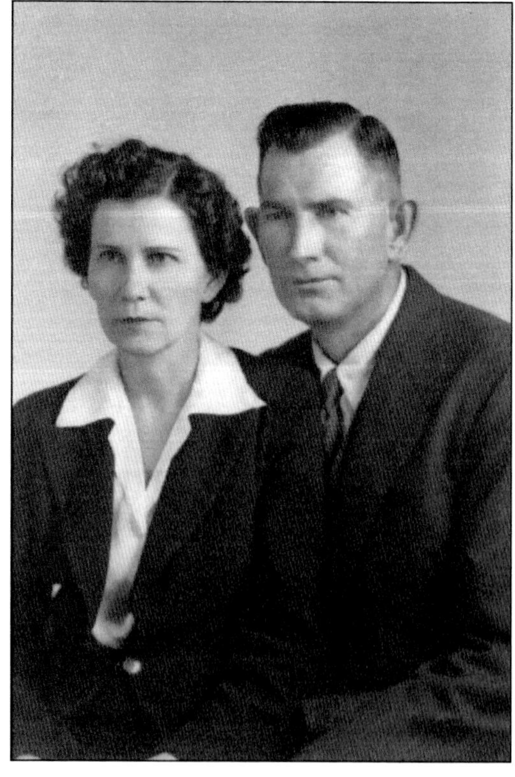

Pictured are Ray and Roxie Pinion Lewis. Ray was born in 1897 and died in 1974. Roxie was born in 1902 and died in 1985. They were married on May 11, 1920. They were honored at their home in Heath on their 50th anniversary. (Courtesy of Charlotte Pinion Krider.)

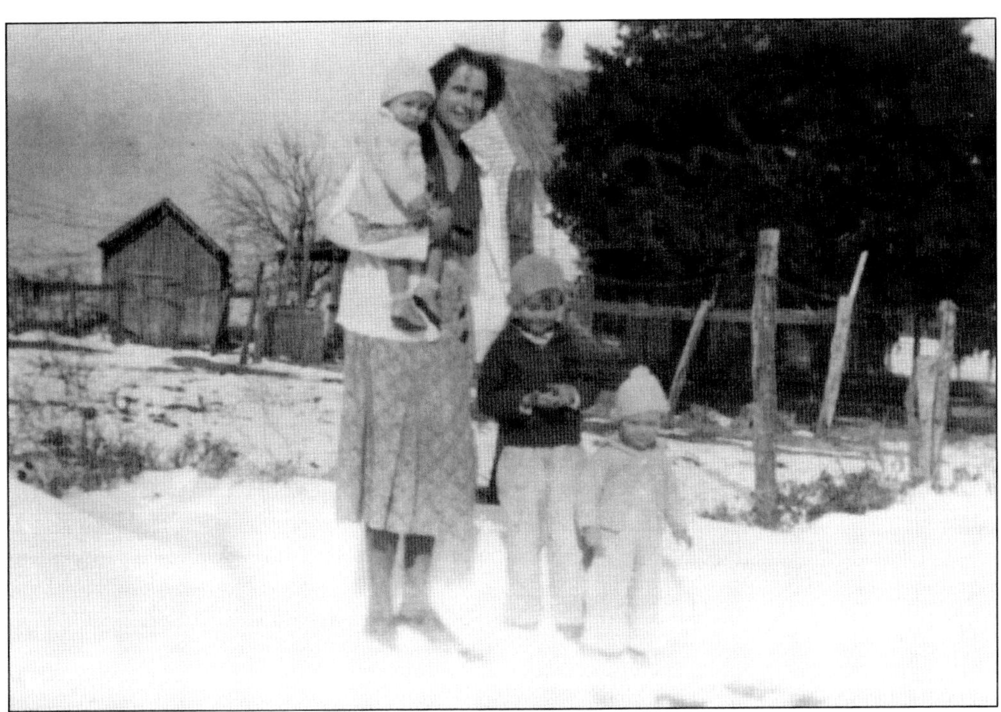

Luke and Ruby Eudy Pinion were married on November 20, 1926, when he was 19 and she was 16. They had one child, Charlotte. Shown above in this image dated sometime in the 1930s is Ruby holding daughter Charlotte with James and John Denton at the Pinion farm in the snow. The image at right, dated in the 1940s, shows Luke and daughter Charlotte sitting on the hood of his car at their home in Heath. Luke died on March 16, 1987, and Ruby died on November 12, 1975. They are both buried in the Heath Cemetery. (Both, courtesy of Charlotte Pinion Krider.)

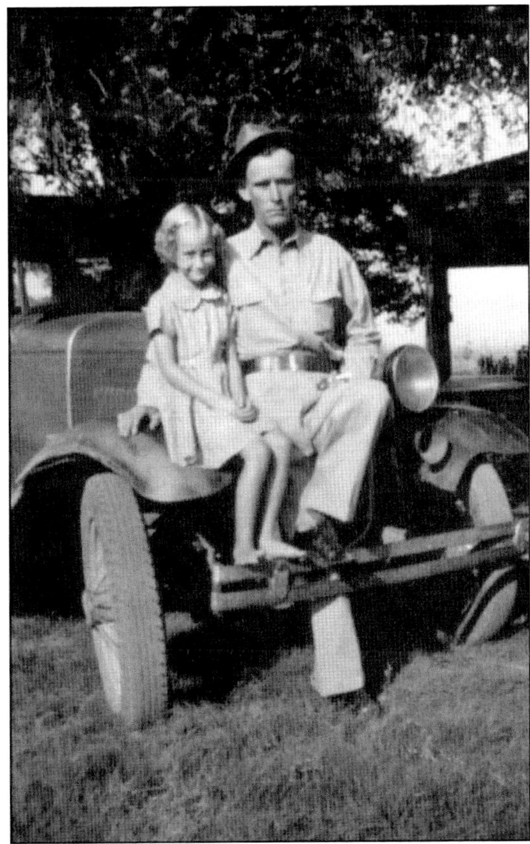

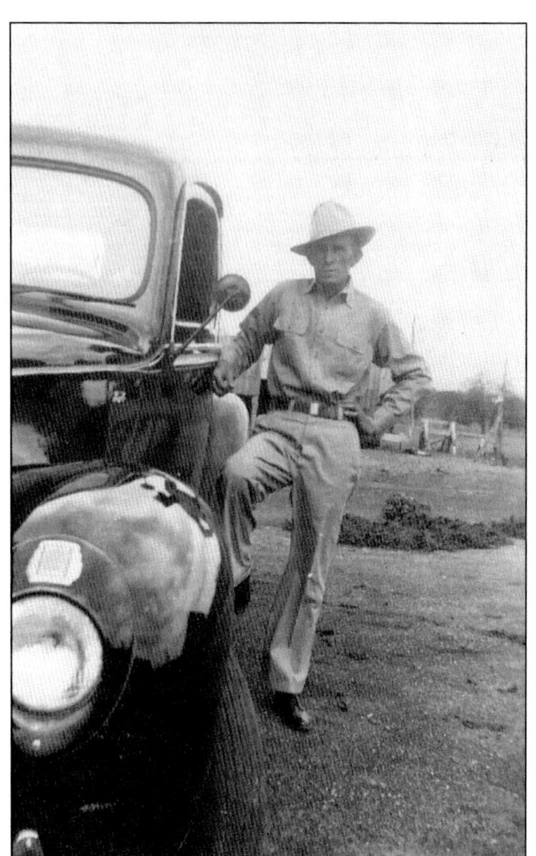

At left, John Pinion stands next to his car on the Pinion farm. John had a large farm in Heath and was one of the more successful farmers in the area. In the 1940s, he owned more acreage than almost anybody else in Heath and mainly raised cotton. He was married to Elizabeth Pinion, the daughter of Minnie and Charlie Cullins. Below is the Pinion family. From left to right are (first row) B.J. Darr, Bertha Pinion Darr, Verna Pinion Denton, and Ruby Pinion; (second row) Roxie Pinion Lewis, Ray Lewis, Elizabeth Pinion, John Pinion, Lonnie Denton, Luke Pinion, and Clora Pinion. (Both, courtesy of Charlotte Pinion Krider.)

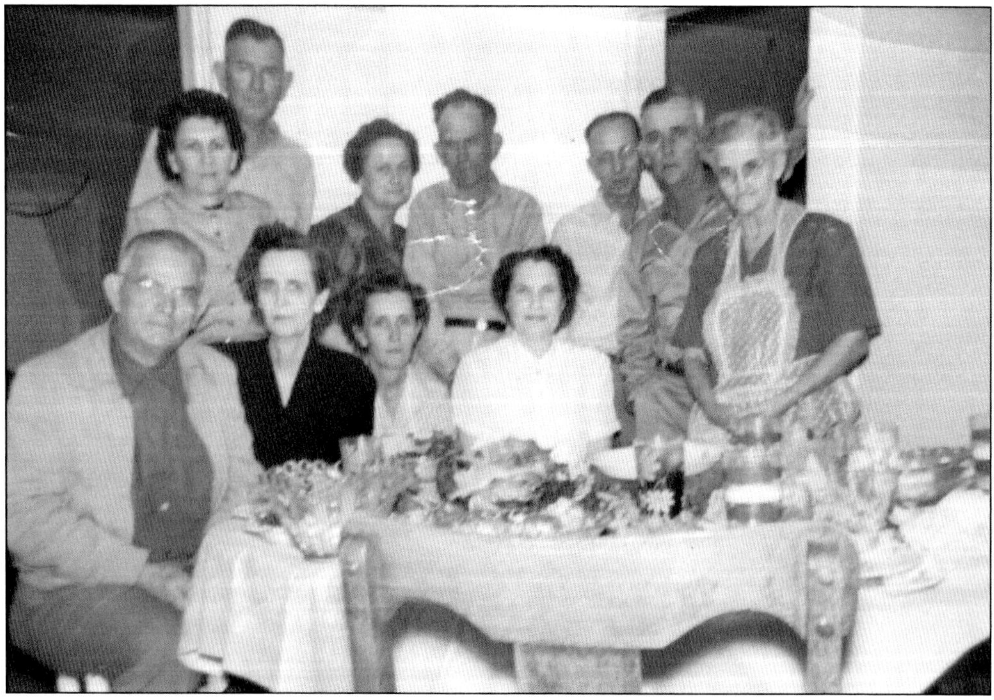

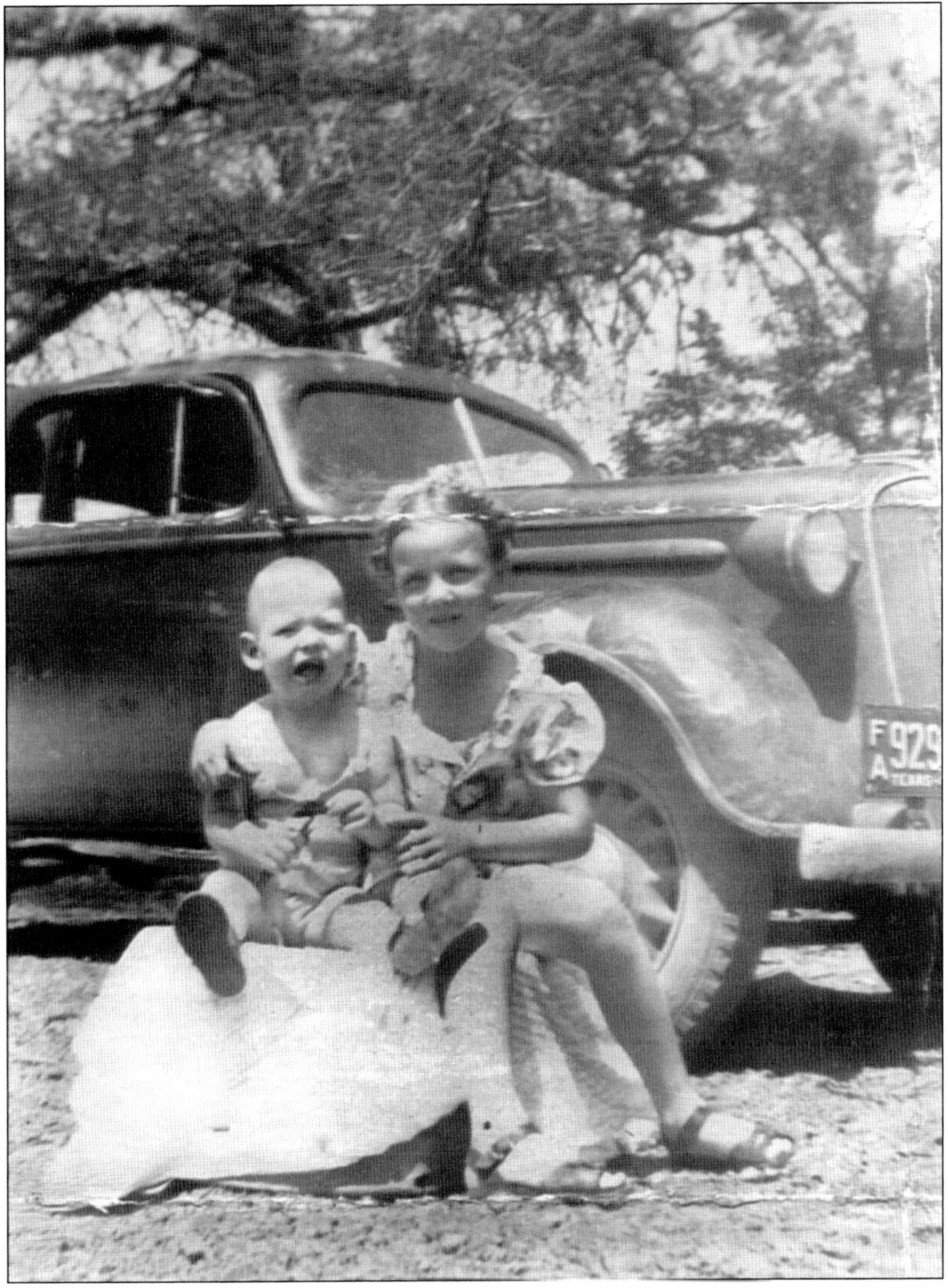

The Seabolts were much later settlers to the Heath area. Pictured here are Ronnie and Sandra Seabolt, the children of Eldon and Hazel Seabolt, in 1946. (Courtesy of Sandra Boyd.)

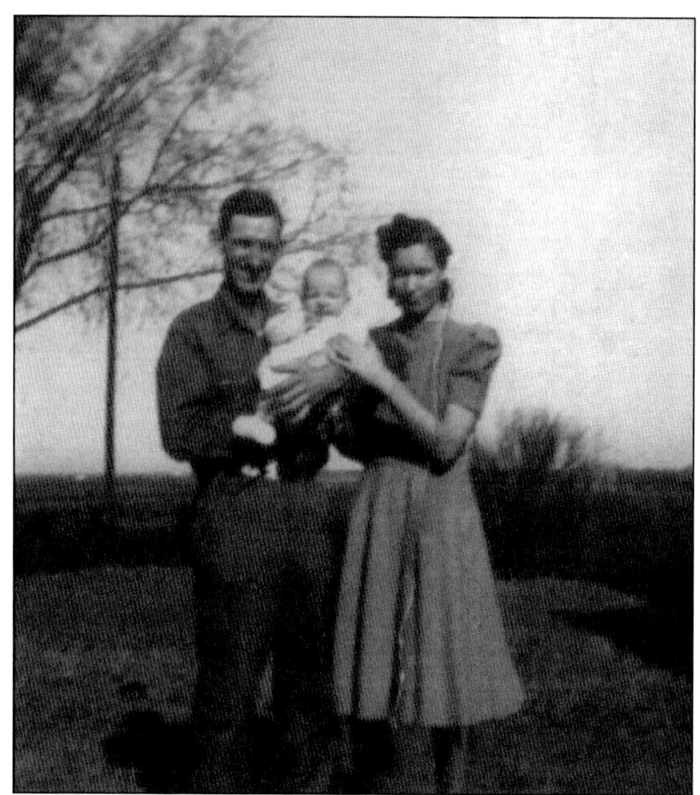

At left are Claudia and Herman Jones. Claudia was born on July 1, 1895, and died on May 2, 1992. She was the daughter of T.D. Lofland and Martha Lou Crawly Lofland. Claudia had a college degree and often was a substitute teacher at the Heath School. Her mother believed her children should be educated and provided the opportunity for them to go to college. Her brothers were James Thomas and Charles Joseph Lofland. Below, Wilkie Boyd, son of Jeff and Bonnie Lee Boyd, stands near their home located on Jeff Boyd Circle in 1956. (Both, courtesy of Sandra Boyd.)

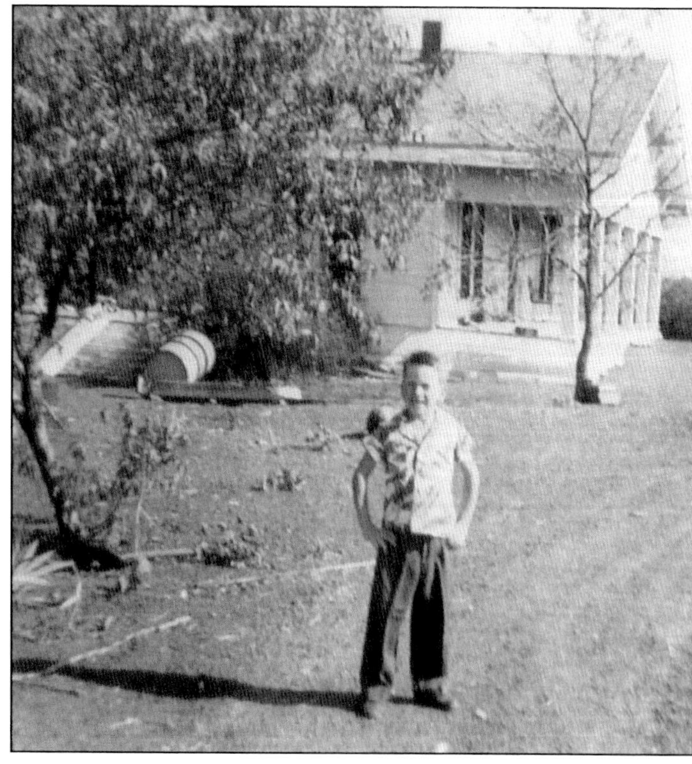

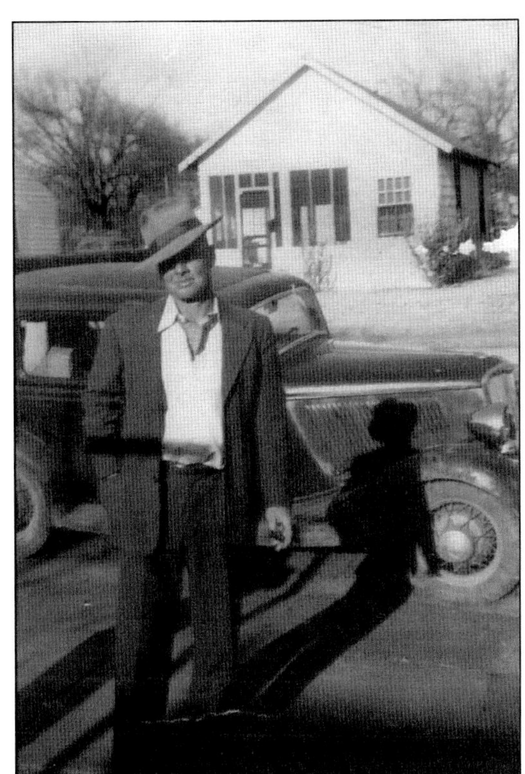

Jeff Boyd (right) owned interesting, often fast, cars. Boyd and his car are marked in the Maon Seabolt drawing of Heath made in 1930. Pictured below, Bonnie Lee Boyd, Jeff's wife, was talented at sewing and machine embroidering. (Both, courtesy of Sandra Boyd.)

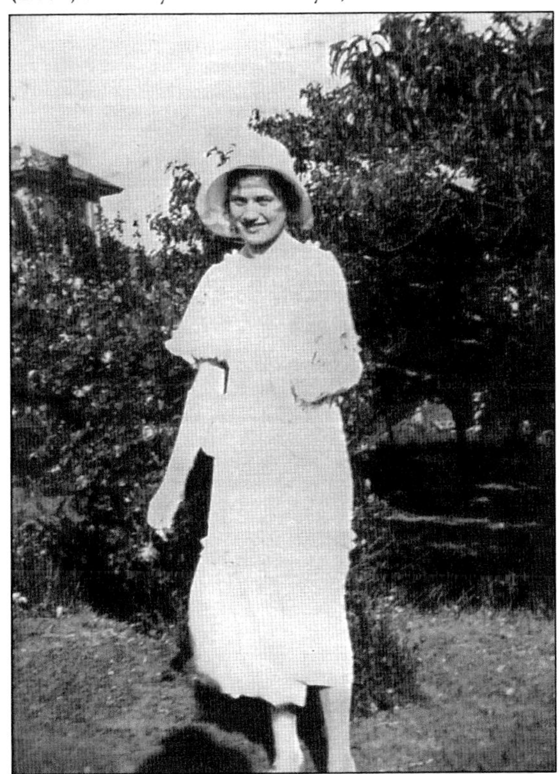

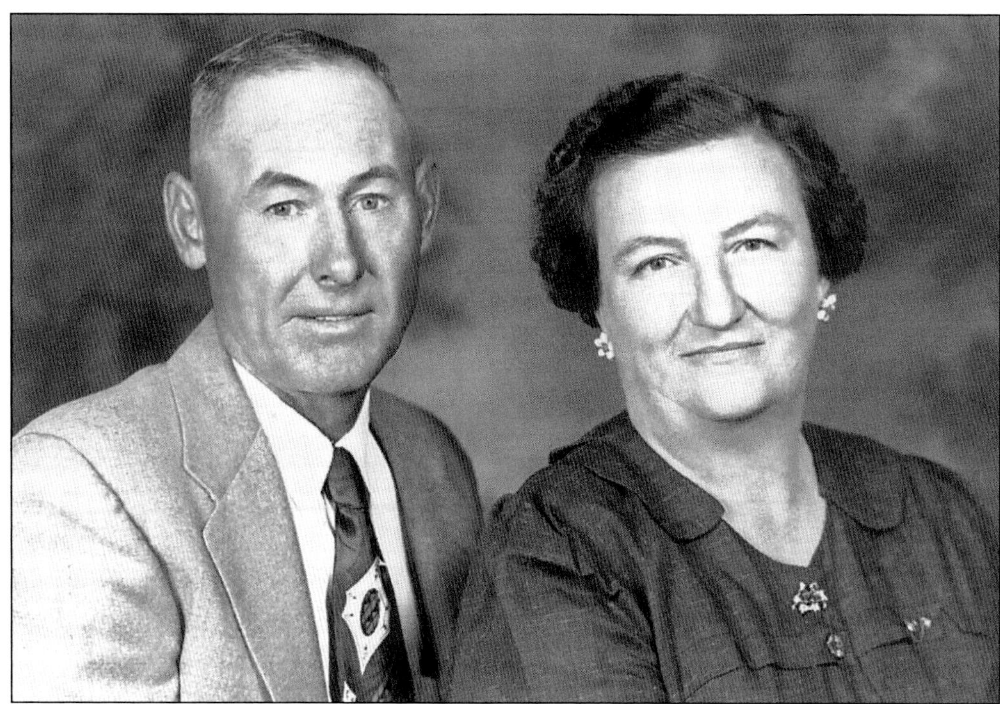

Clarence and Gladys Smirl, pictured above around 1950, had six children, all of whom were born in the three-room house on what is now Smirl Drive. Clarence hunted mink during the winter and would stretch and sell their hides to help keep the family farm afloat. He continued farming until his death in 1968. Gladys passed away in 2000. Pictured below are members of the Smirl family of Heath; from left to right are patriarch Clarence Smirl, matriarch Gladys Smirl, baby Jeffrey Jones, Neta Smirl Jones, Wayne Jones, Theresa Smirl Lindsey, baby Denise Lindsey, Dennis Lindsey, Carolyn Smirl, Claudetta Smirl, Huey Smirl, Clarice Smirl Isbell, and Joe Frank Isbell. (Above, courtesy of Clarice Isbell; below, courtesy of the Smirl family.)

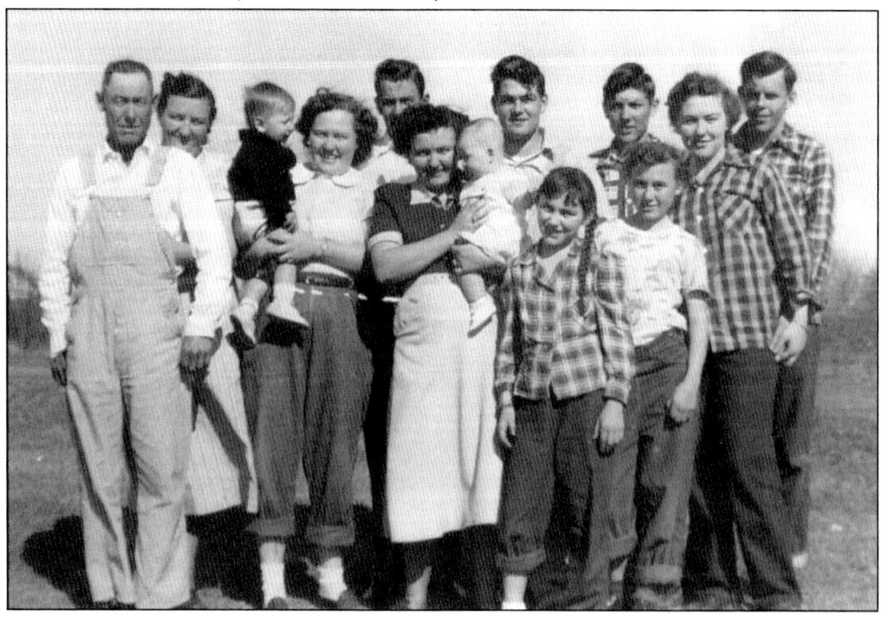

Three

Faces and Activities of Heath

Dig deep into the history of one of the longtime families of Heath, and one is sure to find that each of them connects to one another in some form or fashion, either through marriage, the proximity of their homes, or having children who went to school together in the old two-story Heath School. From the early to mid-1900s, Heath very much painted the picture of a growing community with a small-town vibe, where everyone knew their neighbors quite well and family gatherings were commonplace. Many children attended the Heath School together and were also a part of several clubs together. Today, alumni of the old Heath School hold an annual reunion in the Heath City Hall community room and reminisce about bygone days of family gatherings, church socials, and those fun school field trips across the country.

A closer look into several of Heath's oldest families reveals much about what life was like for those who grew up in Heath around this time period, how tight-knit the families of Heath were (and in many ways still are) in those years, and all the different types of activities found in the community.

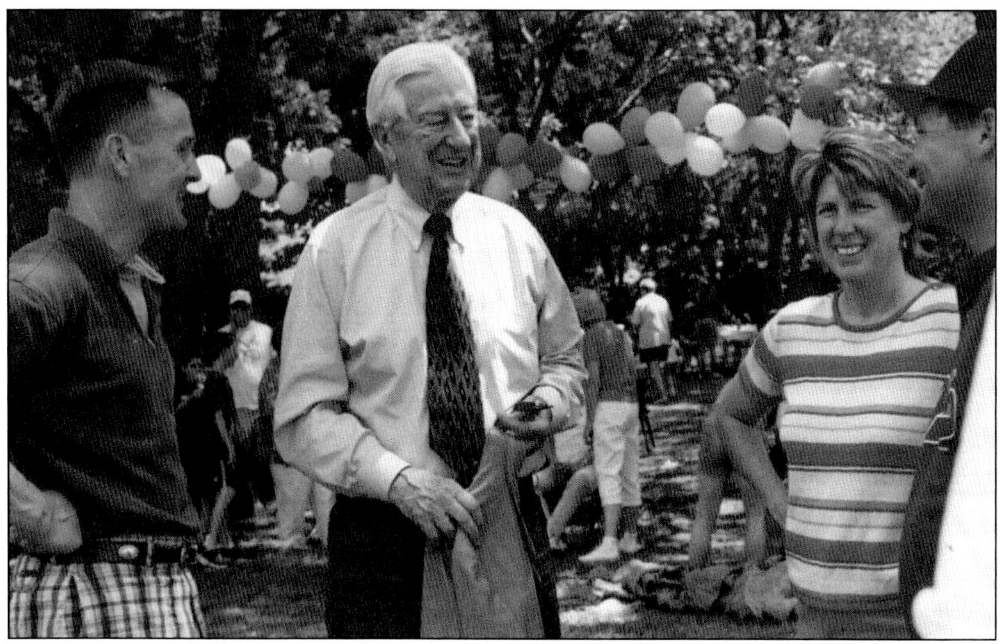

Congressman Ralph M. Hall was born in Fate, Texas, and has represented Rockwall County at the local, state, and national levels of government. On December 25, 2012, Congressman Hall became the oldest member serving in the US House of Representatives in recorded history. In this image, Congressman Hall makes a special appearance during a First United Methodist Church of Heath Fourth of July party at the home of the Conder family. Surrounding Hall are, from left to right, longtime church members Dennis Conder, who also served as the chairman of the Heath Planning and Zoning Commission; his wife, Catharine Conder; and Brett Thames. (Courtesy of the First United Methodist Church of Heath.)

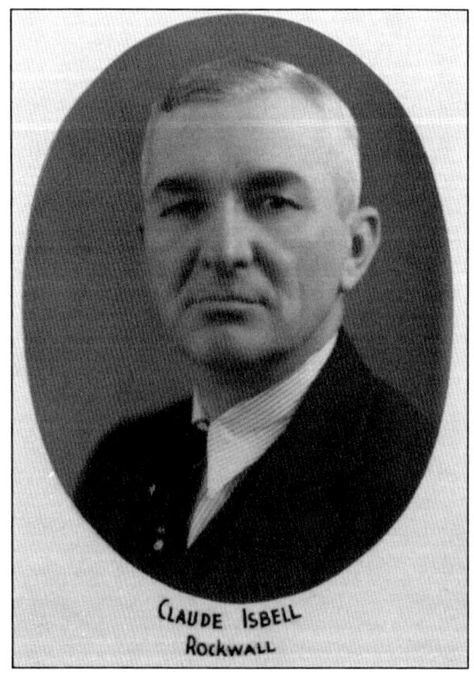

Claude Isbell (raised by his grandmother, Mary Emma Isbell, who lived in Heath) was Rockwall County's first state senator and its only secretary of state to date. In fact, Claude was the first in many areas of Rockwall County politics; he was also the first president pro tempore of the state senate and the first "Governor for a Day" from Rockwall County, an unusual honor that was awarded to him at the end of his very first term in office. (Courtesy of the Stodghill family.)

Lifelong Heath resident James Thomas "Jim" Lofland served as deputy sheriff and tax assessor-collector of Rockwall County for 26 years. Here, Lofland sits at his office desk in the Rockwall courthouse in 1938. He also worked as a bookkeeper at Heath Gin and in banks in Heath and Rockwall and was an active member of the Heath Masonic Lodge for over 50 years. (Courtesy of the Rockwall County Historical Foundation.)

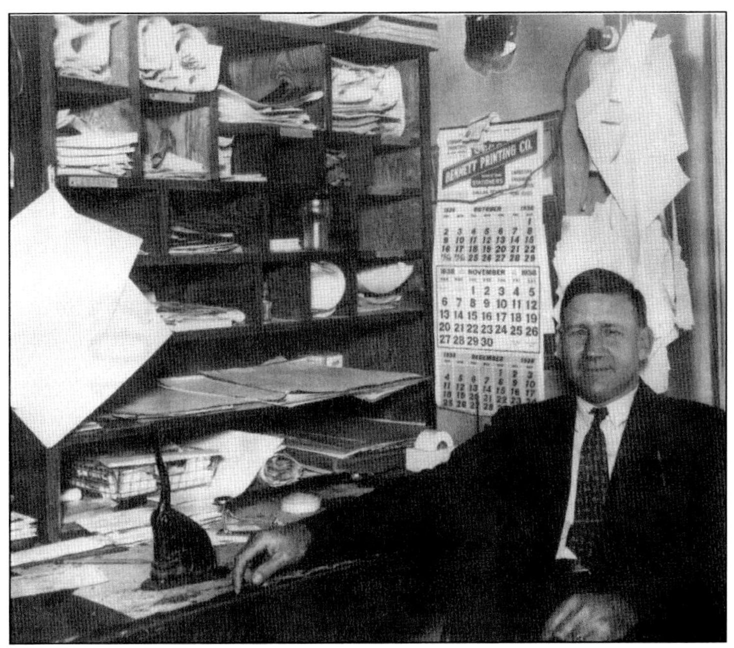

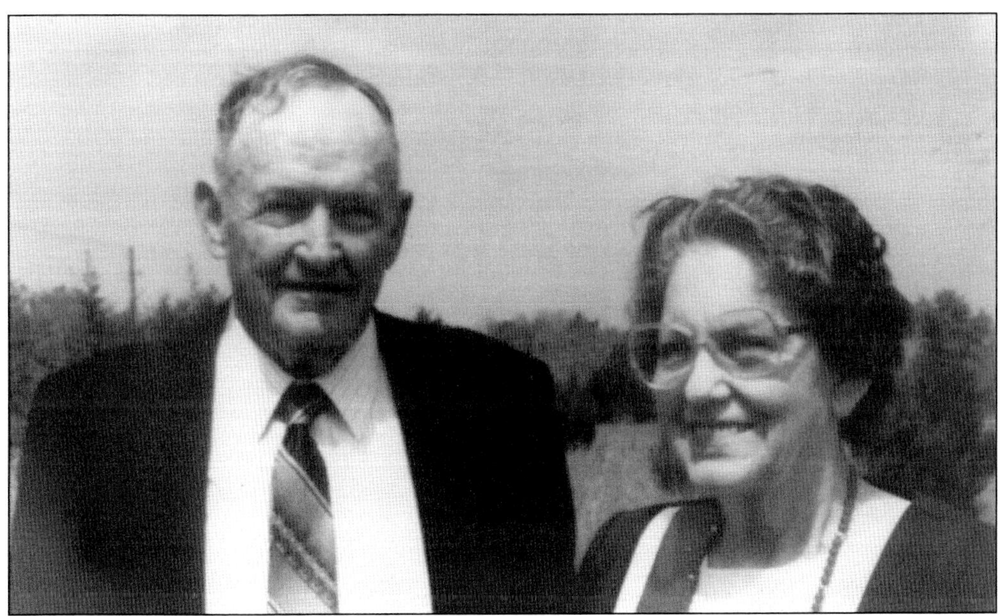

James "Alvis" Nash, pictured above with his wife, Lois, was elected the first mayor of Heath after its incorporation in 1959. A lifelong resident of Heath, Nash served as its mayor from 1959 to 1970, overseeing tremendous growth during his tenure. Heath's population soared from 149 residents at the time Nash was first elected mayor to 520 residents and 192 homes when he stepped down from city government. He was one of six students to graduate from Heath High School in 1929 and served in World War II with the US Navy. (Courtesy of Joyce Nash.)

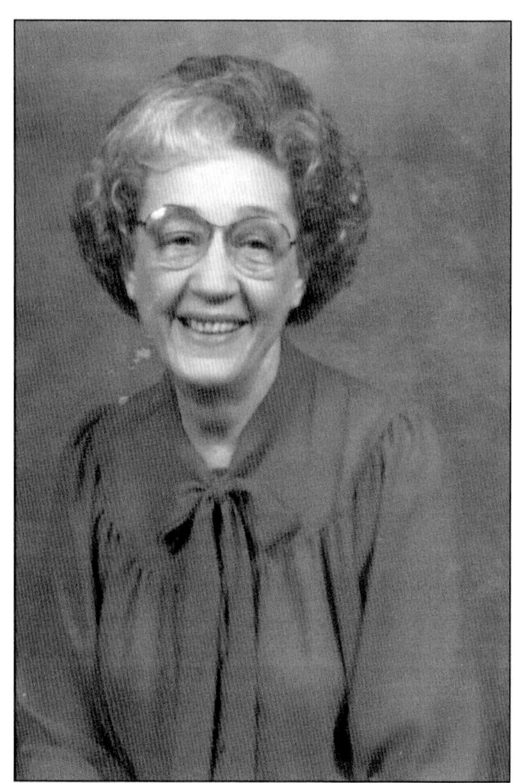

Aileen Terry (left) was a well-known and beloved lady throughout the community of Heath. She served Heath in many capacities, including as city secretary for many years, and was very involved with the Baptist Church. She and her husband, Waymond, built and ran a grocery store in Heath for a time, located at the intersection of FM 740 and what is now Laurence Drive. In the image below, Congressman Ralph M. Hall (left), Terry (center), and Mayor Douglas E. Hall (right) cut the ribbon at the Heath City Hall open house on November 7, 1983. (Left, courtesy of Gale Terry; below, courtesy of Heath City Hall.)

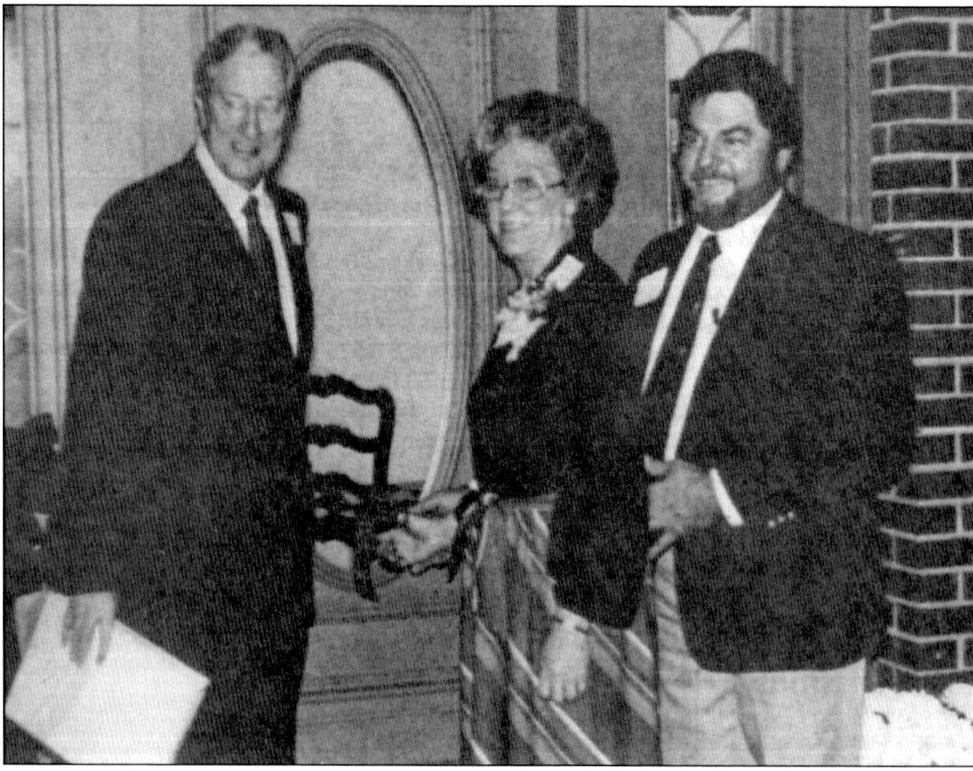

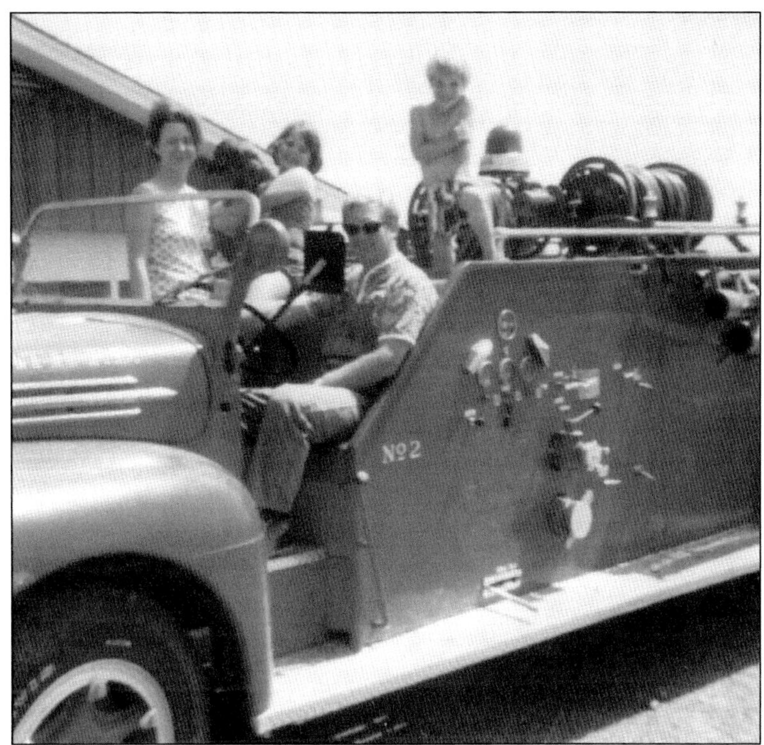

Bill Way became the first fire chief of Heath's volunteer fire department, which was created in 1971. In the image at right, Way mans the steering wheel of the first fire truck, along with his wife, Jerry (far left), daughter Christy, and son Sam. The 500-gallon pumper cost roughly $2,200. Money was raised to purchase the truck by selling raffle tickets and holding suppers and bingo games at the Heath Community Center. (Courtesy of Bill Way.)

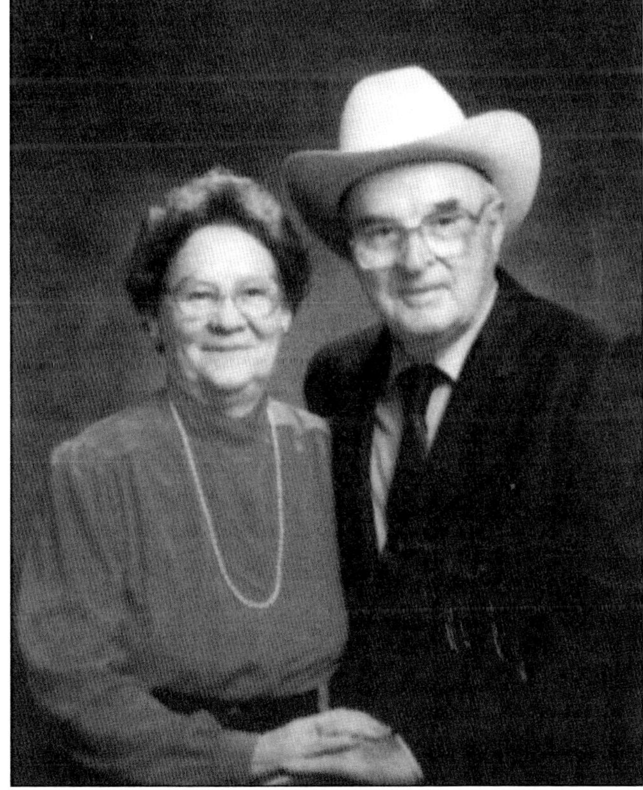

John "J.W." Cullins and his wife, Edna, grew crops and raised cattle on their farm east of Heath. J.W. served as a policeman in Rockwall and later as chief of police in Heath. He was known by many to be a very kind and honest man and always had remarkable common sense and judgement. He often referred to himself as a "peace officer," whose main duty was to keep the peace in the town. (Courtesy of Ila Cullins.)

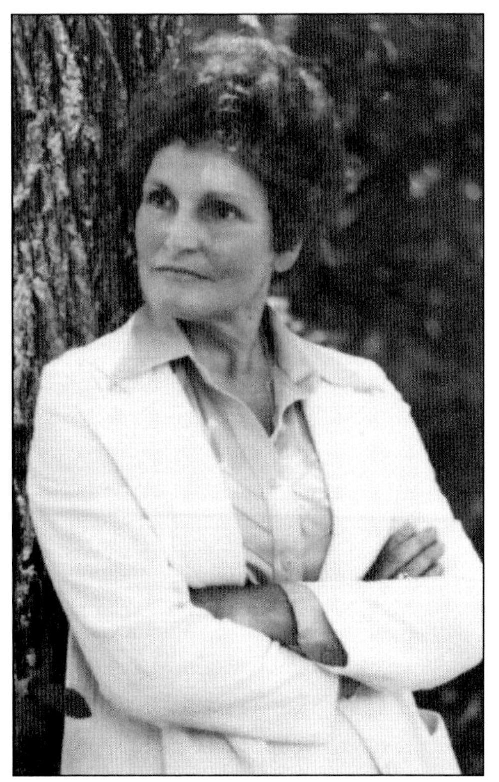

Barbara Venton Montgomery was elected as municipal judge of Heath in 1978 and served in that capacity until 1988. She worked closely with Heath police chief J.W. Cullins and in her book *J.W. and Me* asserts that he taught her that "common sense was more important than a law degree." She has also served as the Rockwall County Democratic chairman on the State Democratic Executive Committee and was a candidate for the US House of Representatives in 1978. (Courtesy of Barbara Montgomery.)

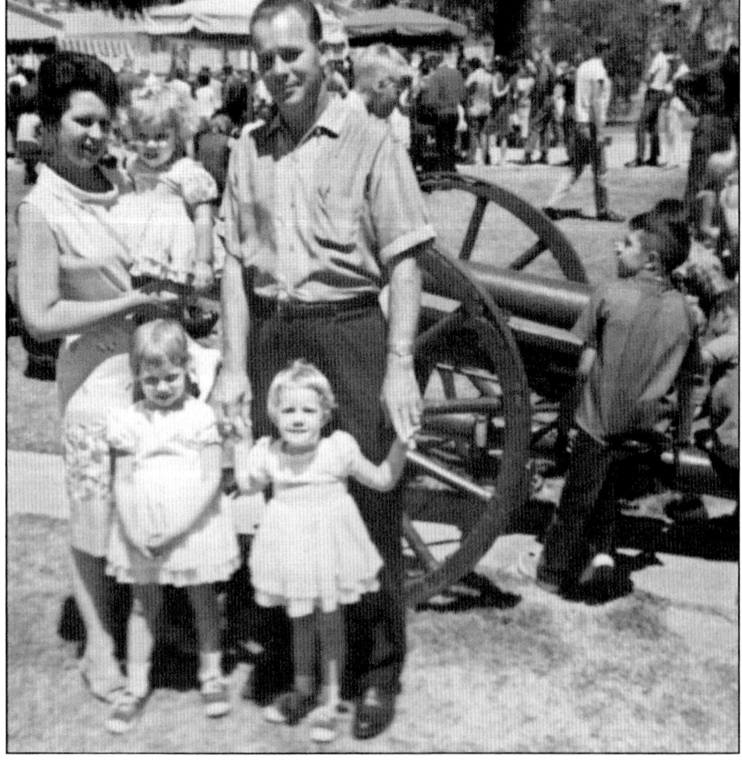

Douglas, son of J.W. and Edna Cullins, served as a constable for 17 years in Heath. He married Ila Phares of Garland, and the couple had three daughters: Danna, Saundra, and Terri. The family is pictured at right. Douglas and John Clem also owned a furniture store in Rockwall for a time. (Courtesy of Ila Cullins.)

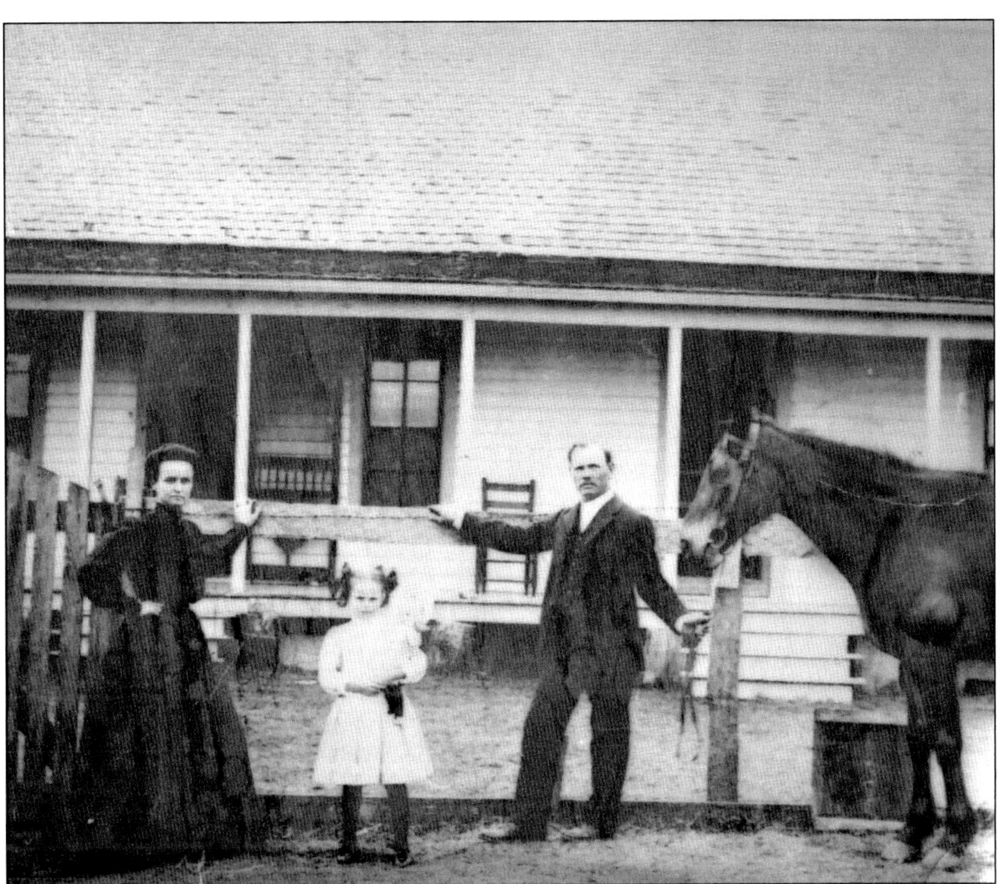

The following images concentrate on the activities and organizations related to Heath's citizens, beginning around the 1900s, through World War I, the Great Depression, World War II and its aftermath, and the prosperity of the 1950s. This photograph, dated in the early 1900s, shows Minnie and Charlie Cullins with their daughter Elizabeth at their home in Heath. Minnie was born in 1878 and died in 1950. Charlie was born in 1869 and died in 1933. Their daughter Elizabeth was born March 11, 1902. She married John Pinion and was the major pianist, later organist, for the First Baptist Church of Heath. Elizabeth died October 12, 1972, in Terrell, Texas. Ruby and Luke Pinion and their daughter Charlotte later lived in the house pictured. (Courtesy of Charlotte Pinion Krider.)

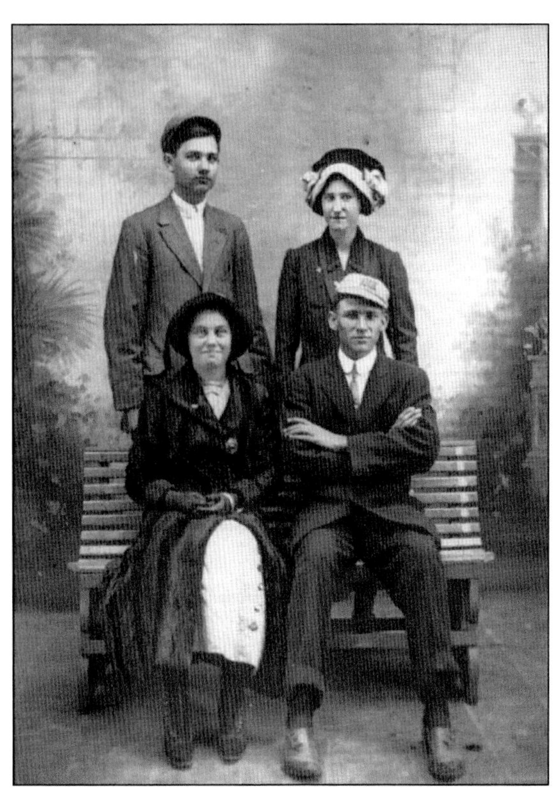

The photograph at left was taken at the Dallas State Fair of Texas around 1919. From left to right are (sitting) Fay Isbell and Jim Lofland; (standing) Clayton Hall and Claudia Lofland. Below is the Heath High School basketball team, referred to as the Heath High School Basketball Bunch. (Left, courtesy of Fay Lofland; below, courtesy of Jerry Deaton.)

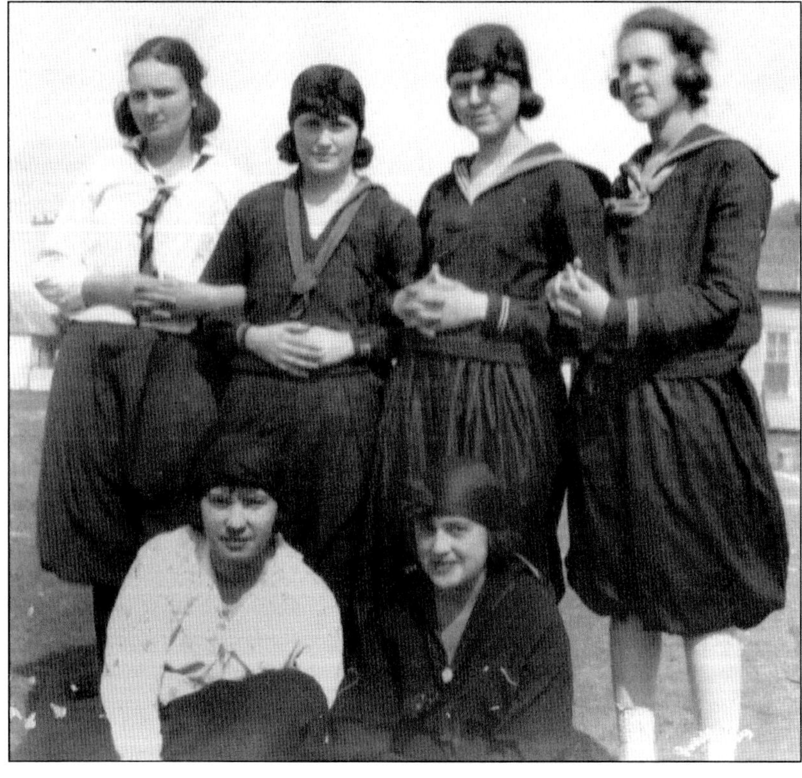

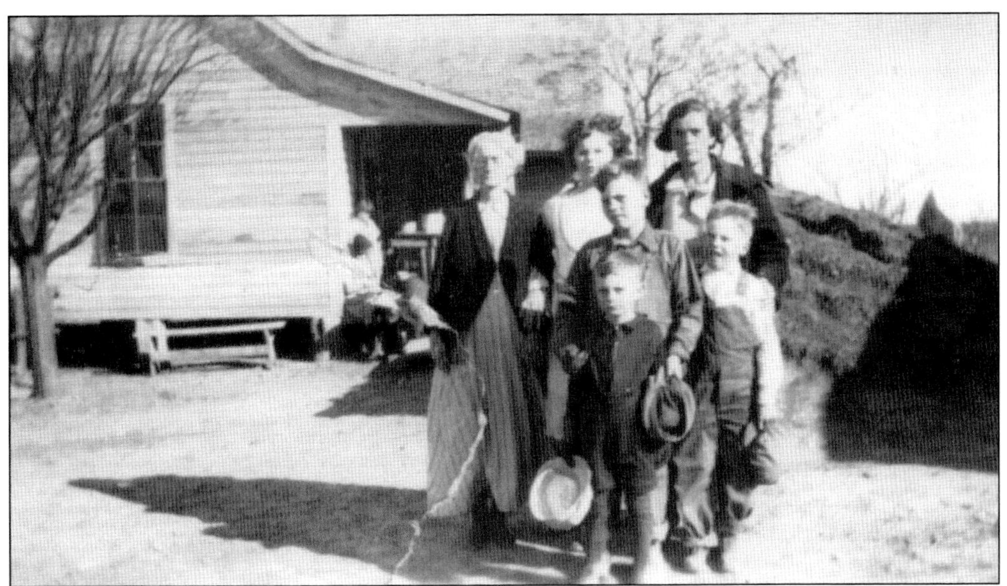

Pictured above are members of the Lemley family outside their home. Among those shown are Nancy Elizabeth Stiles Lemley, Agnes Marie Lemley, William Newman Lemley, and George Lirah Lemley. (Courtesy of Reba Jett.)

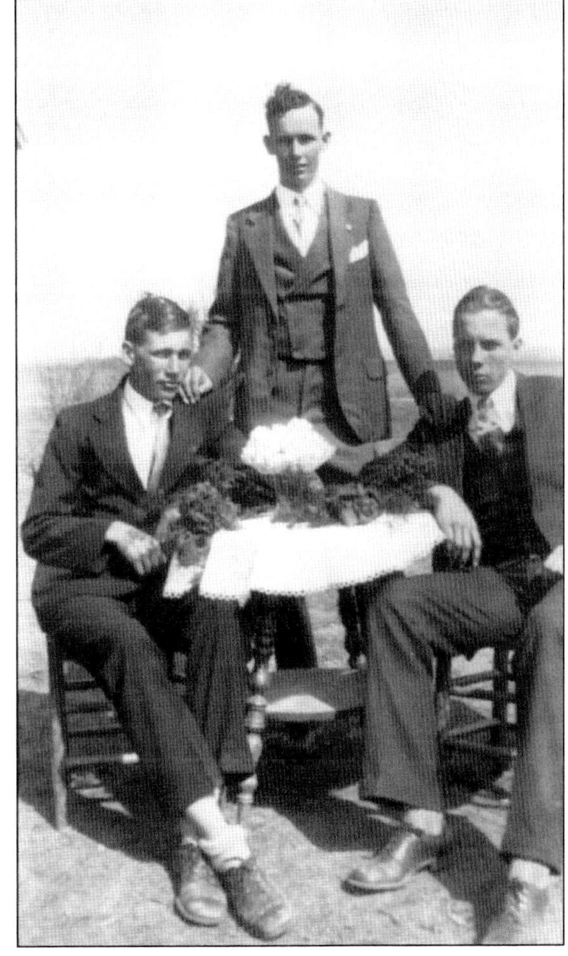

From left to right, Jake Hall, Alvis Nash, and Curtis Hall celebrate at Nash's birthday party. Jake, Curtis, and Alvis were first cousins. Many people during this time period moved furniture outside and used quilts as backdrops to take photograph. (Courtesy of Patsy Stodghill.)

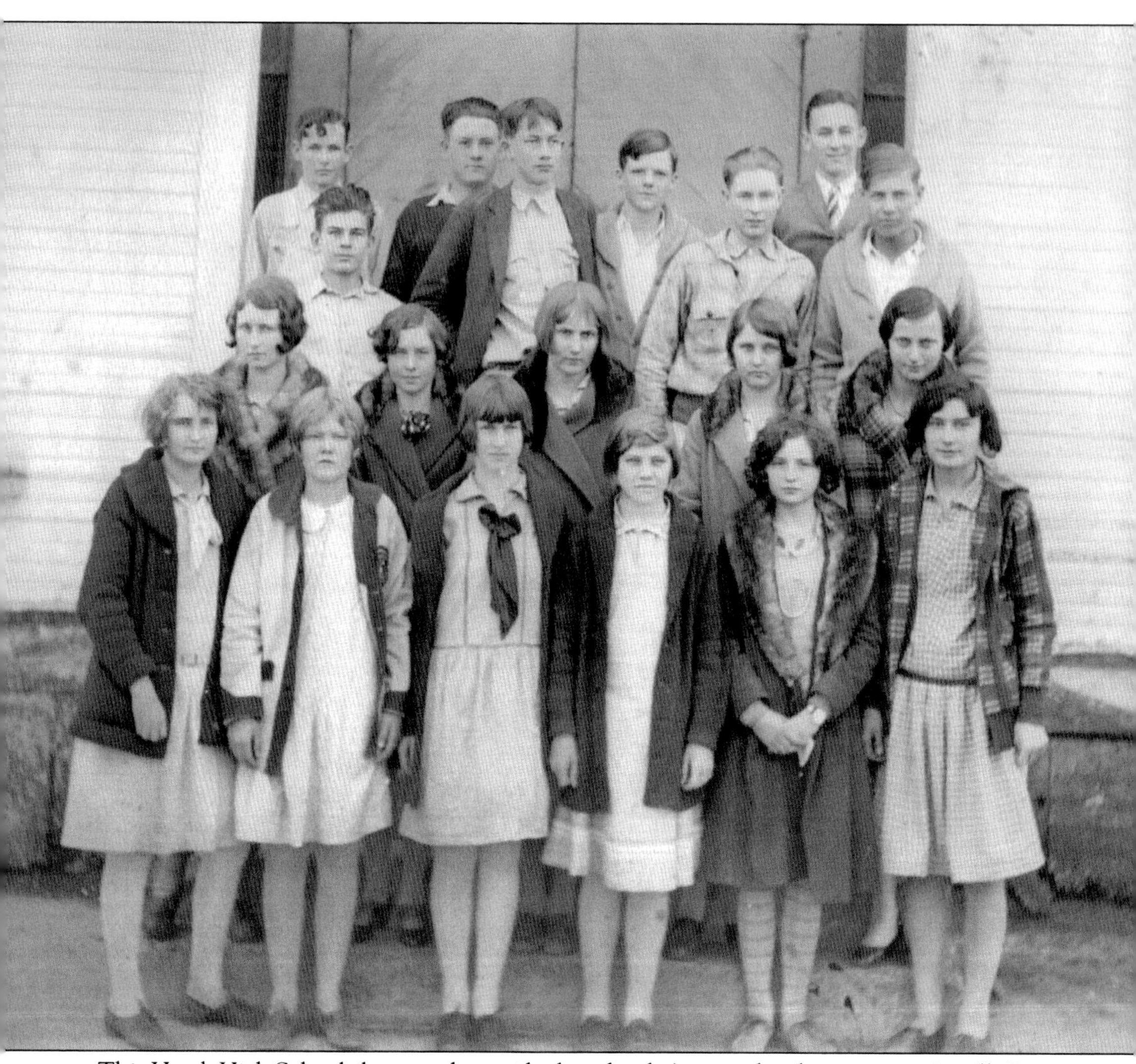

This Heath High School class stands outside the school. Among the classmates are Lucille Bryan, Edith Denton, Emma Lofland, Addie Fay Vaughn, Maxine Vinson, Betty Roach, Ruby Piper, Fay Copeland, Robert Daniels, Curtis Hall, Alvis Nash, and Ray Sellers. (Courtesy of Fay Lofland.)

Good friends Inez Jones (left) and Opal Lindsey (right) sit on grain sacks in the backyard of a local resident in 1927. Later, Inez became Inez Massey, whose daughter was Runell Massey. Opal became Opal Kennerly, and her daughter was Anna Fern Kennerly. In the image below, Patsy Ann Hall (left) plays with Anna Fred Gardenhire (right) amid large piles of wood at the back of the house on the Lofland farm in Heath. The Gardenhires were a well-known family in Heath and ran a store near the Heath School. (Right, courtesy of Runell White; below, courtesy of Fay Lofland.)

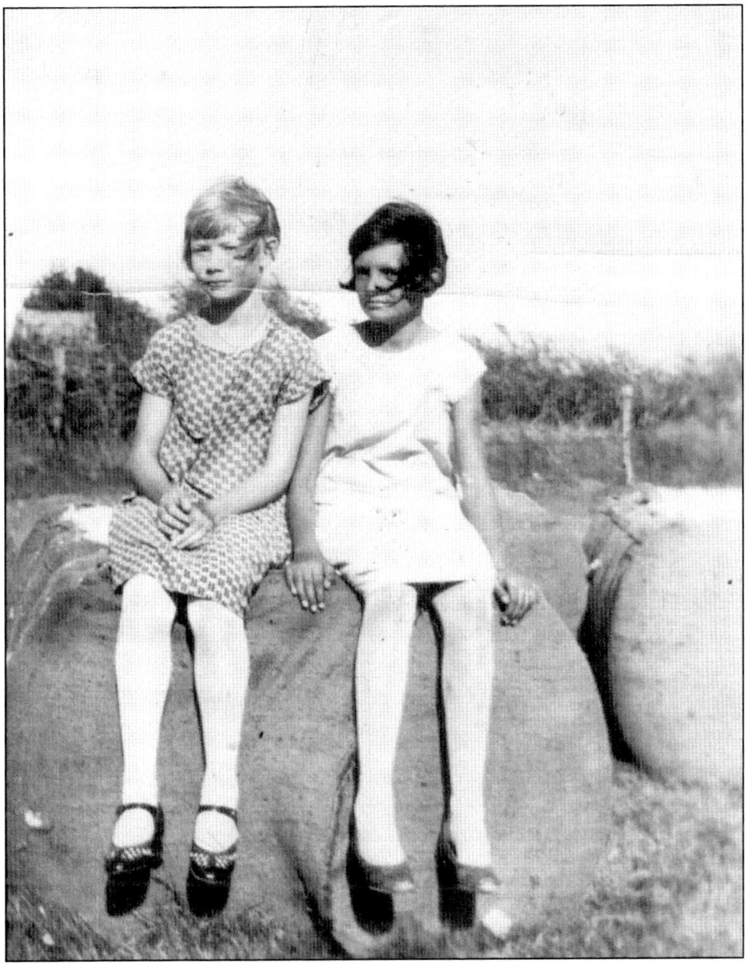

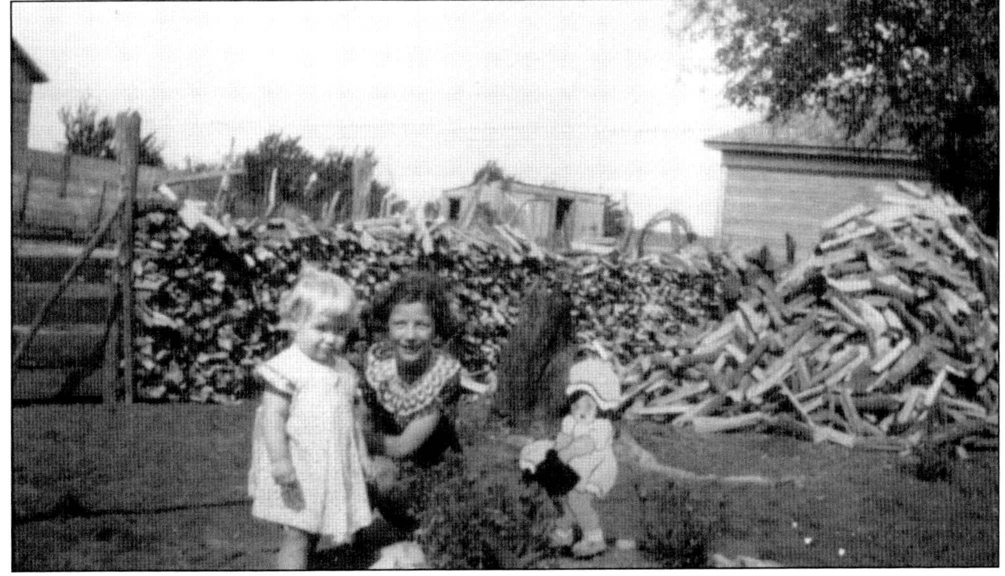

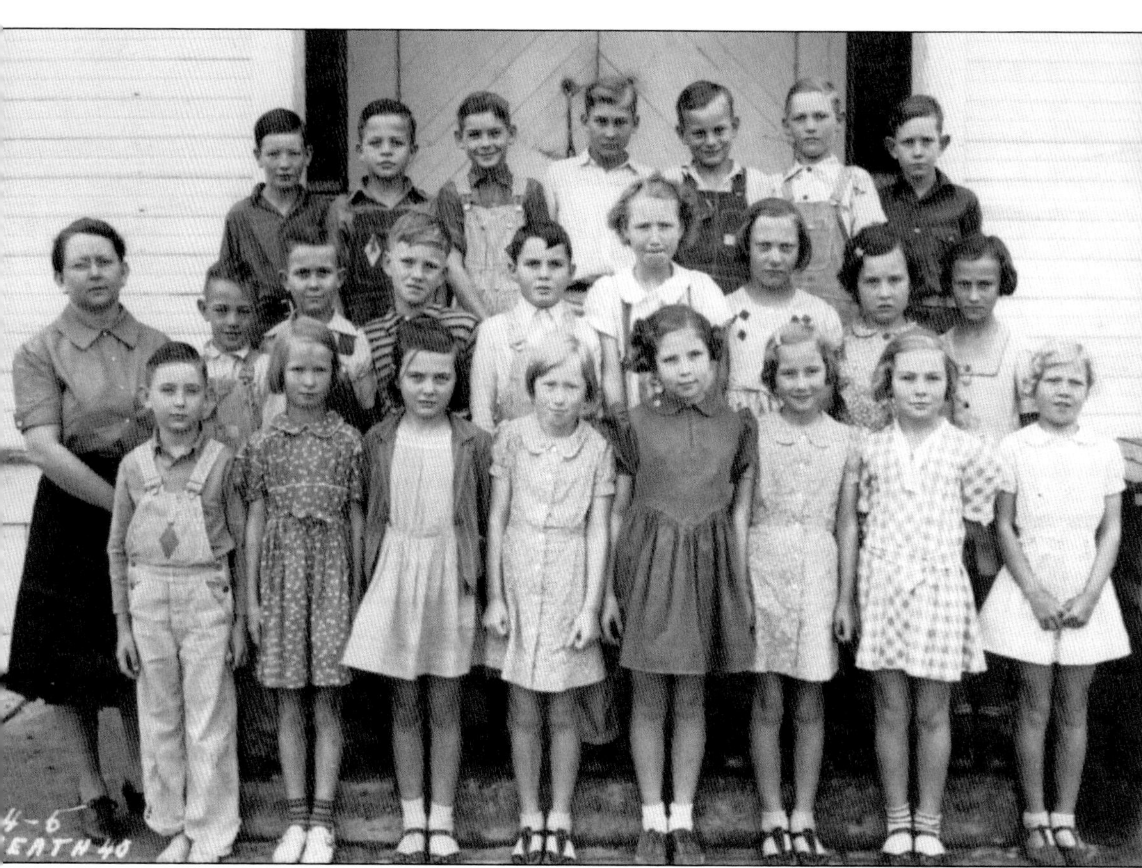

Pictured here in 1940 are third, fourth, and fifth graders at Heath School. The teacher is Mrs. W.D. Drummond. The children are, from left to right, (first row) Jamie D. Drummond, Emma Ruth Shortnacy, Theresa Ann Smirl, Ina Sue Myers, Deldwyn Beth Drummond, Ada Lou Myers, Clarice Smirl, and Lucille Stovall; (second row) Olen Ray Herrell, James Lonnie Denton, Charles Joe Lofland, Lee O. Nalls, Oleta Crawford, Bessie Vank, Peggy Jean Shortnacy, and Clara Lee Henderson; (third row) Charles Berry, Dan McCauly, Harold Lee Shortnacy, Morris Jones, Carl Weant, Virgil Mann, and Harold Evans. (Courtesy of Ada Lou Myers.)

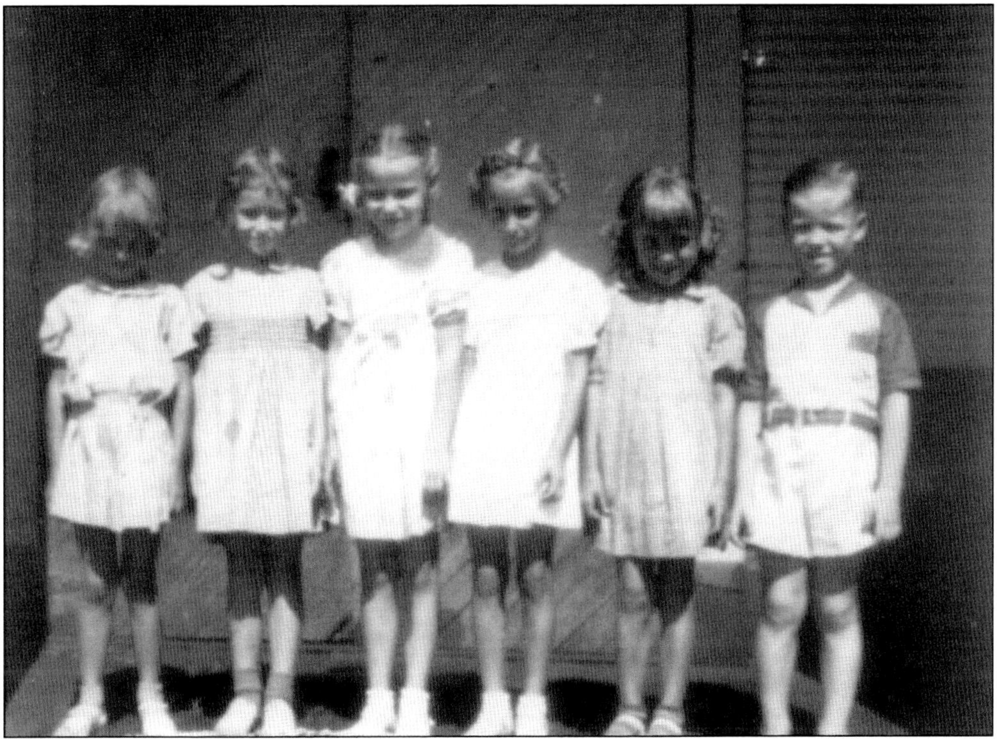

Shown above is the first grade class at Heath School in 1941. Pictured from left to right are Laura Holland, Mary Gwin Piper, Patsy Ann Hall, Charlotte Ann Pinion, unidentified, and Alfred Stovall. Their teacher was Ada Lou Adams. In the photograph at right, four generations of families celebrate the start of school outside the fire escape. From left to right are Emma Lou Hall, Patsy Ann Hall, Fay Lofland, and Emma Isbell. (Above, courtesy of Charlotte Krider; right, courtesy of Fay Lofland.)

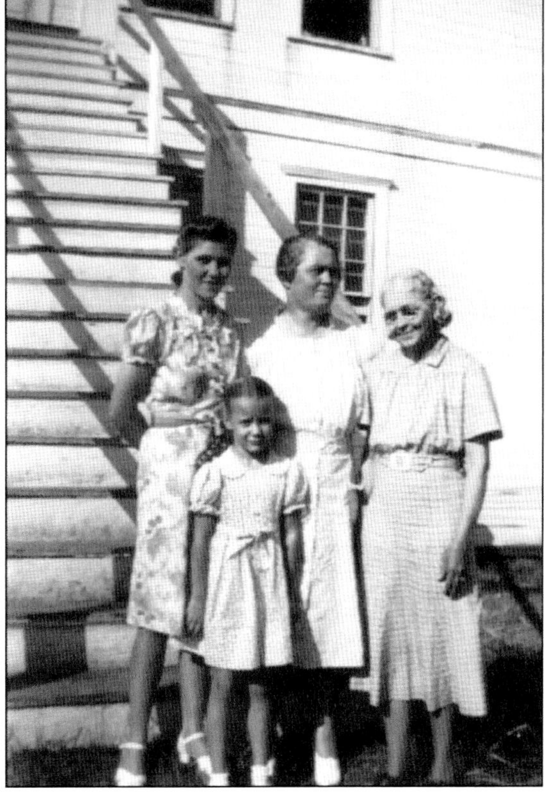

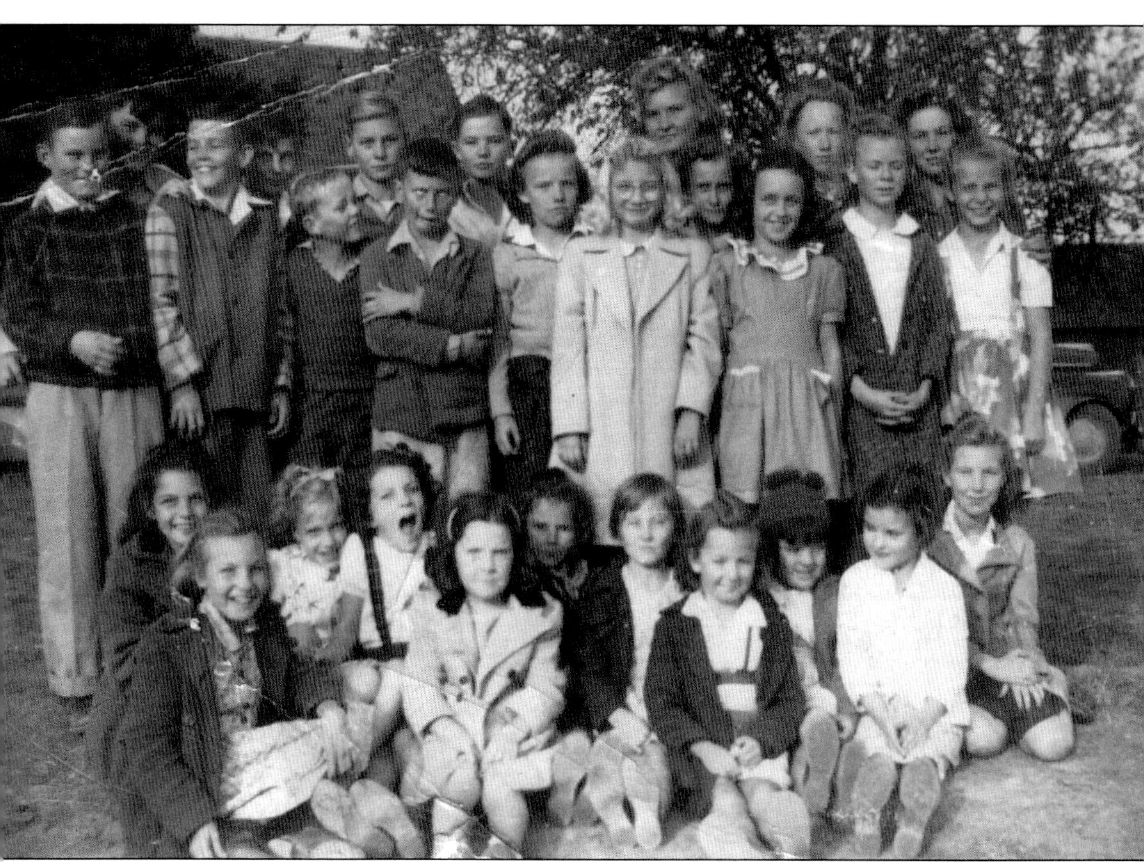

Charlotte Pinion celebrated her 10th birthday party with friends at her home on November 30, 1944. Among those seated are Anna Fern Kennerly, Tommie Sue Hall, Peggy French, Runell Massey, Claudetta Smirl, Louise Jones, Ina Charlotte Terry, Elaine Lasater, Joyce Crawford, and La Delle Lasater. Among the group standing are James Ray Collier, Charles Ray Terry, David Brooks, Joy Faye Terry, Ina Sue Myers, Clarice Smirl, John Austin Denton, Virgil Henderson, Syble Lindsey, Mary Margaret McDonald, Charlotte Pinion, Joy Nash, Margie Shortnacy, and Patsy Hall. (Courtesy of Charlotte Pinion Krider.)

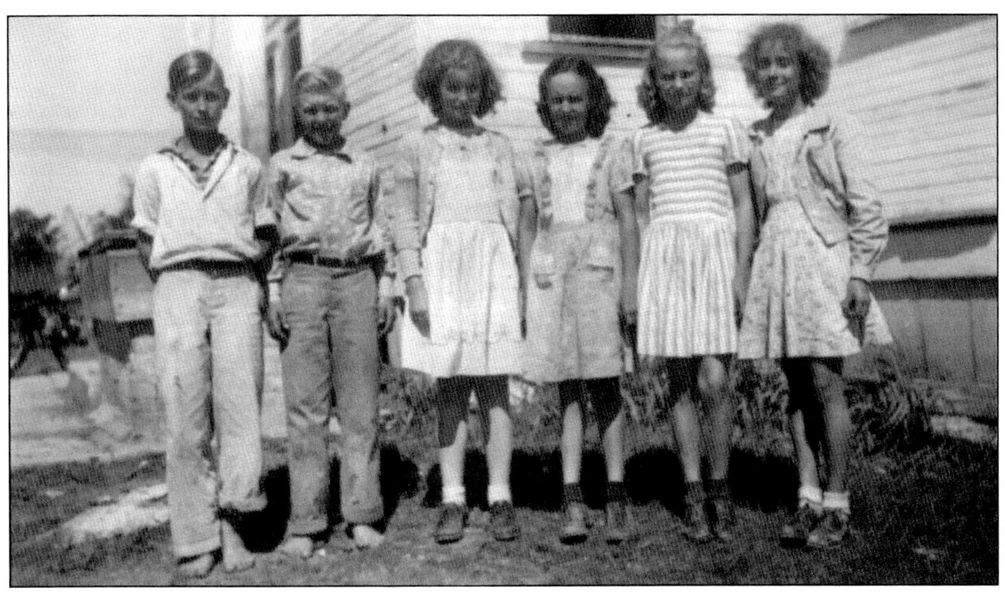

Pictured here are sixth grade Heath School classmates; from left to right are Kent Hunnicutt, Billy Way, Mary Gwin Piper, Joy Nash, Patsy Ann Hall, and Charlotte Pinion. Below is a group of ladies from the Heath PTA; from left to right are J.S. Futrell, Lois Futrell, Edna Lasater, Elizabeth Pinion, Emma Lou Hall, Rhoda Dykes Bowles, Hester Randles, Pauline Vinson, Clarabell Stovall, Claudia Jones, and unidentified. (Above, courtesy of Patsy Stodghill; below, courtesy of Charlotte Pinion Krider.)

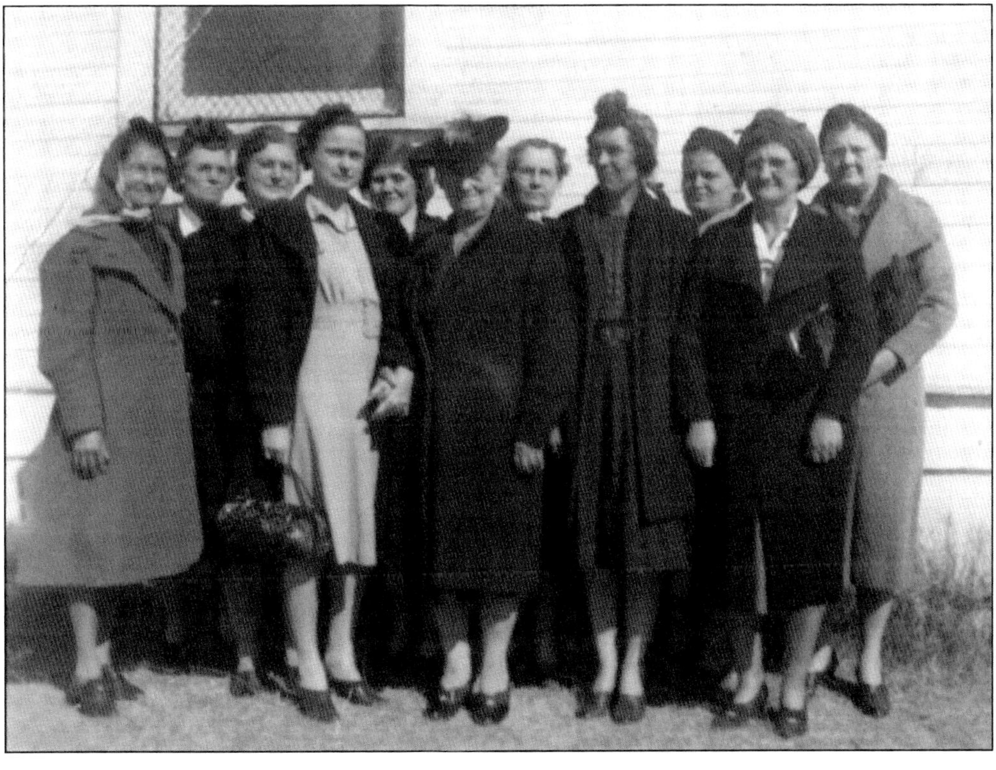

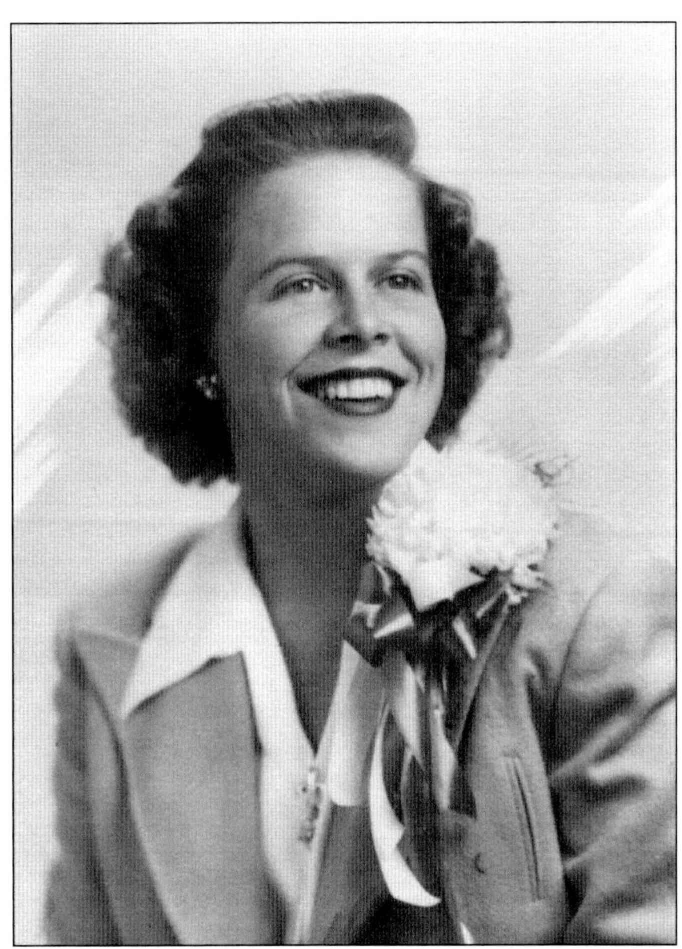

Edna Earle Isbell (left) was a very talented pianist, had a great sense of humor, and was extremely vivacious. Her brother Joe Isbell was married to Clarice Smirl Isbell. Edna Earle's father, Grady, and Grace Vaughn, mother of the Vaughn children, were brother and sister. The Vaughn children pictured below are, from left to right, (first row) Jonnie May Davidson and J.H. Vaughn; (second row) Martha Gray, Isabell Edwards, Mary Dowell, Lena Terry, and Addie Fay Edwards. (Left, courtesy of Fay Lofland; below, courtesy of Maxine and Leslie Gray.)

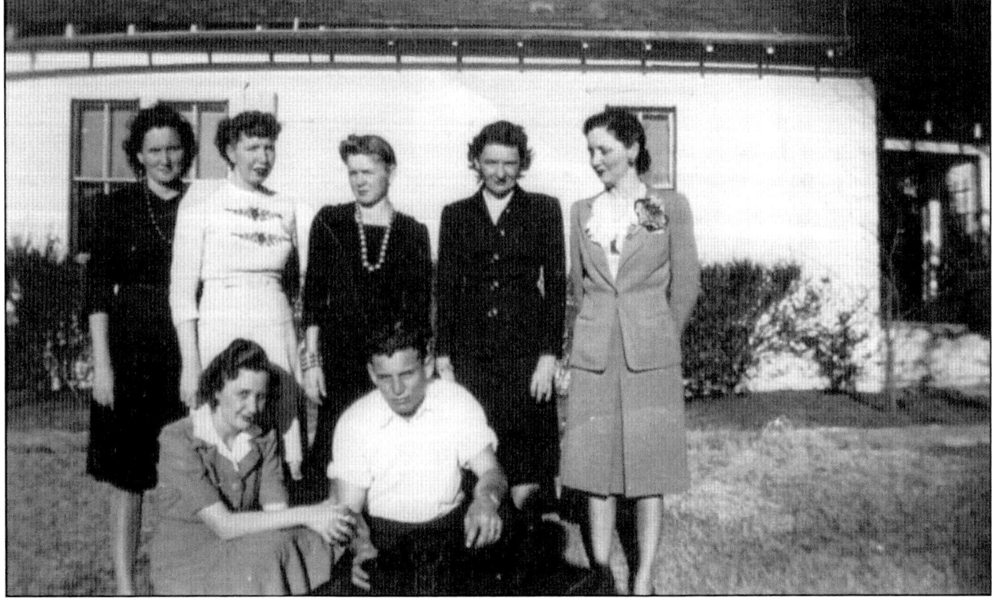

Pictured at right are good friends Claudetta Smirl (left) and Louise Jones (right) in Heath. Below is the birthday party of Sandra Seabolt in 1946. Pictured below are, from left to right, (first row) Gus Seabolt, Phyllis Seabolt, and Linda Berg; (second row) Charlotte Terry, Jerry Lasater, Rosemary Seabolt, and Nelwyn Berg; (third row) Claudetta Smirl, Sandra Seabolt, Libby Peck, Carolyn Smirl, and unidentified; (fourth row) Carolyn Williams, unidentified, Kenneth Kendall, and Elaine Lasater. (Right, courtesy of Runell White; below, courtesy of Sandra Seabolt.)

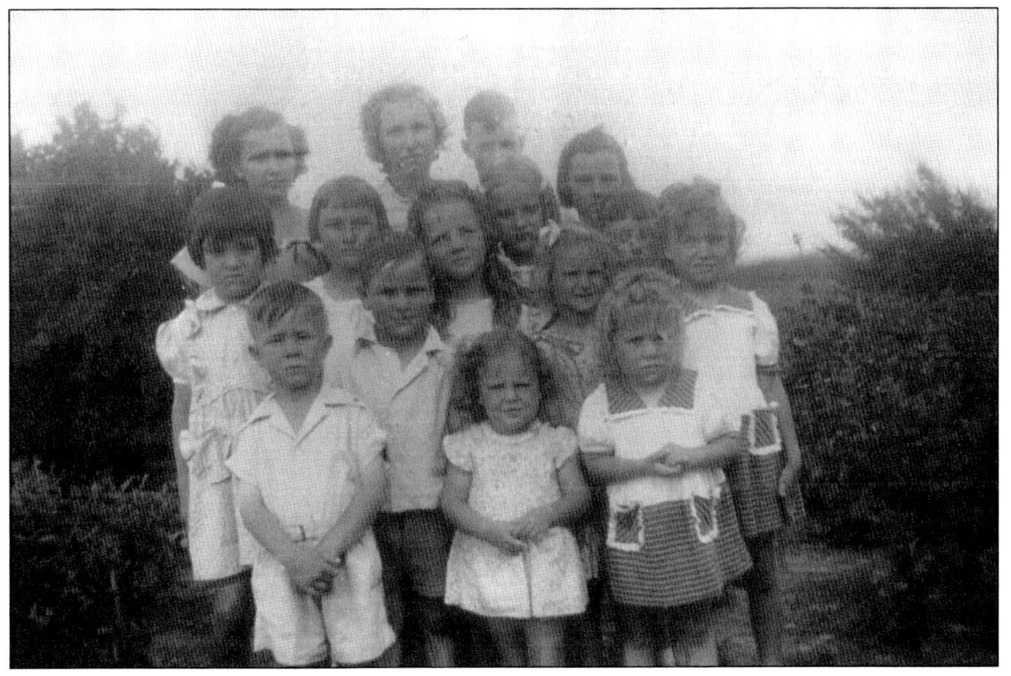

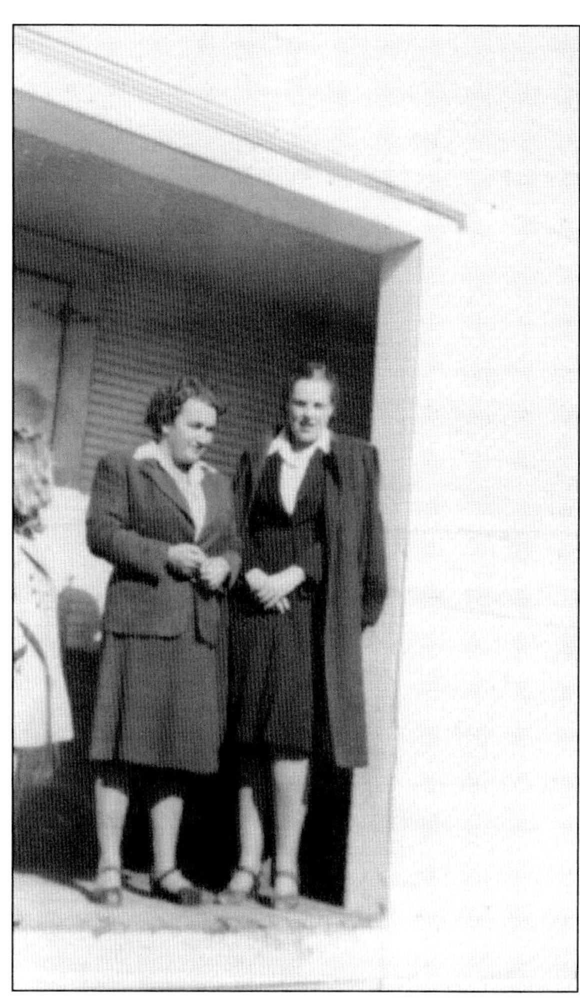

Two teachers at the Heath School stand outside the school in the 1940s. They are Edna Earle Scott (left) and Ada Lou Adams (right). Below, the girls of the Heath School class of 1947 are playing on the swings at the back of the school. Among the girls are Patsy Randles, Runell Massey, Peggy French, Mary Lou Boshears, Ina Charlotte Terry, Ella Fay Henderson, Mary Roselyn Lofland, and Ruby Daniels. (Left, courtesy of Charlotte Krider; below, courtesy of Runell White.)

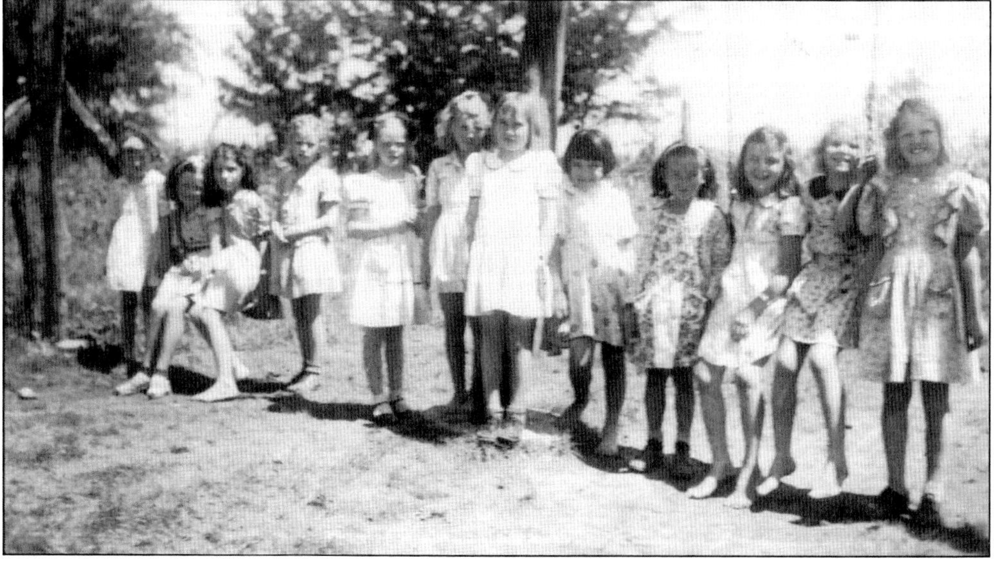

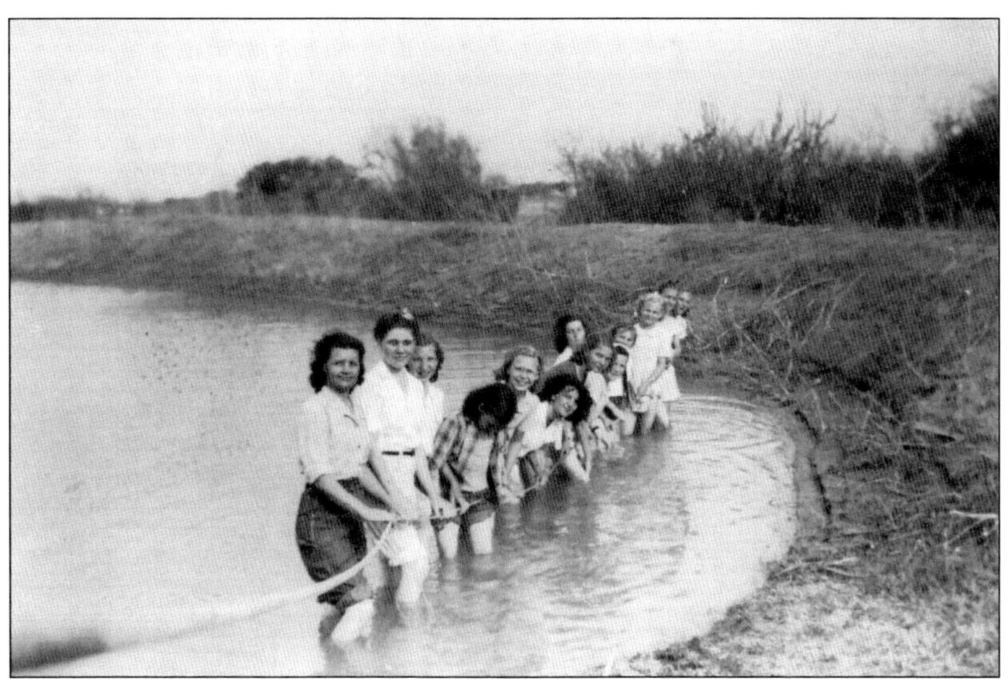

These Camp Fire Girls play tug-of-war during a meeting outside the Pinion home in 1947. The Heath Camp Fire Girls were founded by locals Emma Lou Hall, Ruby Pinion, and Eunice Way. The first two women holding the rope are Eunice Way and Emma Lou Hall, and among the girls shown are La Delle and Elaine Lasater, Patsy Hall, Anna Fern Kennerly, Peggy French, Betty Jo Cummings, Claudetta Smirl, Tommie Sue Hall, Charlotte Pinion, and Betty Terry. The Camp Fire Girls visited the balloon factory in Forney in 1947. Pictured below are, from left to right, Ruby Pinion, Emma Lou Hall, and Eunice Way. (Both, courtesy of Charlotte Pinion Krider.)

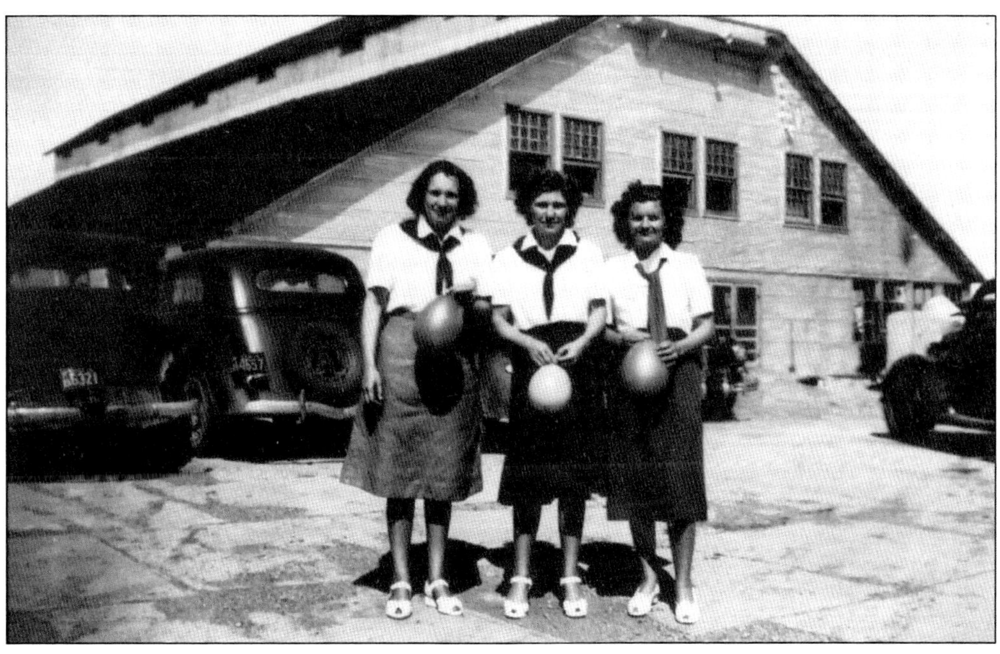

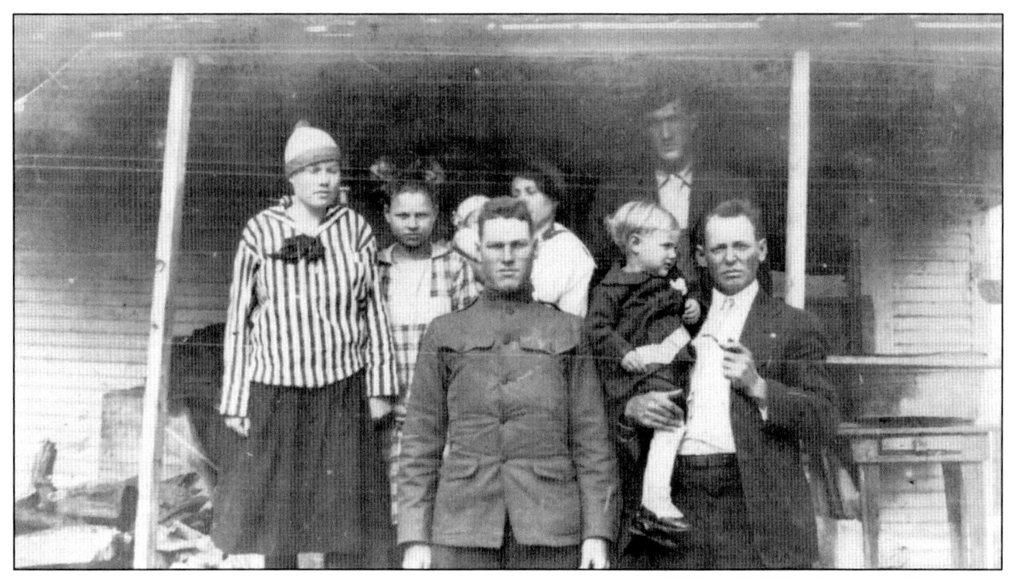

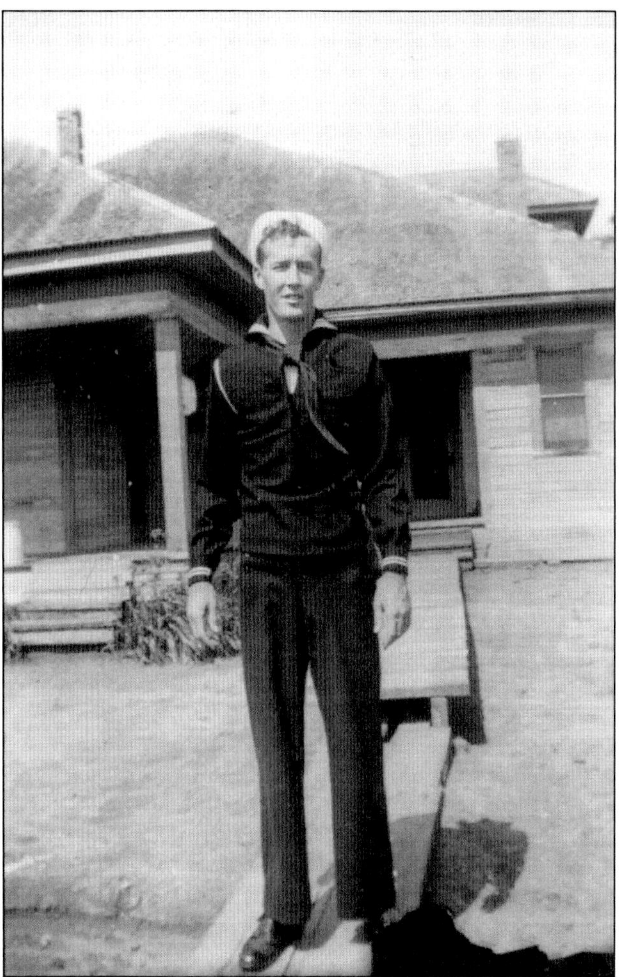

Although Heath seemed a long way from the battlefields of World War I and World War II, residents of Heath still participated in both wars and in military service afterwards. One of the heroes of World War I with ties to the Heath community was John Robert Lasater, pictured above (center) at the home of Marye Randles on New Year's Day in 1919. He married Edna Lee Butler, a direct descendant of Robert E. Lee. Their children were Anna, La Delle, Elaine, and Gerald Ray. John had been in the 111th Field Signal Battalion in the Meuse-Argonne Sector of France. Gen. John J. Pershing presented him with the Medal of Honor. He later served in the US Navy on the battleship USS *Pennsylvania*. At left is Buck Piper in his US Navy uniform outside the Piper residence in Heath. (Above, courtesy of Reba Jett; left, courtesy of the Rockwall County Historical Foundation.)

At right is J.H. Vaughn, son of Grace and John "Rusty" Vaughn. He was the youngest of their seven children. He was the main pitcher of the championship-winning Heath softball team, and his talents were recognized by the US Navy; he was recruited to play for its team. Wayne Jones (below, right) was the son of E.C. and Lois Jones. He served in World War II and married Neta Fay Smirl. They had one child, Jeffery. Wayne's twin brother, Fayne, was killed in the war in 1946. (Right, courtesy of Fay Lofland; below, courtesy of Runell White.)

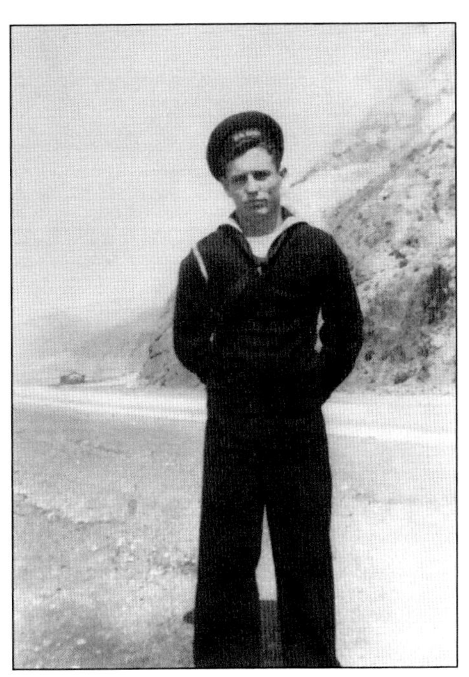

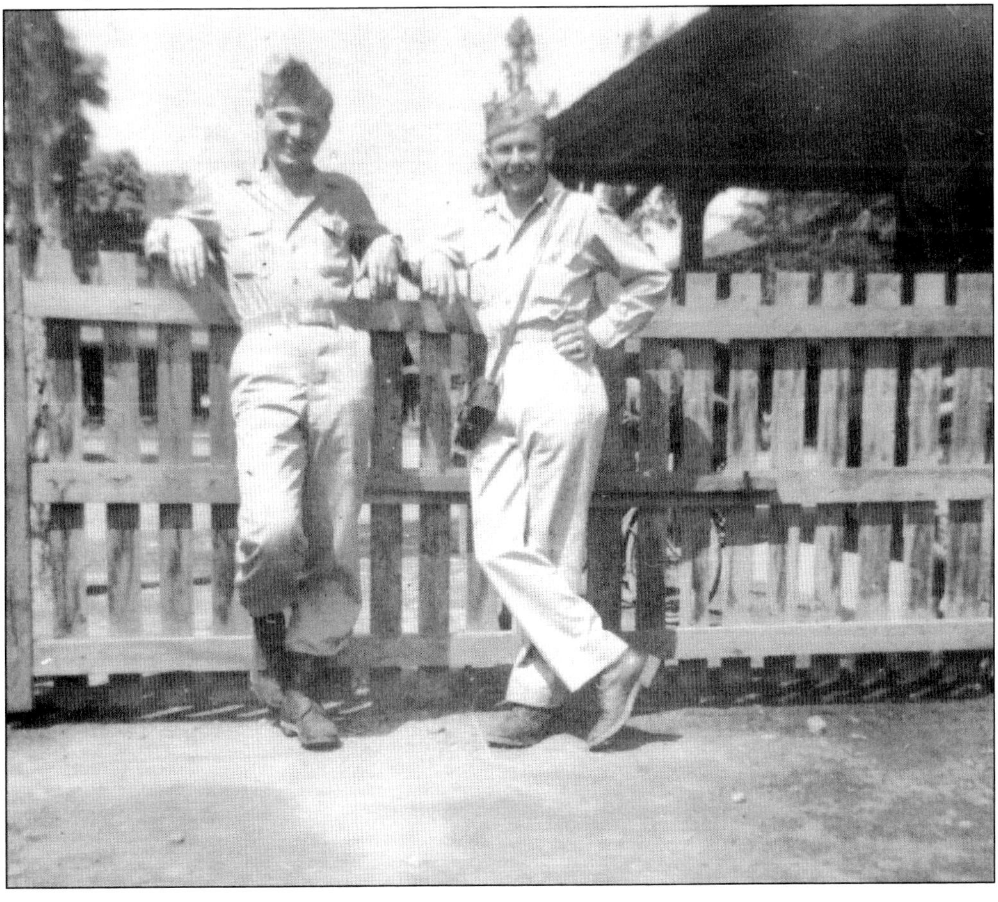

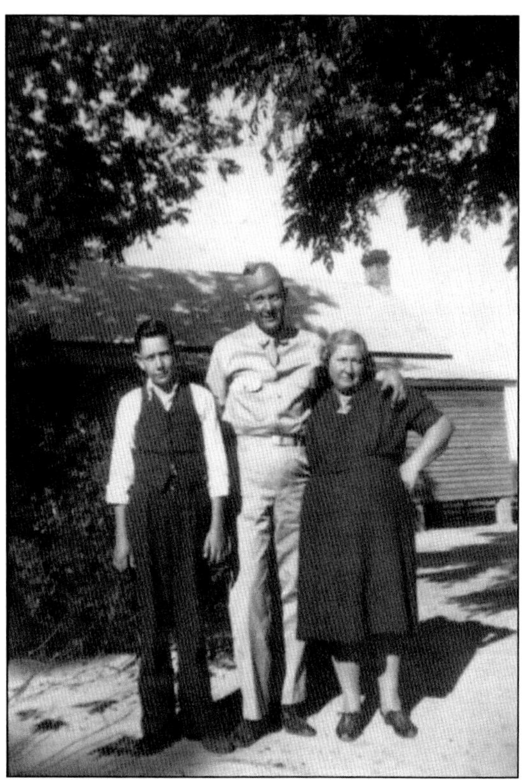

Pictured at left are Harold Evans (left) with his brother George "Dub" (center), who served in World War II, and their mother, Alice Evans. Harold and Dub's father was George W. Evans. (Courtesy of Gale Terry.)

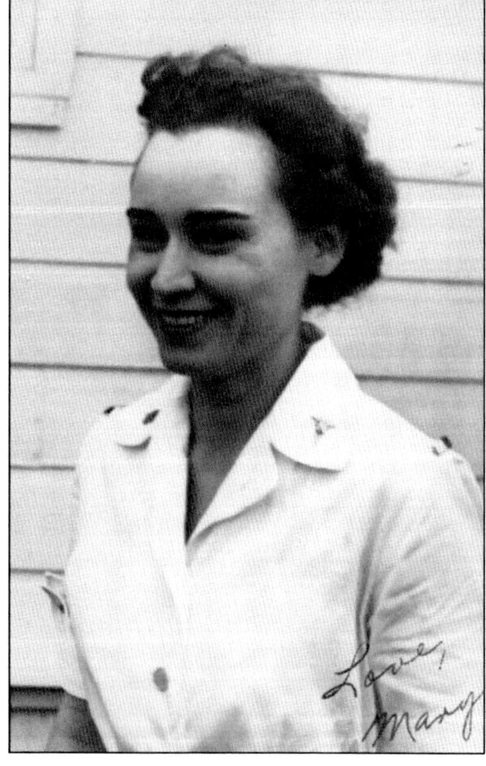

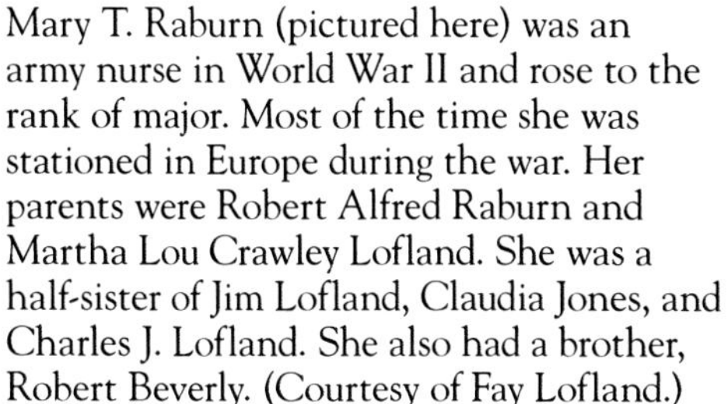

Mary T. Raburn (pictured here) was an army nurse in World War II and rose to the rank of major. Most of the time she was stationed in Europe during the war. Her parents were Robert Alfred Raburn and Martha Lou Crawley Lofland. She was a half-sister of Jim Lofland, Claudia Jones, and Charles J. Lofland. She also had a brother, Robert Beverly. (Courtesy of Fay Lofland.)

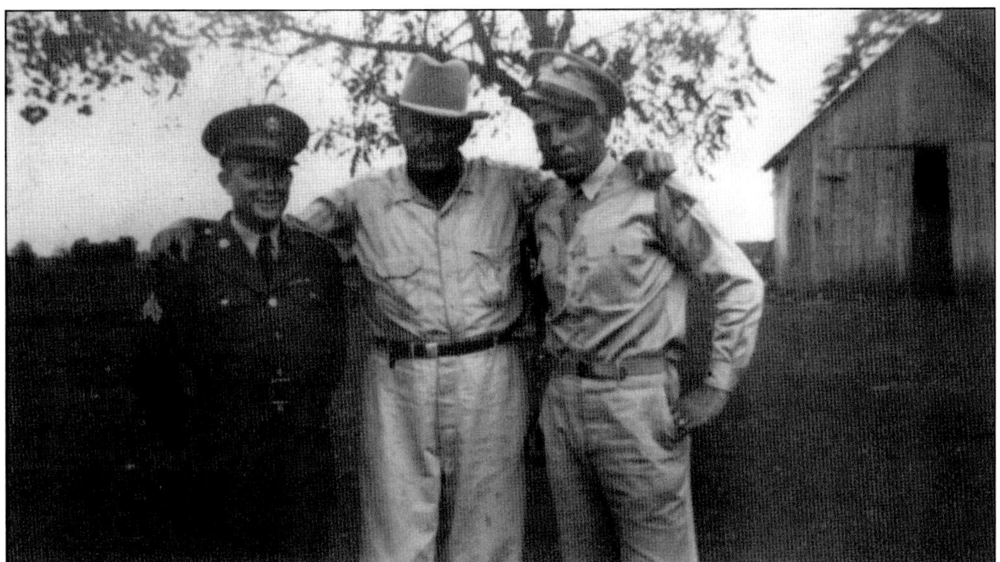

From left to right in the above image are Mack Denton, John Thomas "Tom" Hall, and John Thomas "Jake" Hall Jr. Jake and Mack were on furloughs. Jake served in World War II as a staff sergeant in the 12th Armored Division of the US Army, and he received a Bronze Star due to "heroic achievement for crossing a heavily-shelled area to maintain urgently needed contact between forward observers and the supporting artillery." Below are Wayne Massey; his wife, Angela; and a friend Paul. Wayne was much younger than the other soldiers mentioned and served at a later time. (Above, courtesy of Patsy Stodghill; below, courtesy of Runell White.)

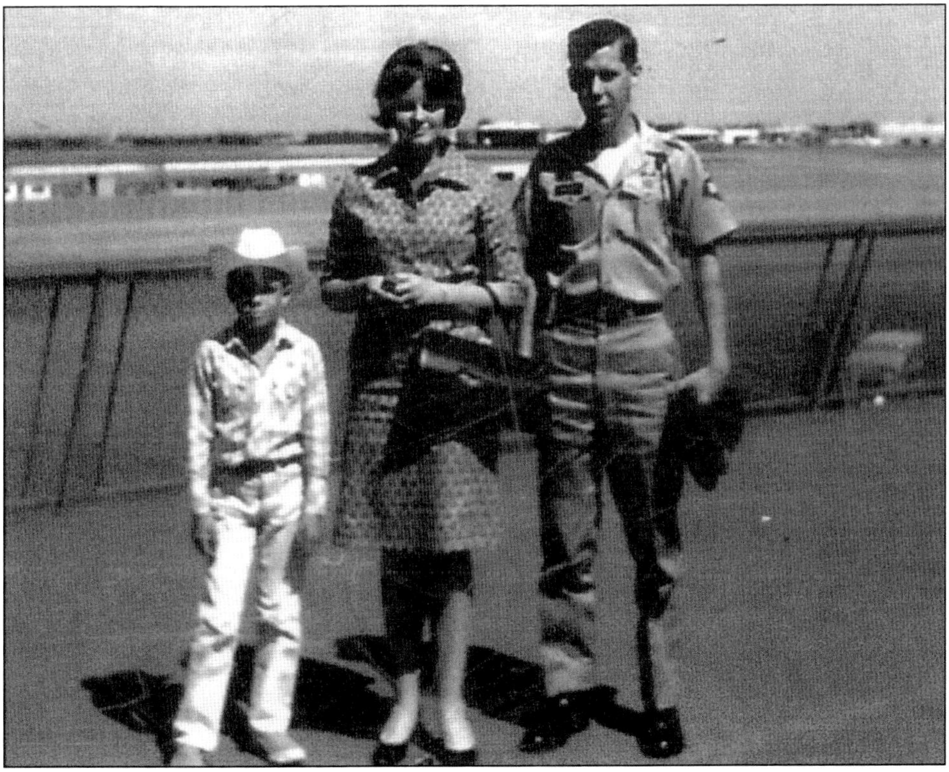

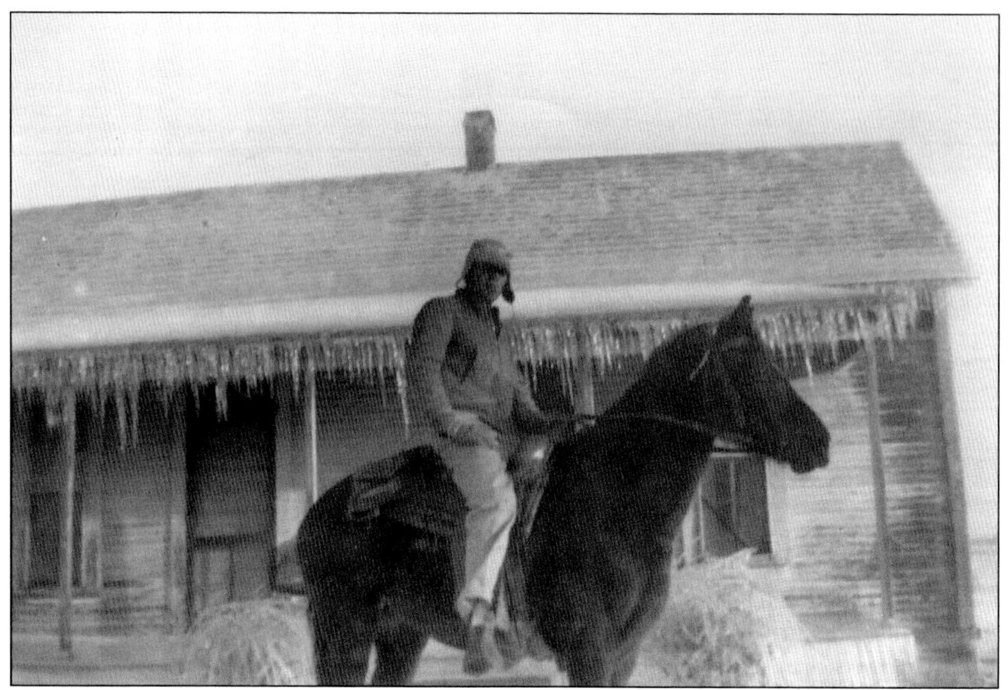

Horseback riding was a favorite pastime for many in Heath. Clifford Hall and his horse Sugar trudge through the snow on a wintry day at the Way family farm in 1951. During this time, the road now known as FM 3549 was unpaved, which made it impossible to drive a car through the mud from the Hall house three miles east of Heath. At these times, Clifford would ride Sugar to Heath and leave the horse in the shade of the gin with food and water until he returned from work. Below are, from left to right, Charlotte Pinion, John Austin Denton, and Gilbert French on Charlotte's white horse Tilley outside the Pinion home in Heath. (Above, courtesy of Bill Way; below, courtesy of Charlotte Pinion Krider.)

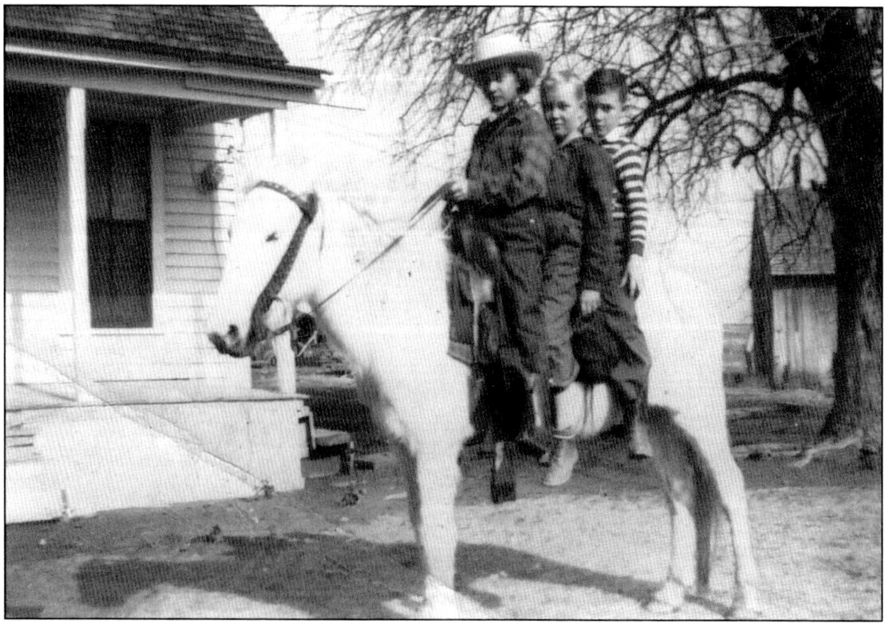

At right is Frank Jefferson with his horse Rusty. Son of Charlie and Annie Mae, Jefferson married Lois Marie Boren (1916–2002) on September 25, 1935. Frank was a real cowboy and made a living buying and selling cattle for many years. He and Lois had one son and one daughter, both born in Rockwall County. In 1968, he and Lois purchased the Dairy Queen, and on Wednesdays they served fried chicken—all one could eat for $1.25. Frank died in 1972 at 55 years old. Below from left to right are Patsy and Tommie Hall on their horse Nellie, Joy Fay Terry on her horse, and Charlotte Pinion on her horse Tilley. (Right, courtesy of Carolyn Holt; below, courtesy of Patsy Stodghill.)

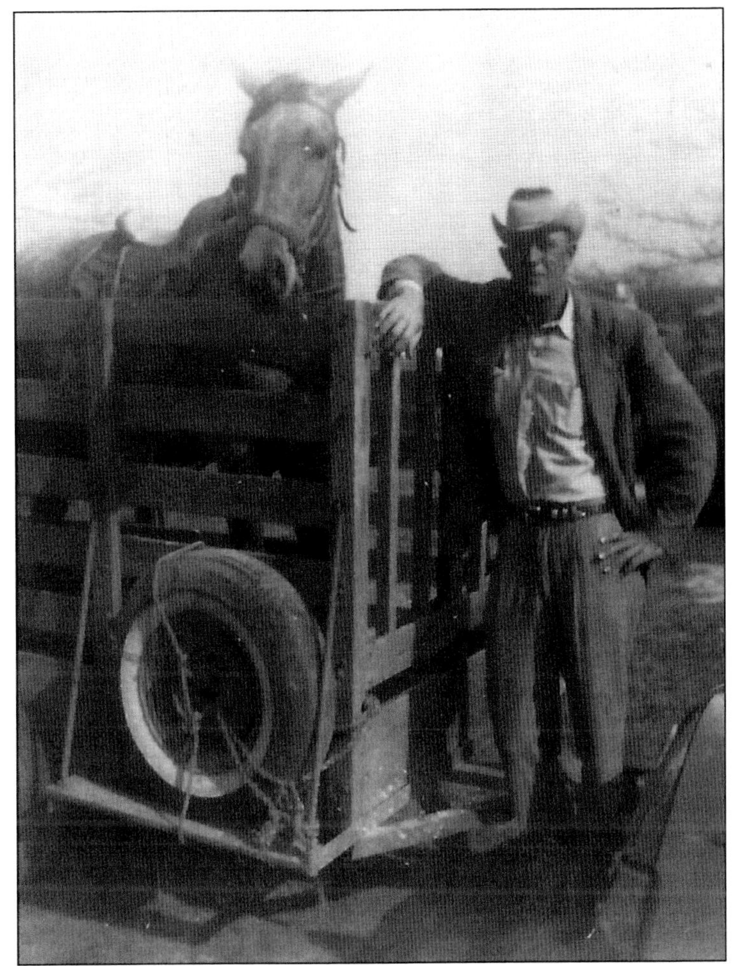

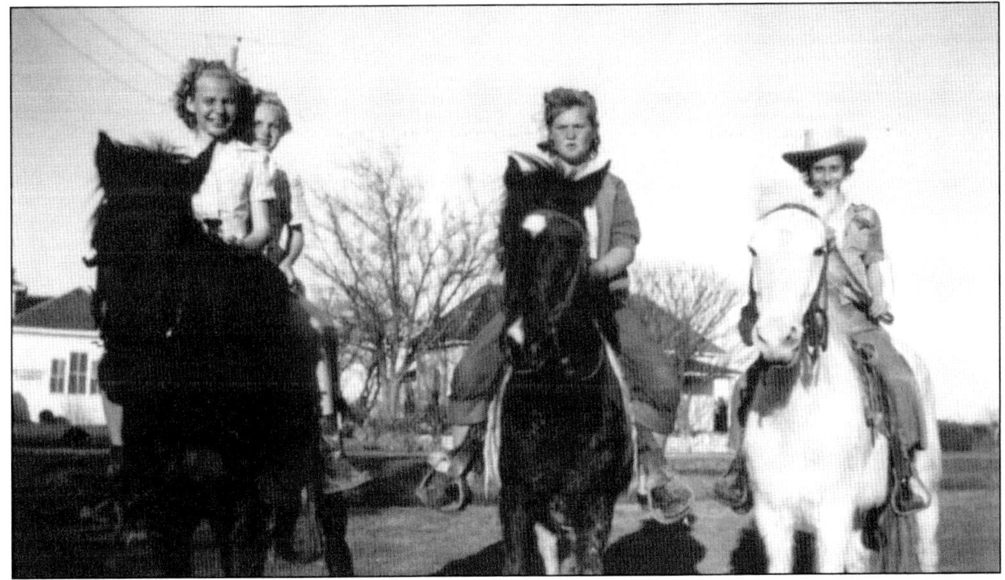

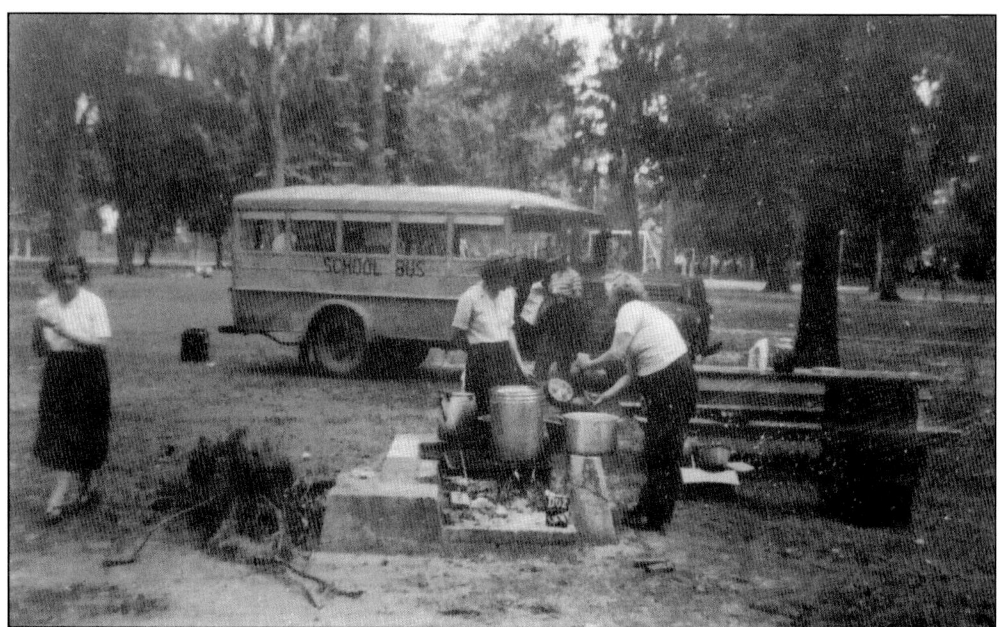

Under Heath School principal Tom Seely, the seventh and eighth grade classes took a school trip to Houston to the San Jacinto Battlefield and Monument in 1947. They camped out on part of the trip, and the above image shows the old school bus used for traveling during the trip. On their next trip, in 1948, they visited Austin and also enjoyed a lovely and informative visit to the Rose Window of the San Jose Mission in San Antonio. Pictured below are, from left to right, (first row) Bill Way and Jerry Bettingfield; (second row) Peggy French, unidentified, and Tommie Sue Hall; (third row) Patsy Hall, Joy Nash, Betty Terry, and unidentified. (Above, courtesy of Bill Way; below, courtesy of Patsy Stodghill.)

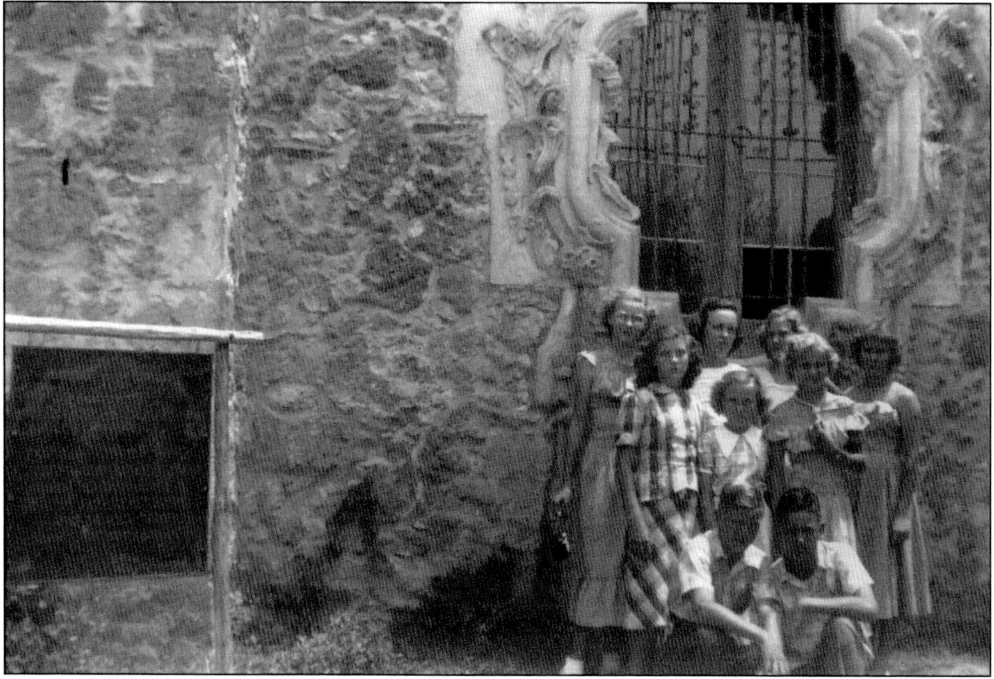

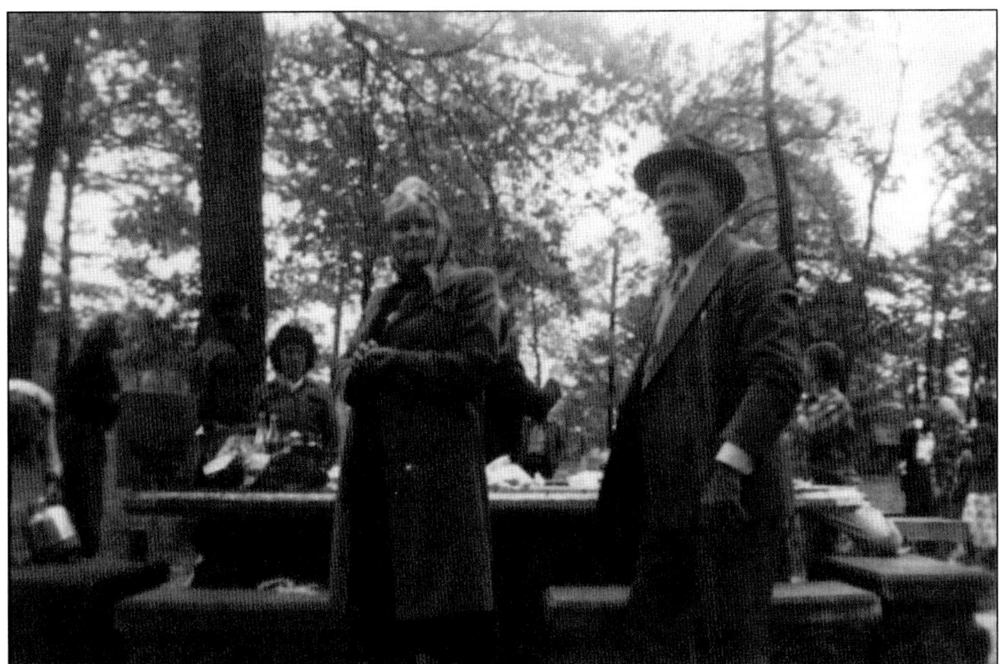

Pictured above are Grace and Tom Seely on a Heath School trip in 1948. Tom was the principal of the old Heath School and would take the students on trips across Texas during the summer. At right, Bill Way is holding up a nice-sized goose, which he often hunted down near the old stock tank on the Way farm. (Both, courtesy of Bill Way.)

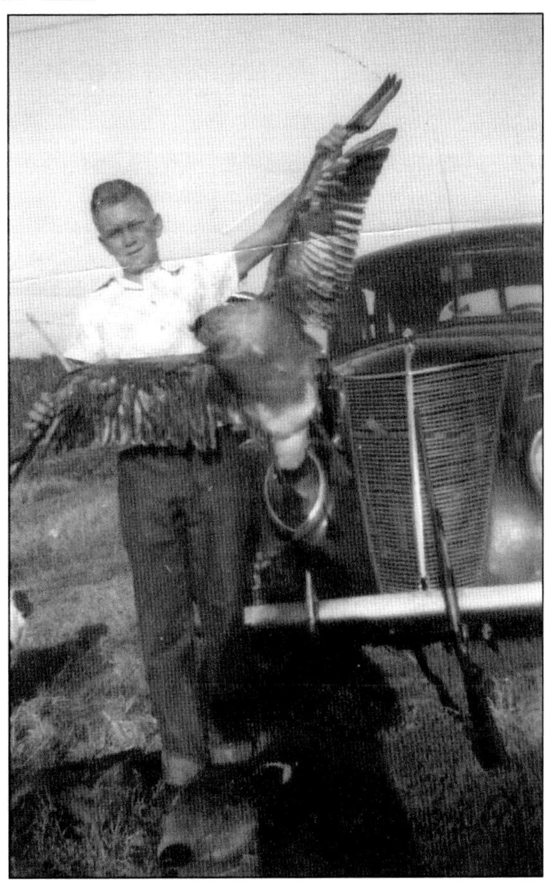

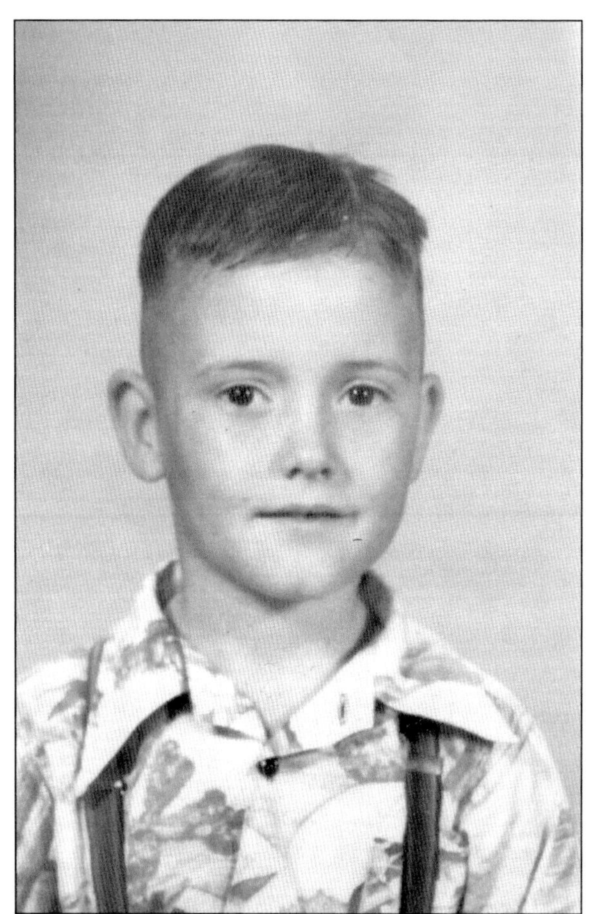

Pictured at left is John Dan Myers back in his first year at the Heath School. He later went on to become a county commissioner in Rockwall. He was born on November 11, 1934, and died at the age of 34 on January 7, 1978. He is buried in the Heath Cemetery. Below, posing on Barnes Bridge are, from left to right, Clara Lee Henderson, Theresa Smirl, Ima Jo Jones, twins Ina Sue and Ada Lou Myers, and Emma Ruth Shortnacy. (Left, courtesy of Bill Way; below, courtesy of Ada Lou Abernathy.)

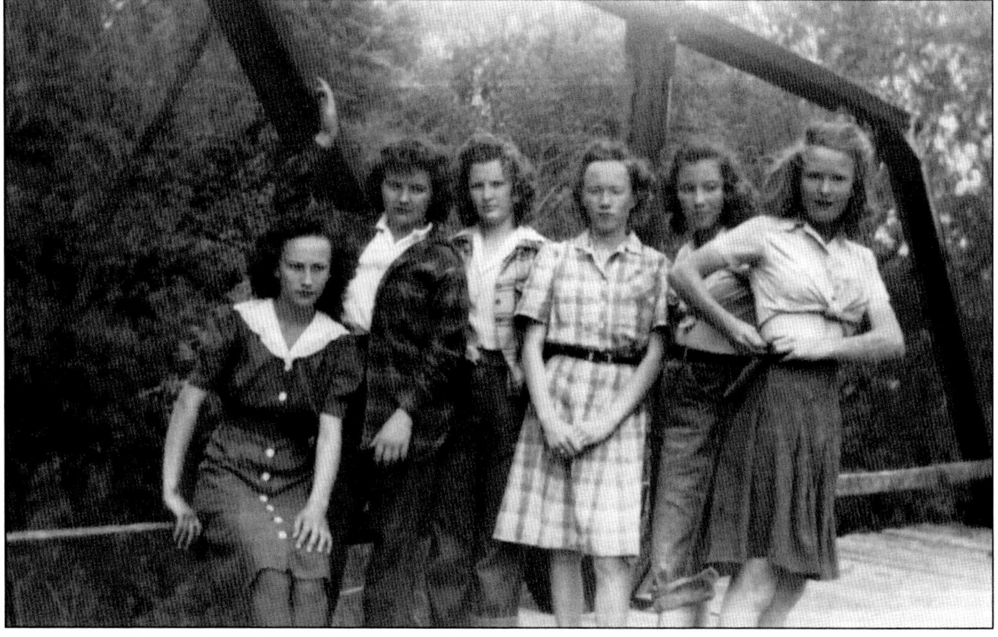

At right is Will Seabolt's son W.L. Seabolt posing in Western wear on the dusty streets of Heath. Below is a photograph taken at an engagement luncheon for Lynda Jones at the Century Room of the Adolphus Hotel in Dallas in 1950. The ladies are, from left to right, Theola Barnes, Claudia Jones, Ada Lou Adams, Emma Lou Hall, Tommie and Patsy Hall, Lynda Jones, and five ladies who are relatives of Lynda's fiancé, Homer Hopkins. Lynda and Homer were married in June 1950, about two months after this picture was taken. (Right, courtesy of Rosemary Seabolt Klutts; below, courtesy of Patsy Stodghill.)

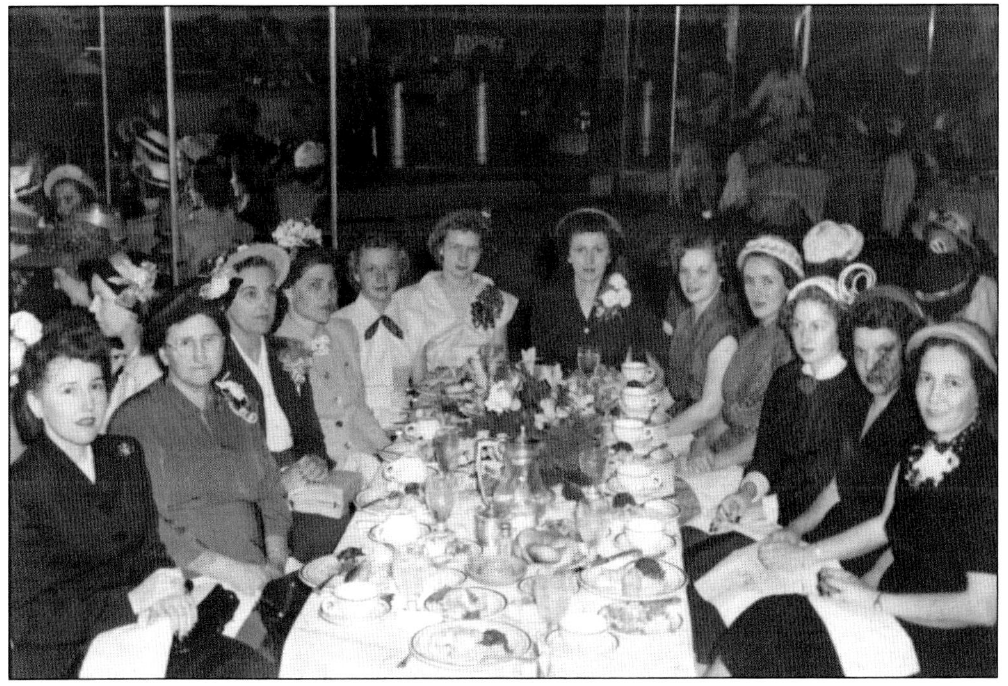

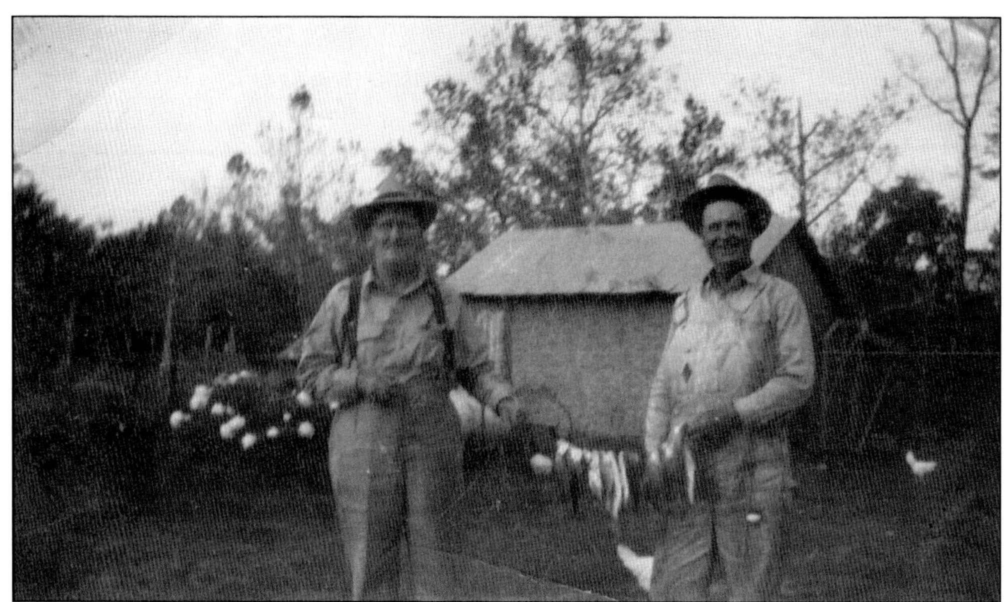

Theo Poindexter (left) and his brother Tilmon Ernest Poindexter (right) show off some great catches from a fishing trip on the Poindexter farm. The farm contained three stock ponds full of crappie, bass, and catfish. The chickens seen in the background also served as a food source for the Poindexter family. Rockwall fire chief Mark Poindexter is seen below as a boy riding around on the family farm about 1960. At age six, Mark learned to drive his grandfather's tractor and would help plow the fields. Mark also loved to hunt squirrels, rabbits, and raccoons. According to Mark, at age six, he and his father, Gene Poindexter, killed a raccoon that weighed a whopping 46 pounds. (Both, courtesy of Mark Poindexter.)

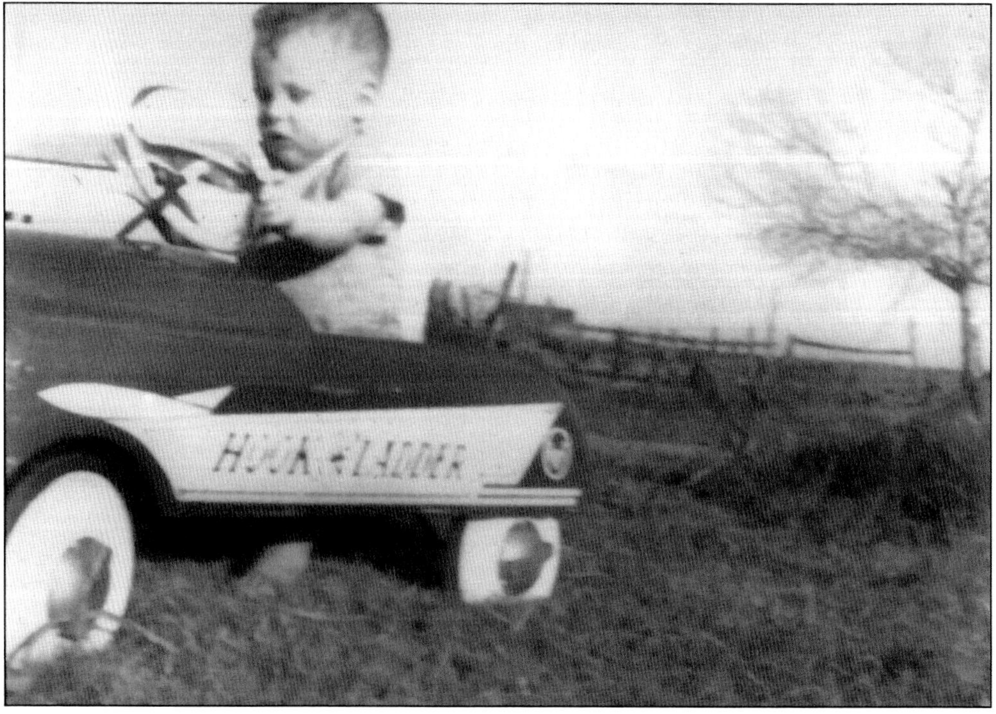

At right, Max (front) and George "Dub" (back) Evans pose outside the home of their parents, George W. and Alice, which was located where city hall is now. (Courtesy of Gale Terry.)

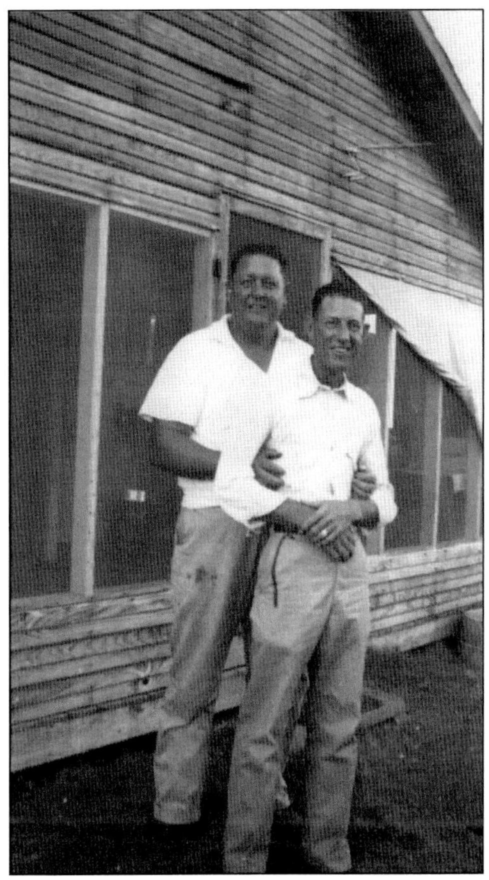

From left to right are Harvey Way, Kent Hunnicutt, Clifford Hall, Mildred Hall, Eunice Way, Hillary Watley, and Florence Way enjoying an afternoon on the porch of the old Way family home in Heath. (Courtesy of Bill Way.)

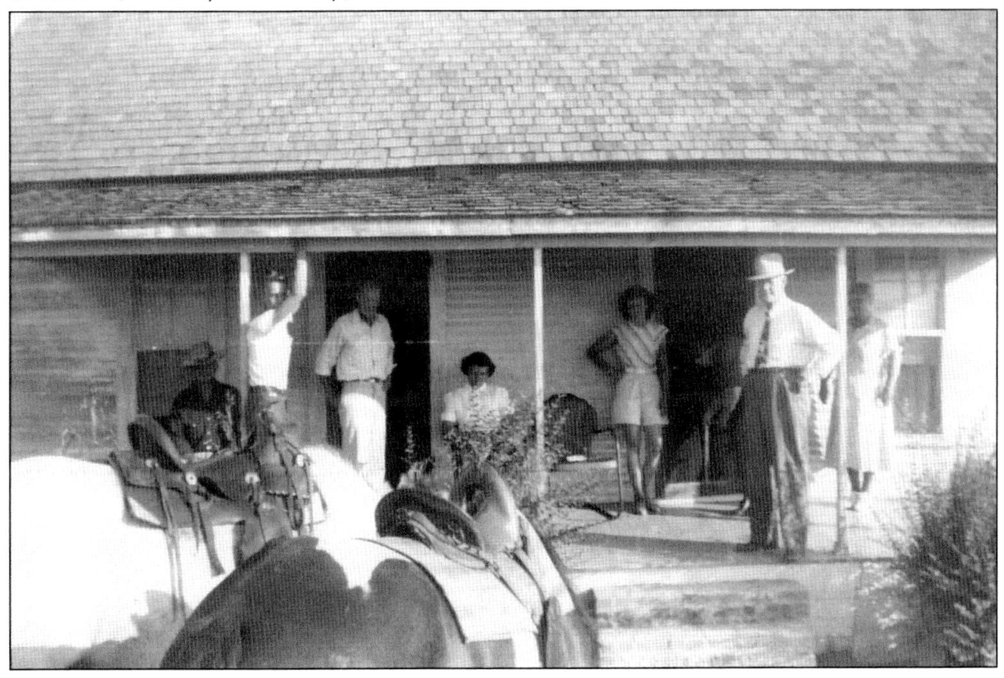

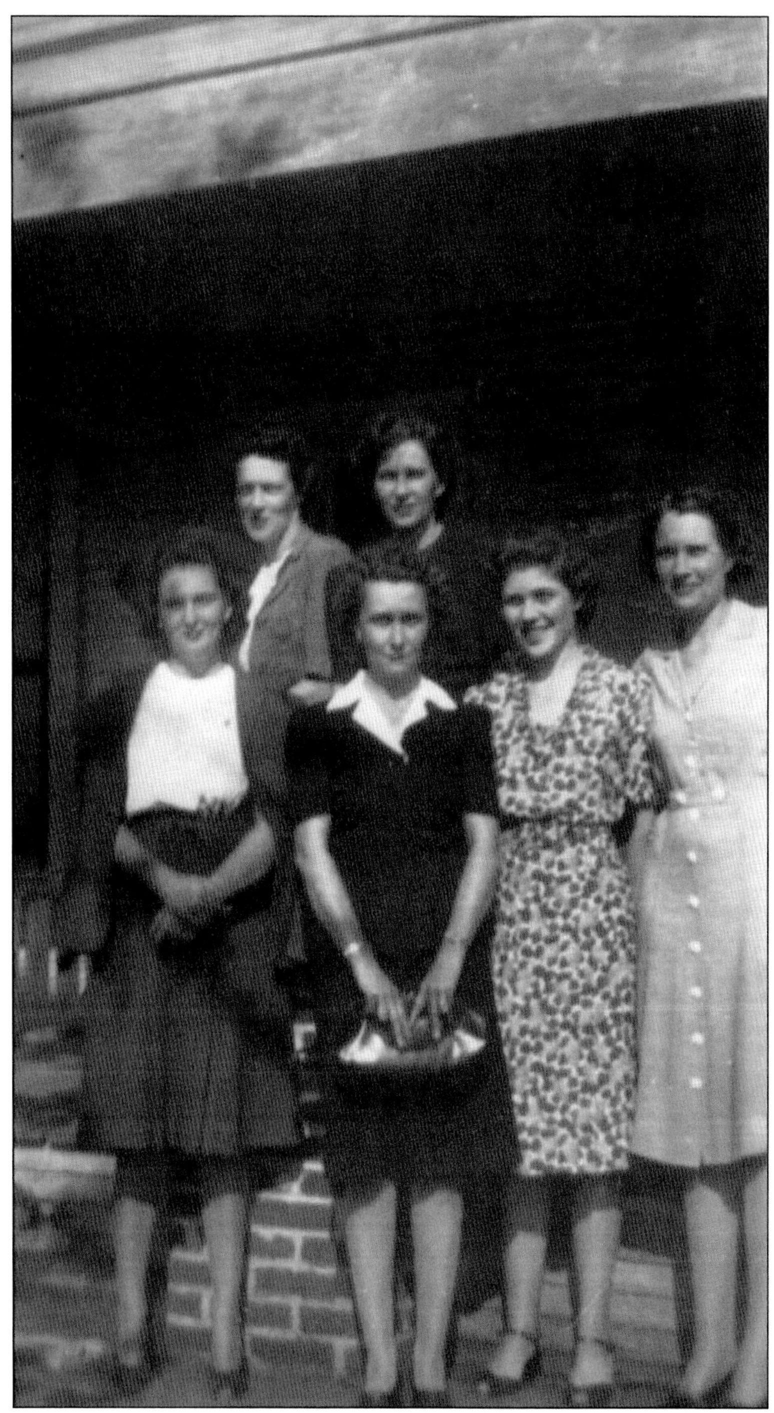

Shown here are members of a group of ladies in Heath who called themselves the Black Cat Club. From left to right are (first row) Martha Gray, Verna Denton, Emma Lou Hall, and Ruby Pinion; (second row) Anna Gardenhire and Roxie Lewis. The club would usually go into Dallas to eat, go shopping, or see a movie. Once a month they held parties and dances at each other's homes where their husbands were invited and games of canasta were played. (Courtesy of Charlotte Pinion Krider.)

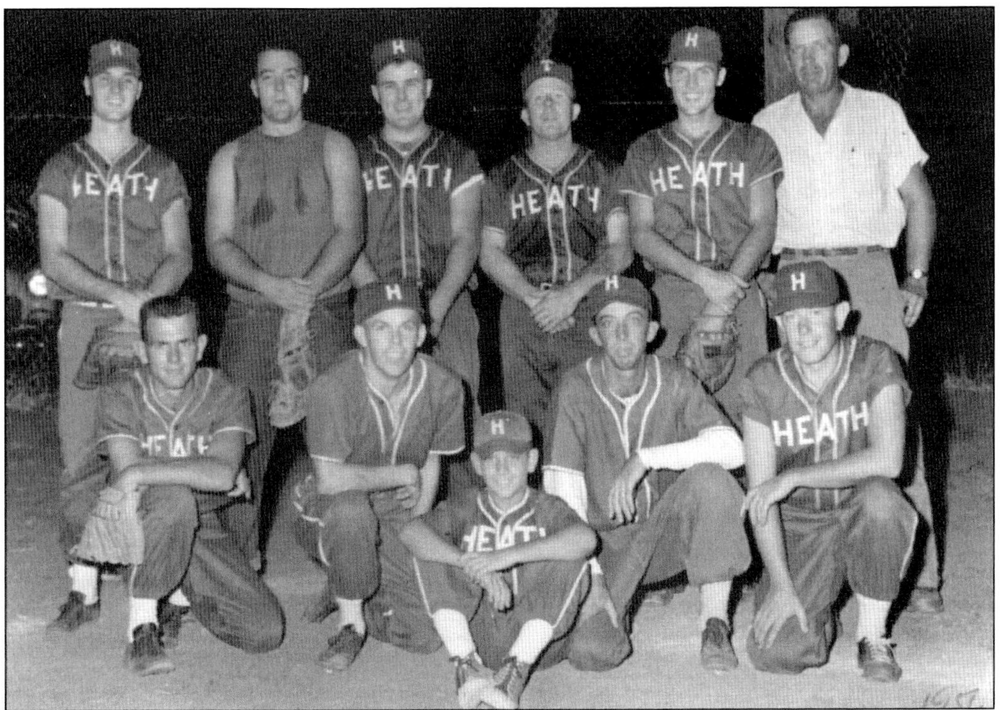

Nothing brought the town of Heath together like a good old-fashioned game of baseball. In fact, Heath residents were so passionate about the sport they would show up in droves to the town ball field, located near the middle of downtown Heath, to cheer on their family members and friends, who so often in those days made up the Heath baseball teams. Folks would line their cars almost bumper to bumper along the road and sit on the hoods to watch the action. Pictured above is the 1956 Heath traveling baseball squad made up of many local men from the area. From left to right are (first row) A.R. Seabolt, Joe Frank Isbell, mascot and batboy Kenny Terry, Roy Gene Mitchell, and Harold Evans; (second row) Charles Terry, Lloyd Oakley, James Terry, Grady Isbell Jr., Huey Smirl, and coach Jake Hall. Below is the Heath Ladies Softball Club in the summer of 1971. Pictured are (first row, no particular order) Virginia Smirl and three unidentified ladies; (second row, from left to right) Peggy French, Doris Cox, Neta Jones, Joy Nash, Clarice Isbell, Anna Vank, and Joyce Jones. Joe Isbell was the manager of the club. (Both, courtesy of Clarice Isbell.)

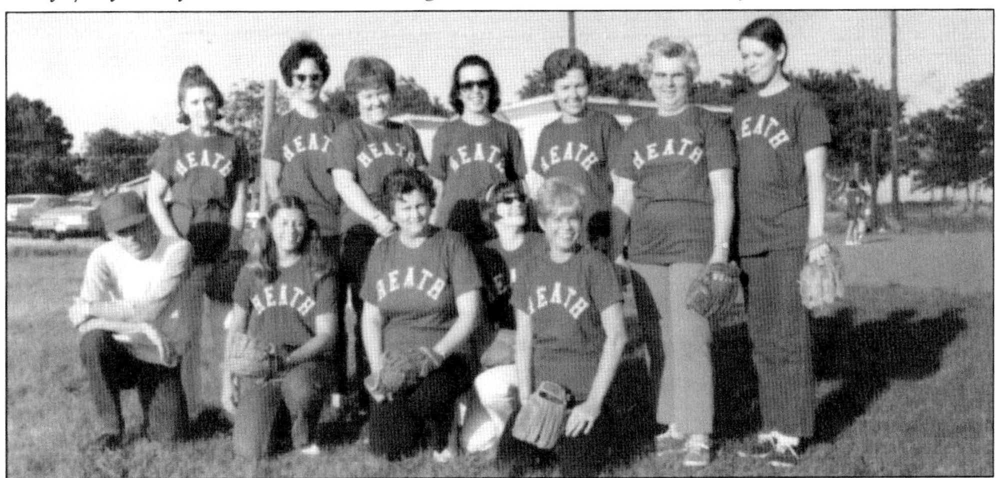

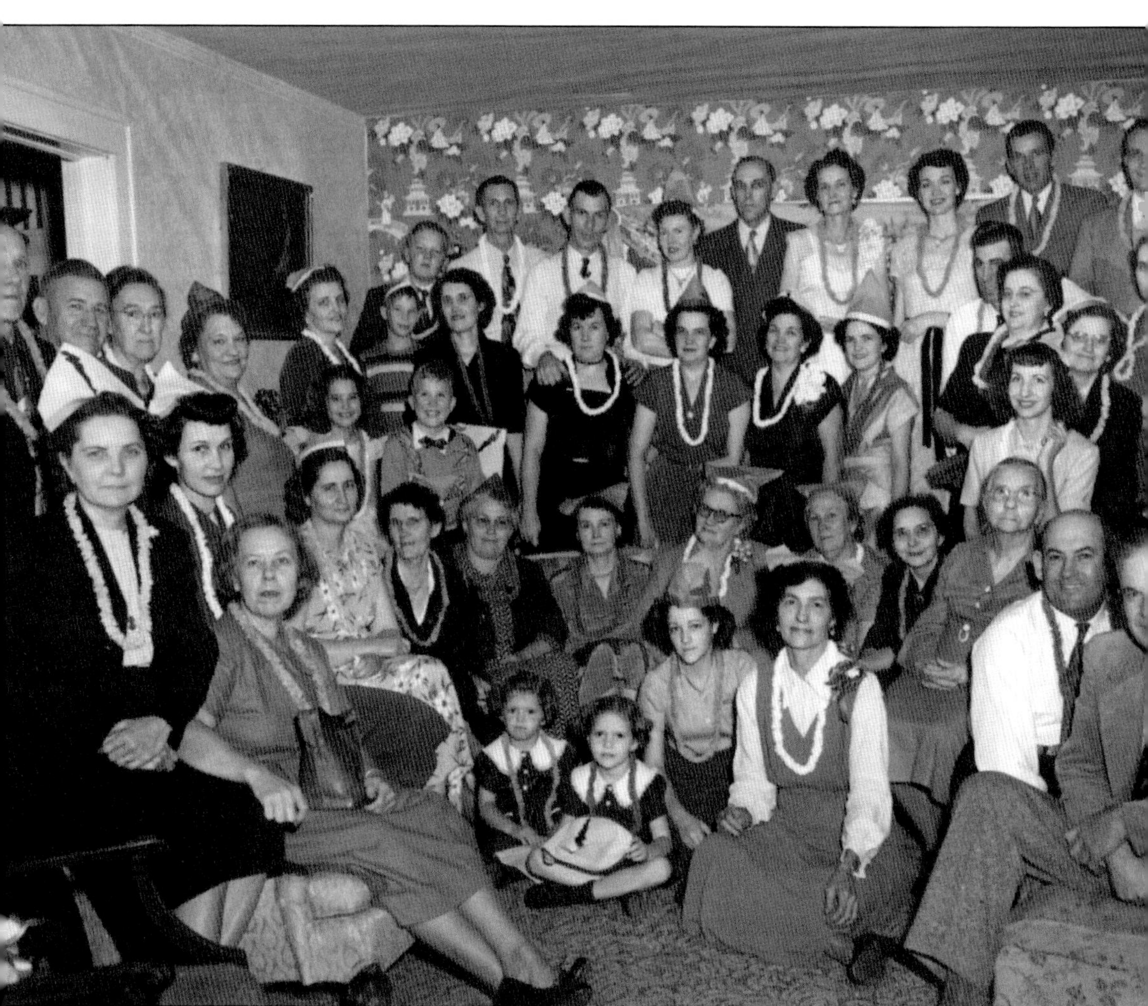

This group of women, originally from Heath, now living in Dallas, made up the Heath Club. The club lasted over 20 years. They had special parties on occasion where they invited their husbands. Among those pictured are Anna Bradford, Maggie Bratcher, Mildred Bryan, Annie (Keely) Burns, Elizabeth Campbell, Lou Cheek, Estelle (McMahon) Chenault, Catherine (Evans) and Weldon Collier, Lucille Copeland, Peggy Gauthier, Allene Hall, Fay and Jim Lofland, Doris (Bryan) Hall, Floy Lewis, Oriole (Brannon) Lozano and husband Fred, Anna (Brooks) Mayers, Genevieve Meggs, Winnie (Hall) Middings, Evelyn and Bob Smallwood, Dorothy Stuart, Paulina Vinson, Roxie (Spillman) Wilson, Hattie (Byrd) Knight Vittrup, Anna Brooks Wilson Bradford Mayers, Maurine Lamm and son Milton D., Marie and Jack Wendt, Sallie Piper, Georgia McFarland (guest), Dorothy and Clayton Hall, Buellah Bryan, Sue Davis, S.H. Holt, and Nora Chenault. (Courtesy of Fay Lofland.)

Four

Lake Ray Hubbard and the Founding of the Rush Creek Yacht Club

Rush Creek Yacht Club (RCYC) was founded on the shores of Lake Ray Hubbard in 1969. The yacht club was built on the grounds of the old Futrell farm. Years before Lake Ray Hubbard became a lake, it was a river bottom known to locals as the Bottom, a popular place to picnic, camp, and fish. When White Rock Lake in Dallas began to dry up for a time around 1957 and the pressure was on to find another water supply for the city of Dallas, then mayor R.L. Thornton and Dallas Parks board member Ray Hubbard decided to form a new lake in Rockwall County and were backed by state-issued permits to do so in 1959.

Dallas annexed 22,745 acres for water coverage and then purchased additional lakefront parcels. The largest purchased land was 6,000 acres from EBS ranch, which covers the southwest area of the lake up to approximately the Elgin B. Robertson Park area. By 1967, work on the dam was complete.

Although the engineers predicted it to take around three to five years for the lake to completely fill, Mother Nature had other ideas. Heavy rains swept across the area and flooded the lake faster than construction crews could clear out the trees on the lake bottom, and in 1968, the lake reached its capacity. The filling of the lake set in motion some very expansive growth for the city of Heath, including the development of lakefront homes, which drew more and more people to the community.

With a promising new lake to attract more boaters, fishermen, and sailors, the RCYC quickly became a vastly popular and cutting-edge yacht club in the Dallas area as well as the Southwestern region of the United States. Home to some of the most skilled yacht racers around, the RCYC today offers organized competition for all ages. Its facilities operate year-round and include wet- and dry-slip storage, a swimming pool, an expansive deck with attached playground, a full-service dining room, and a bar.

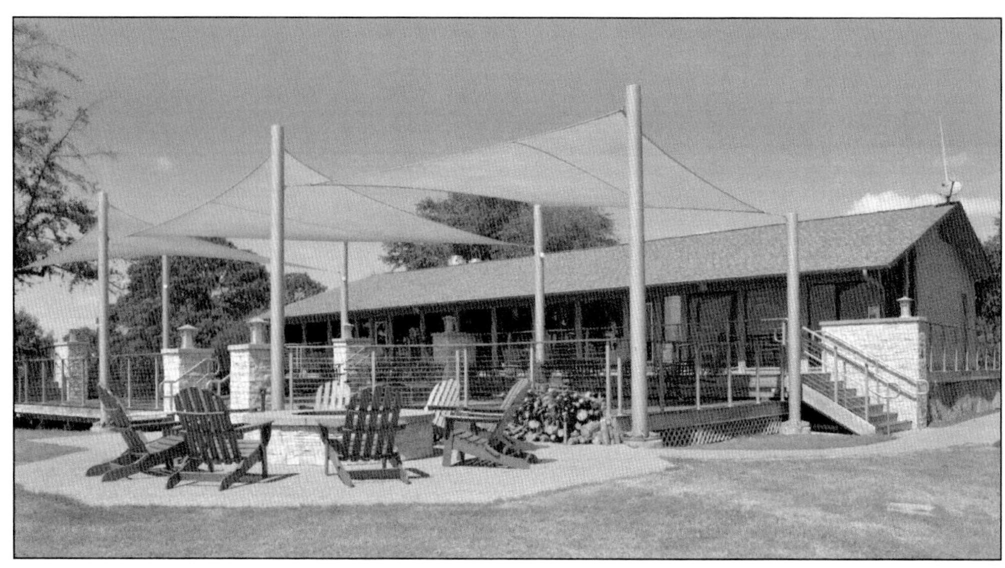

Founded in 1969 by a group of avid sailing enthusiasts from the White Rock Lake area in Dallas, Rush Creek Yacht Club began with a philosophy dedicated to sailboat racing. Originally called the Dallas Olympic Sailing Club, the name changed to Rush Creek—derived from a nearby creek on the designated site—due to a discovered copyright on the name Olympic. (Both, courtesy of the RCYC.)

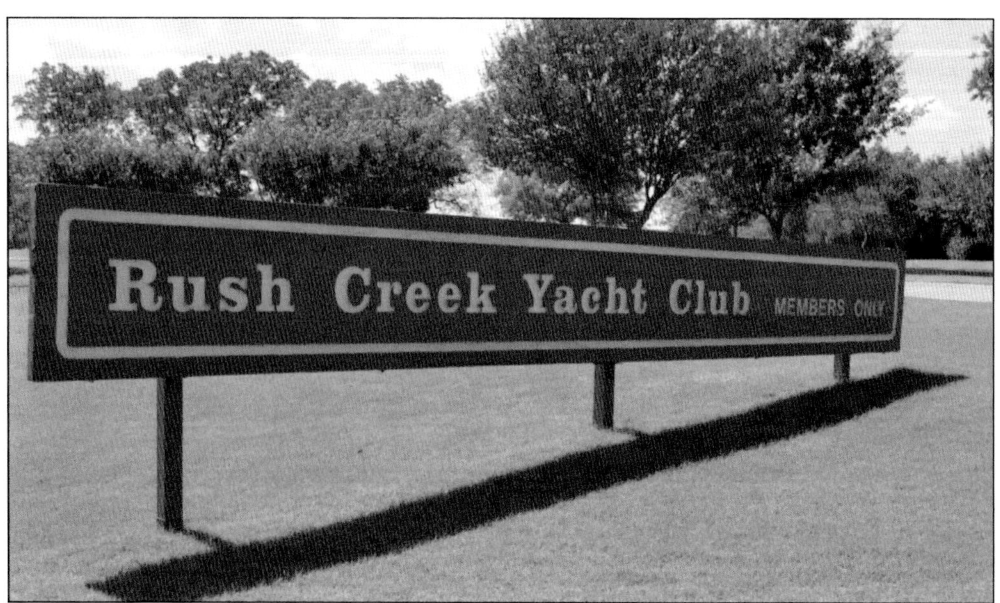

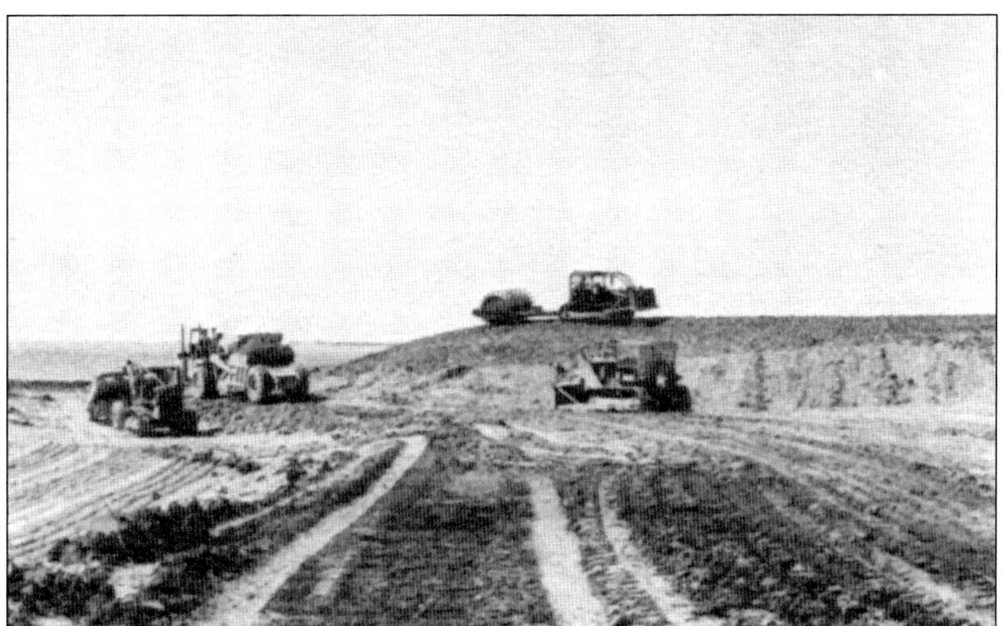

Pictured above is a view from the harbor floor toward the breakwater during the initial construction of the yacht club in 1970. The 1970s saw a concerted drive to increase membership of the yacht club while facilities were being planned and built, with the hope of beginning a racing program later that summer. The first short breakwater was built, and by February 1970, membership of the club had reached 84. An official ground breaking for the clubhouse was held in March of that year. Below is an image depicting the yacht club's original charter members viewing the club's master plan during the ground-breaking ceremony. (Both, courtesy of the RCYC.)

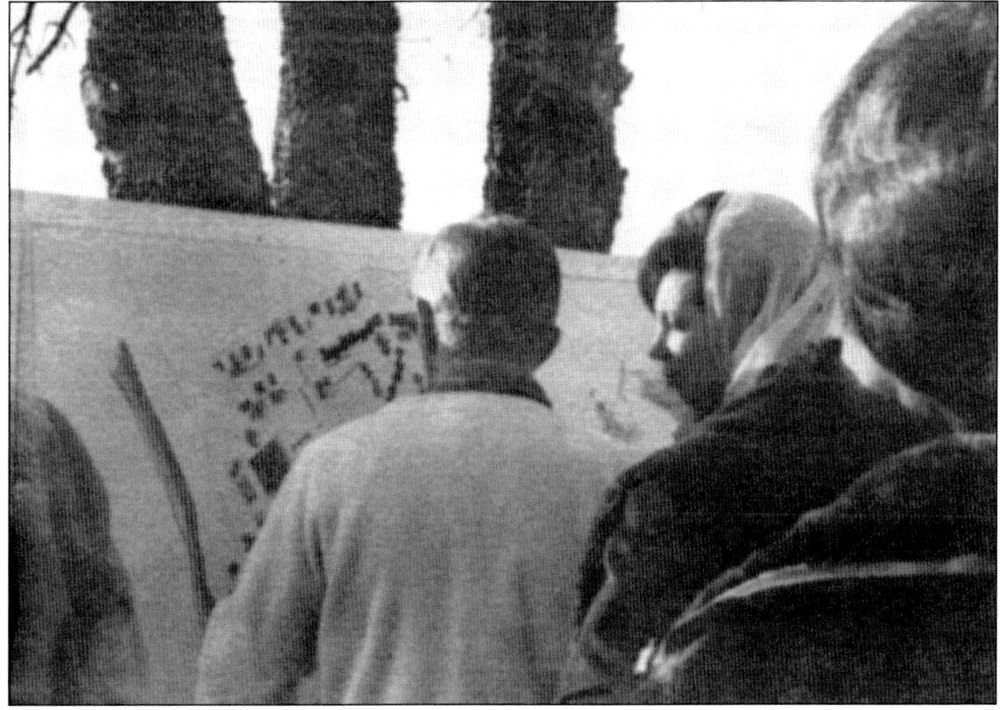

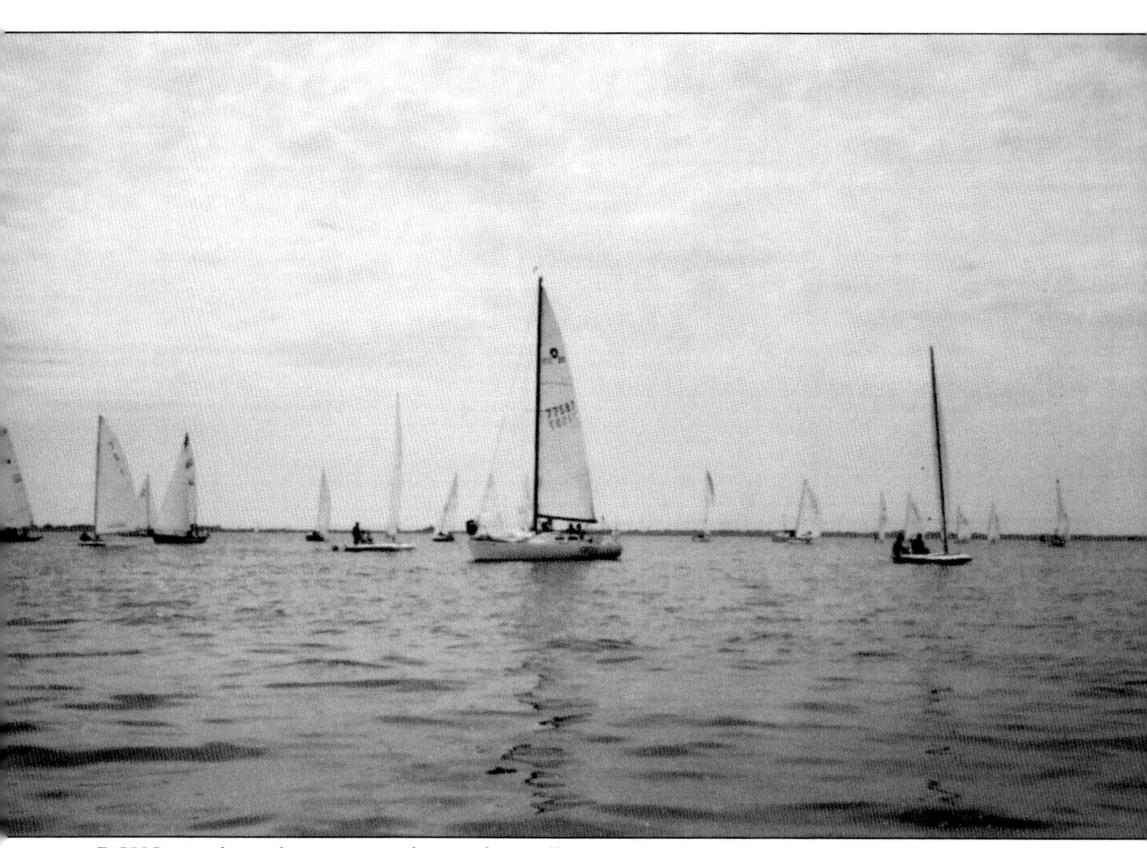

RCYC members always enjoyed some fun sailboat racing every Sunday, such as the race shown in the above image taken sometime in the early 1990s. Sunday racing was made especially popular by local sailors once Lake Ray Hubbard filled; its size was much larger compared to the smaller White Rock Lake. The lake saw as many as 50 sailboats racing at one point in time. The club now holds weekly racing events on Wednesday evenings. The club has hosted a number of big championship races in its history and has a reputation for providing a great venue, spirited camaraderie, and excellent race management. RCYC members placed first, second, or third as either skipper or crew in 70 championship events between 1972 and 2009. (Courtesy of the RCYC.)

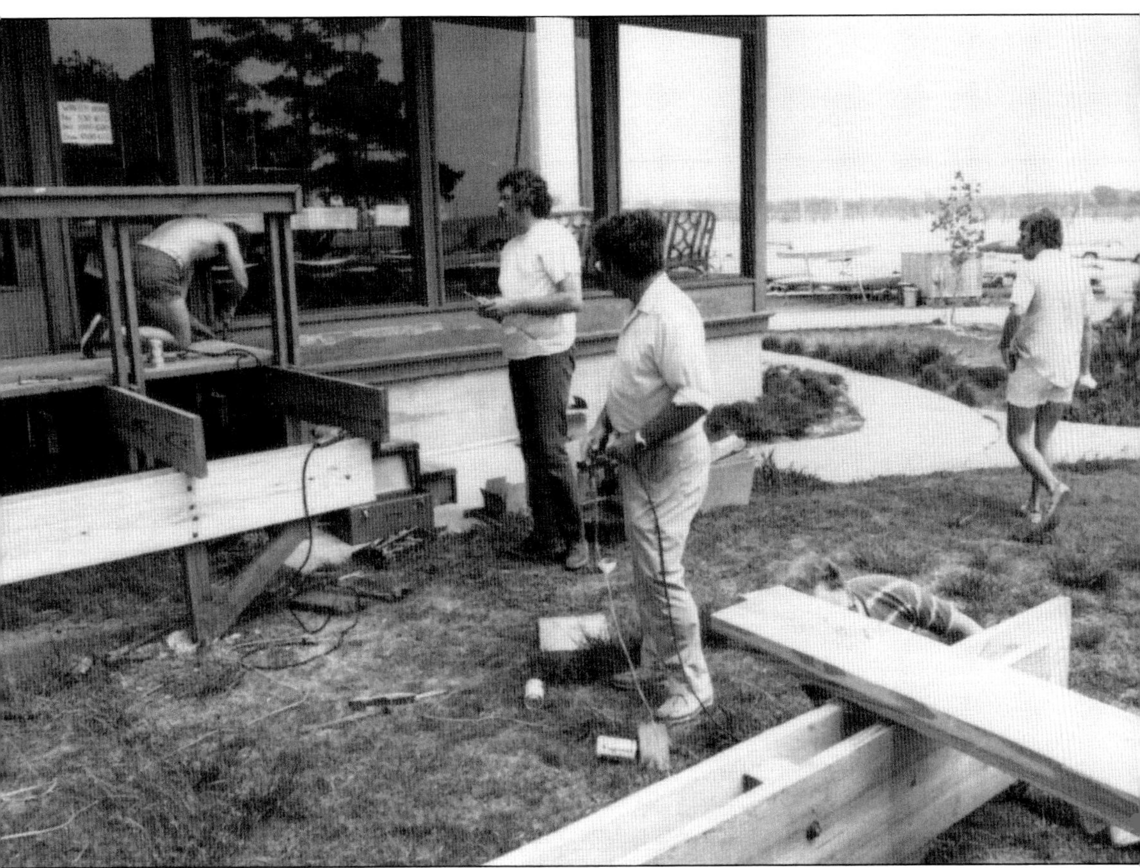

The year 1971 saw the completion of the clubhouse, condos, and keeper's house for the RCYC. A couple of years later, a tennis committee was appointed, and plans were made to erect tennis courts for the club. Other improvements to the clubhouse included the construction of a deck by member volunteers. In the above image, RCYC members Tony Seeley (second from left) and Jim Anderson (holding cord) work with other members on the construction of the original deck of the yacht club in 1973. (Courtesy of the RCYC.)

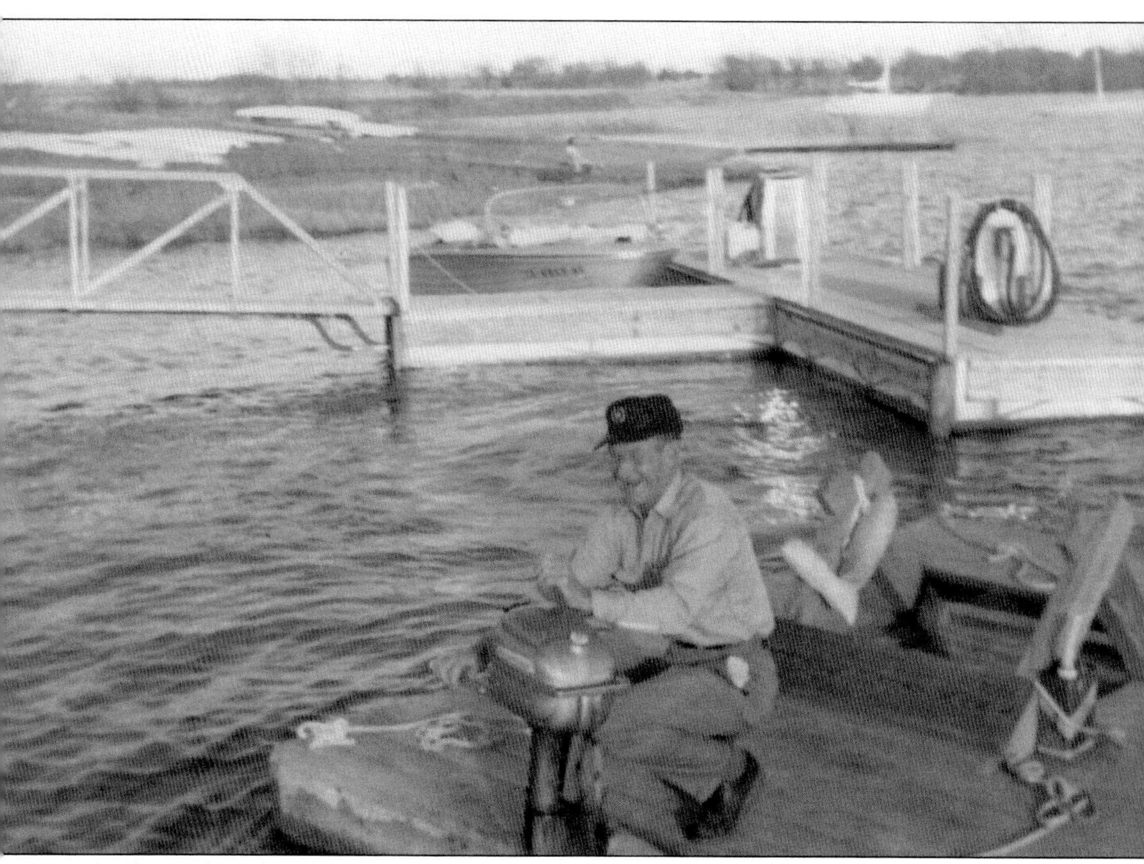

Rush Creek Yacht Club's first club manager, Charles Yates, also acted as groundskeeper. Here, he operates the work barge near the club's original gas dock seen in the background, shuttling sailors to and from the club docks. (Courtesy of the RCYC.)

The year 1985 saw major financial breakthroughs for the RCYC. In the photograph at right, the RCYC holds its annual banquet with Rockwall mayor and RCYC charter member George Hatfield (left) introducing Manning Grinnan (right)—one of the original founding members of the yacht club—as its new commodore. Under Grinnan's leadership, club facilities were improved with the addition of a 21,000-square-foot concrete parking ramp east of the club manager's house along with the acquisition of 50 new chairs for the clubhouse. The RCYC board also instituted the capital reserve fund to ensure future improvements without the need to borrow money from the bank. Below, members of the RCYC also celebrated the retirement of the club mortgage after it was able to buy back the land from pioneer member Jim Anderson (with microphone), pictured next to Commodore Manning Grinnan (left). (Both, courtesy of the RCYC.)

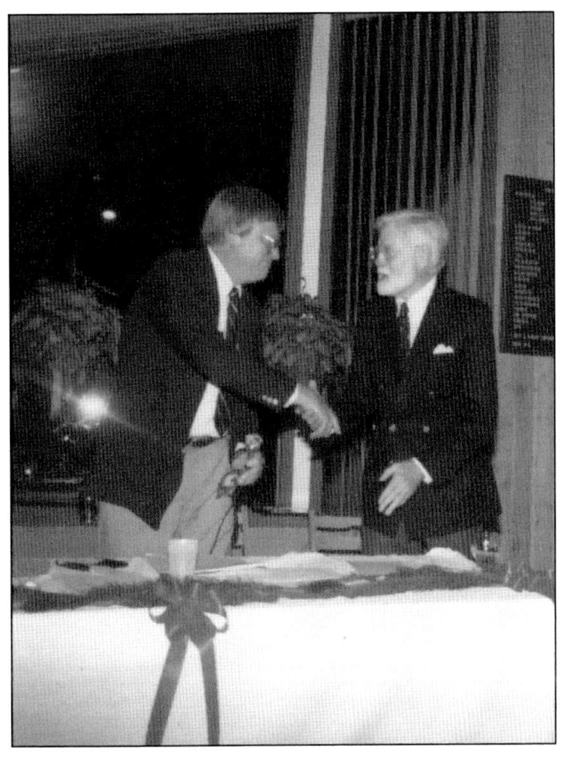

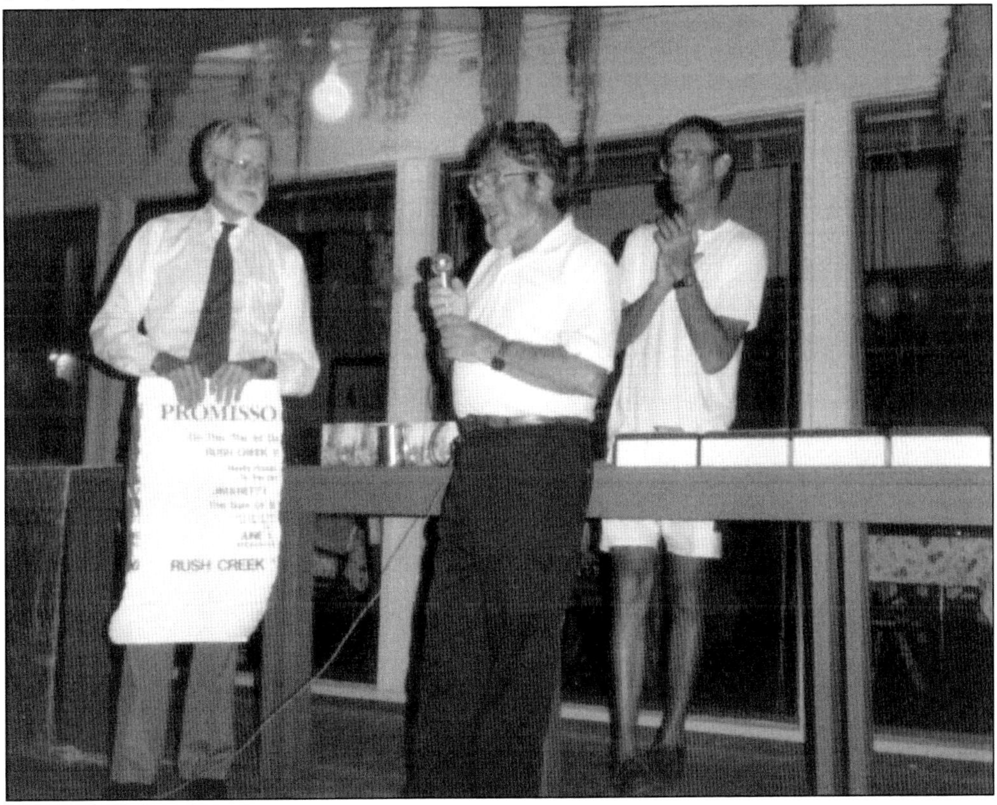

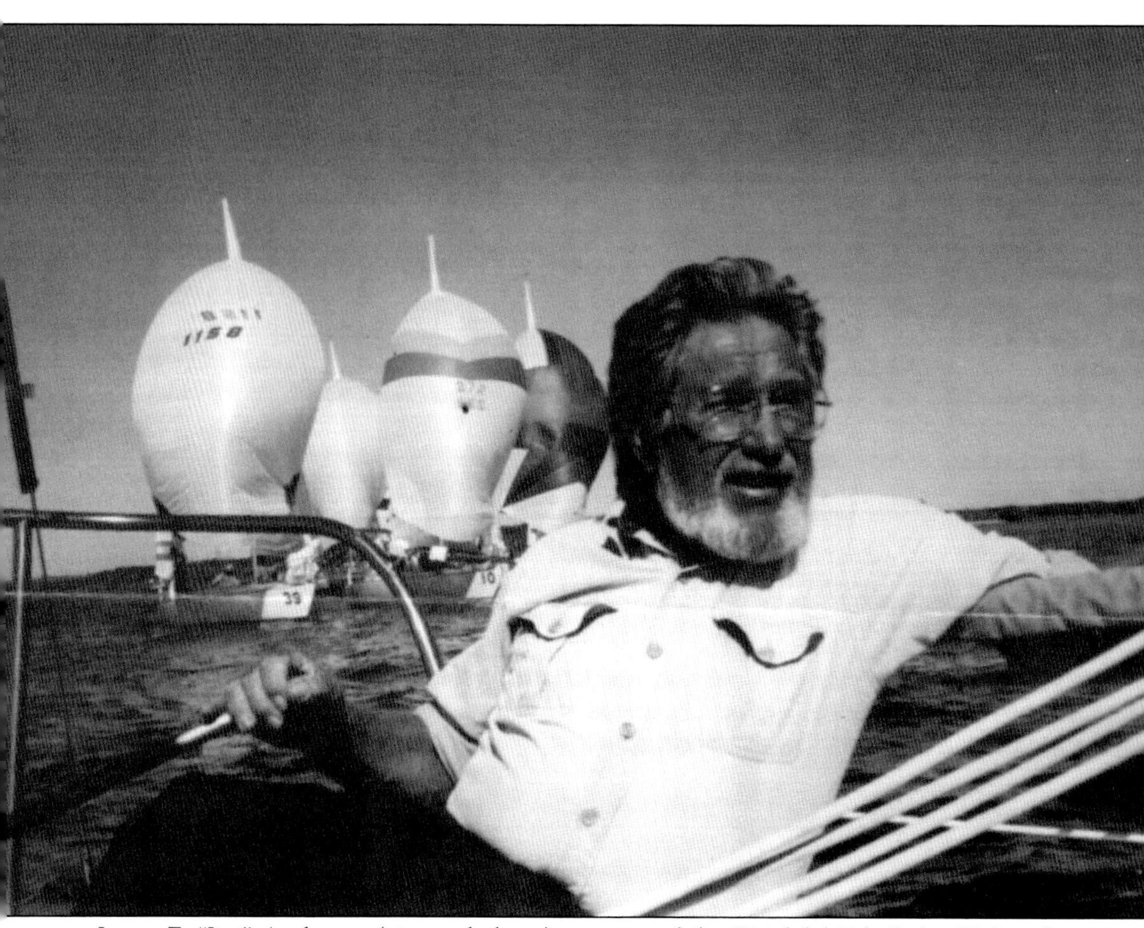

James E. "Jim" Anderson (pictured above) was one of the "Faithful Fifty," the 50 founding members of the RCYC. He bought and sold the original 13.8 acres of land for the club on very favorable terms. Anderson served as chairman of the board of governors for the club during its earliest years when much of the facilities were still being planned and built. Anderson also served as commodore in 1979 and 1991 and was bestowed the title of commodore of the fleet along with fellow RCYC founding member Bob Chilton in 1976 for his sailing accomplishments and promotional activities on behalf of the RCYC, as well as other contributions to the growth of the club. (Courtesy of RCYC.)

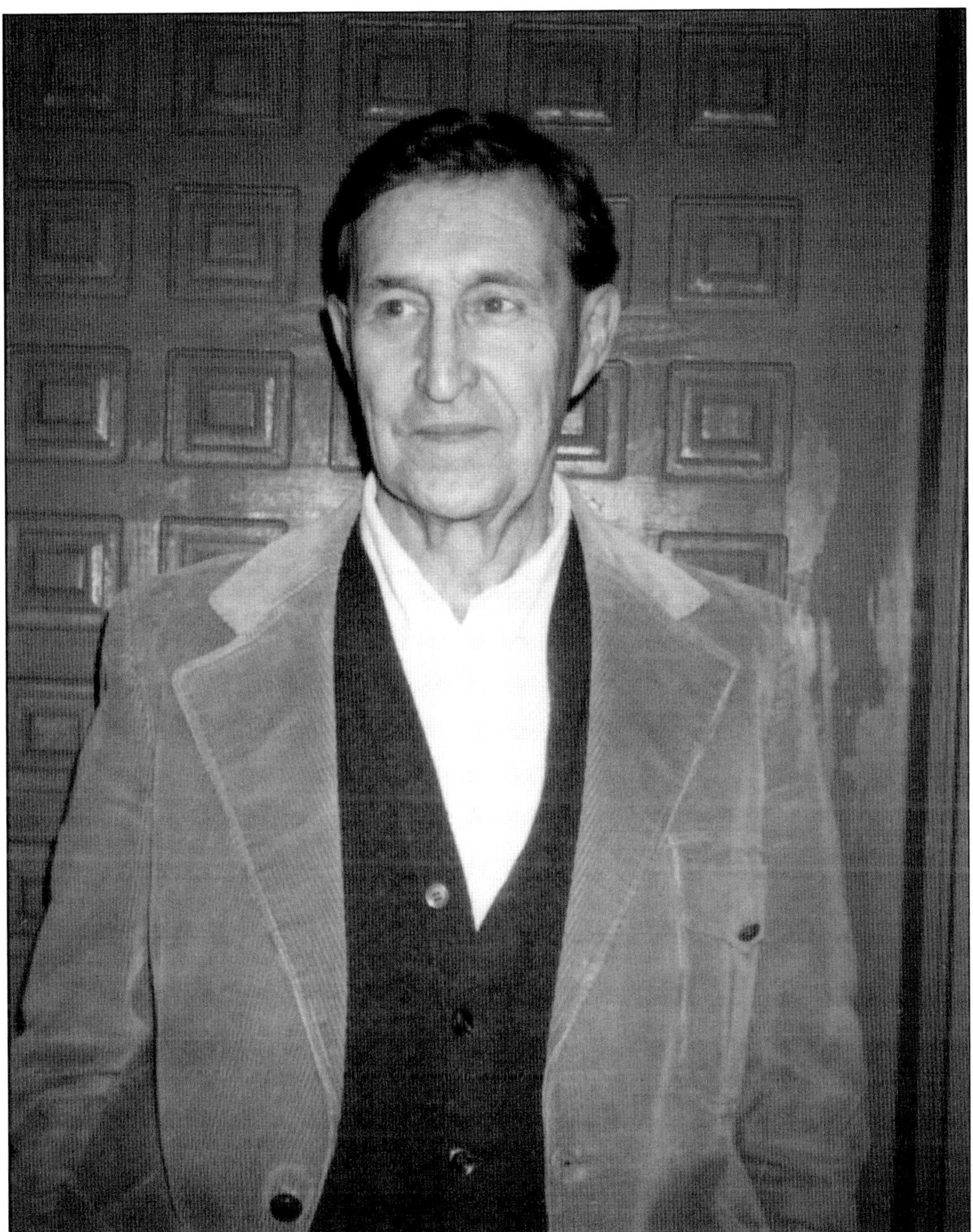

John Sellon was one of the original founding members and a past commodore of the RCYC. He founded the original 14 acres of land on which the RCYC is located today. Sellon and his racing committee of Jim Craig, Duncan Porter, and Dick Prokup helped establish a full sailboat-racing program, including racing policies and fleet organization, for the club's first year of racing in 1971. Sellon was presented with an honorary life membership in appreciation of his years of service to the club in 1986. (Courtesy of the RCYC.)

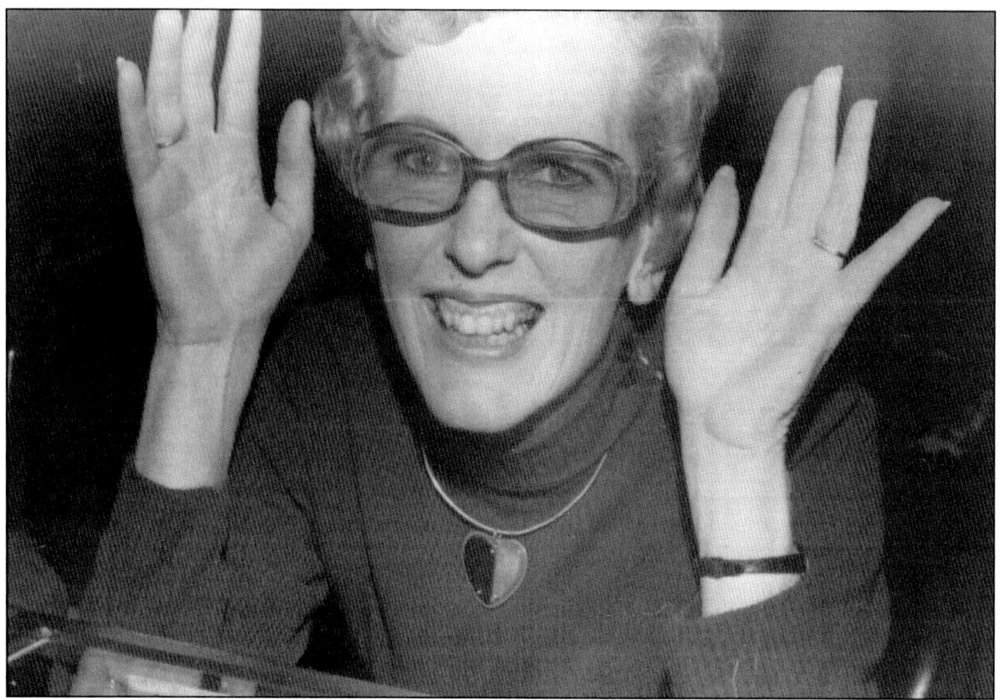

Pictured here is Betty Anderson, wife of RCYC founding member Jim Anderson. The club's first race committee boat—the *Betty A I*—was named in her honor. The original *Betty A* was eventually replaced by a new boat and named *Betty A II*, but serious problems with that vessel led the club to purchase a new boat. Research and recommendations by Jim Anderson and Richard Guinan resulted in the ordering of a custom-built boat with a 60-horsepower diesel engine, and *Betty A III* (shown below) was launched in 1979. (Both, courtesy of the RCYC.)

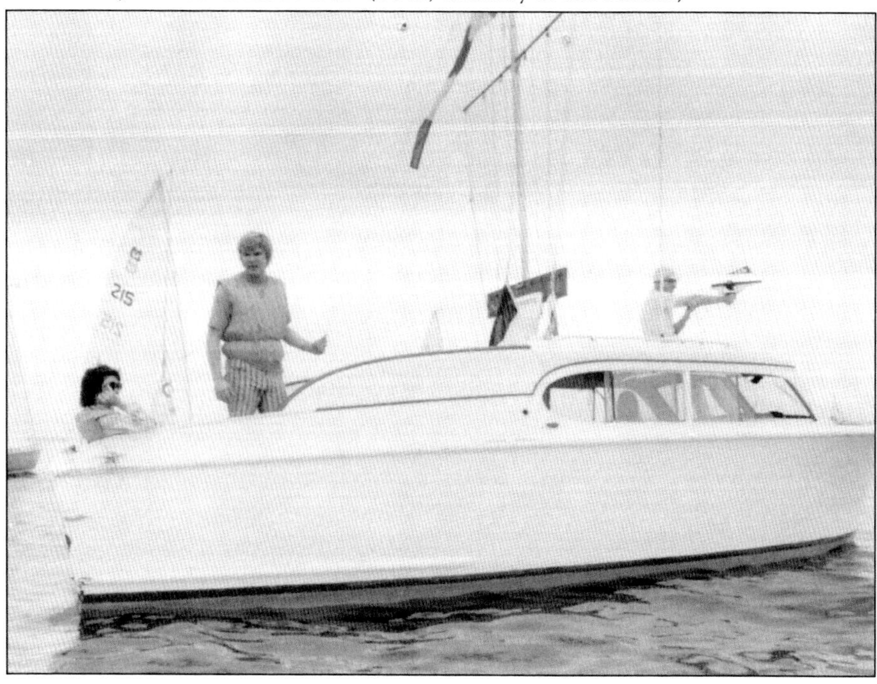

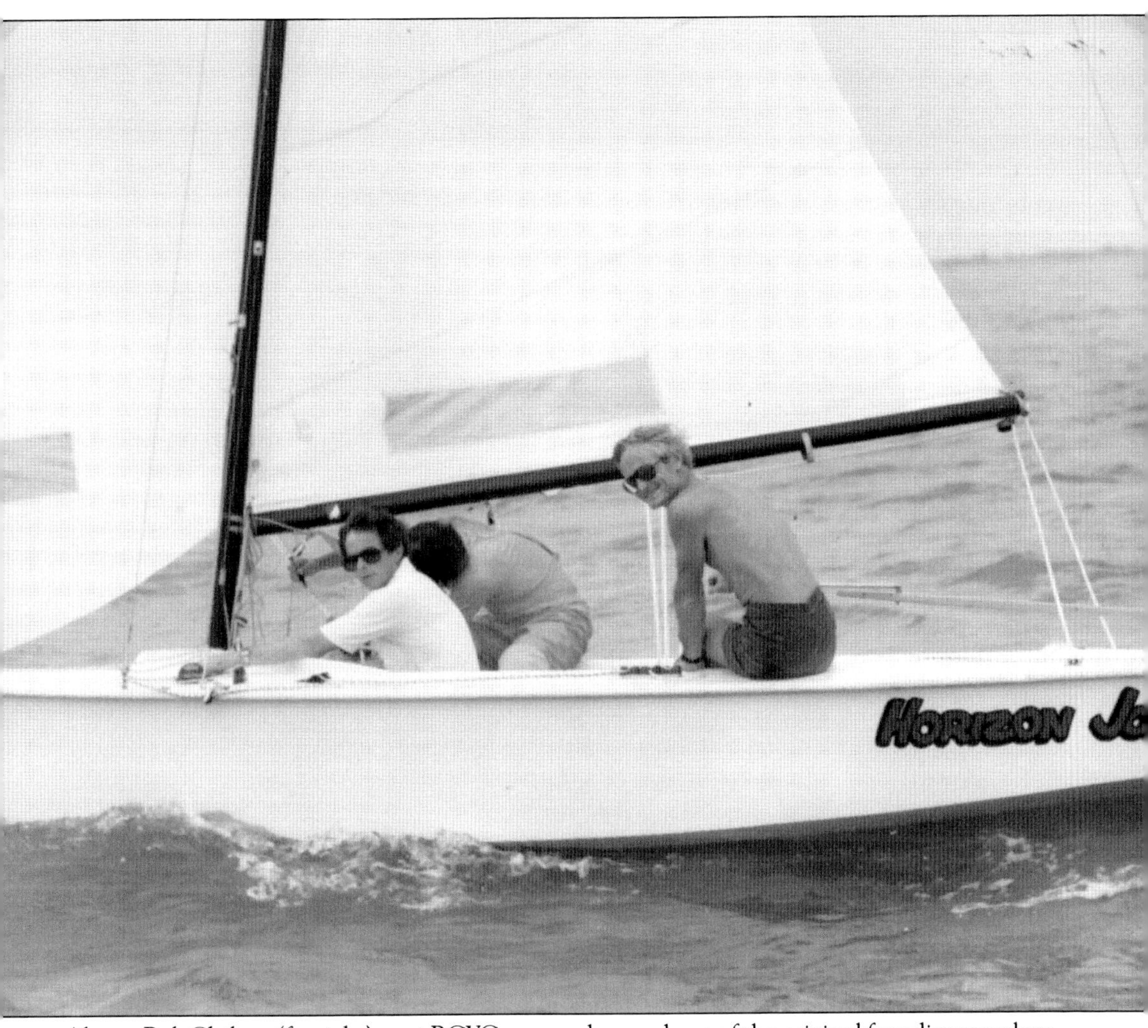

Above, Bob Chilton (far right), past RCYC commodore and one of the original founding members of the club, and fellow crew member Jim Craig (white shirt) take Chilton's lightning boat, *Horizon Job*, out for a sail prior to the 1979 Lightning World Championships, hosted by the RCYC. The event saw a total of 53 teams from across the globe take part in the event. Listed then as five feet, nine inches and 150 pounds, Chilton was also one of the oldest to participate in the championships at 46 years old. Most of the participants in the event were in their mid-20s. In 1990, Chilton made a transatlantic crossing on his 100-foot yacht, *Royal Eagle II*, in an attempt to break a record. Chilton, along with Rockwall-area sailors Bryan Davis and Rusty Jackson, made their voyage using the route pioneered by Christopher Columbus from Las Palmas in the Canary Islands to the West Indies in 13 days and 6 hours, just shy of the record-setting 12.5 days set by a similar yacht. Towards the middle of the trip, Chilton and his crew experienced 30-foot waves, and no one was able to eat on tables or sleep in bunks for the majority of the voyage. (Courtesy of the RCYC.)

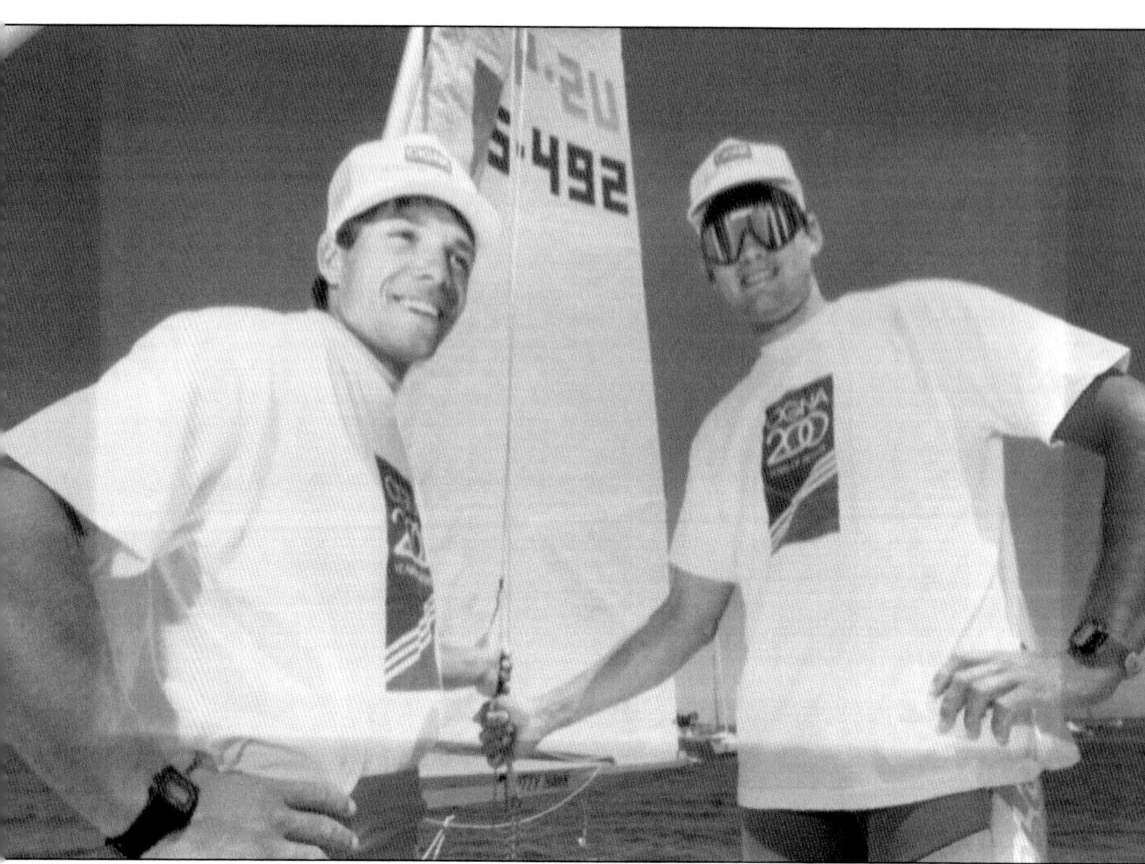

RCYC sailing sensation and skipper of Team CompuCom/Kitty Hawk Paul Foerster (pictured left) and teammate Bob Merrick (right) won a silver medal in the Men's 470 at the 2000 Olympic Games in Sydney, Australia. Foerster, who was inducted in the National Sailing Hall of Fame in October 2015, has won medals (two silver, one gold) in two different classes in three Olympic events, four world championships in three different classes, seven national championships in Flying Dutchman, and is a three-time college All-American. (Courtesy of the RCYC.)

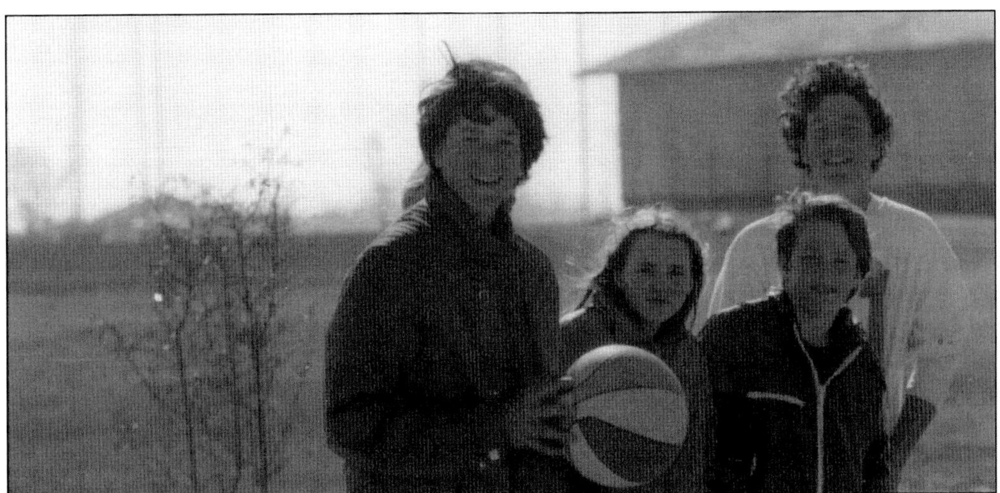

Before the RCYC launched its Junior Youth Sailing Program in 1979, kids would all sail with their parents and enjoy other recreational activities at the club. Pictured in the above image are, from left to right, club youth Jeff Grinnan, Cindi Craig, Stephen Craig, and Kevin Fuller on the grounds of the RCYC in 1974. In the photograph below, boys and girls of the 1992 RCYC Summer Sailing Program pose on the dock of the yacht club. The program was led by longtime RCYC member and 1983 commodore Stephen Andre (back row, second from the right). Today, the RCYC offers a year-round sailing program for boys and girls ages 8 to 17 with an interest in developing racing skills in boats ranging from single-handed dinghies to keelboats. The program also focuses on developing future leaders, as the older juniors help coach and mentor beginning sailors. (Both, courtesy of the RCYC.)

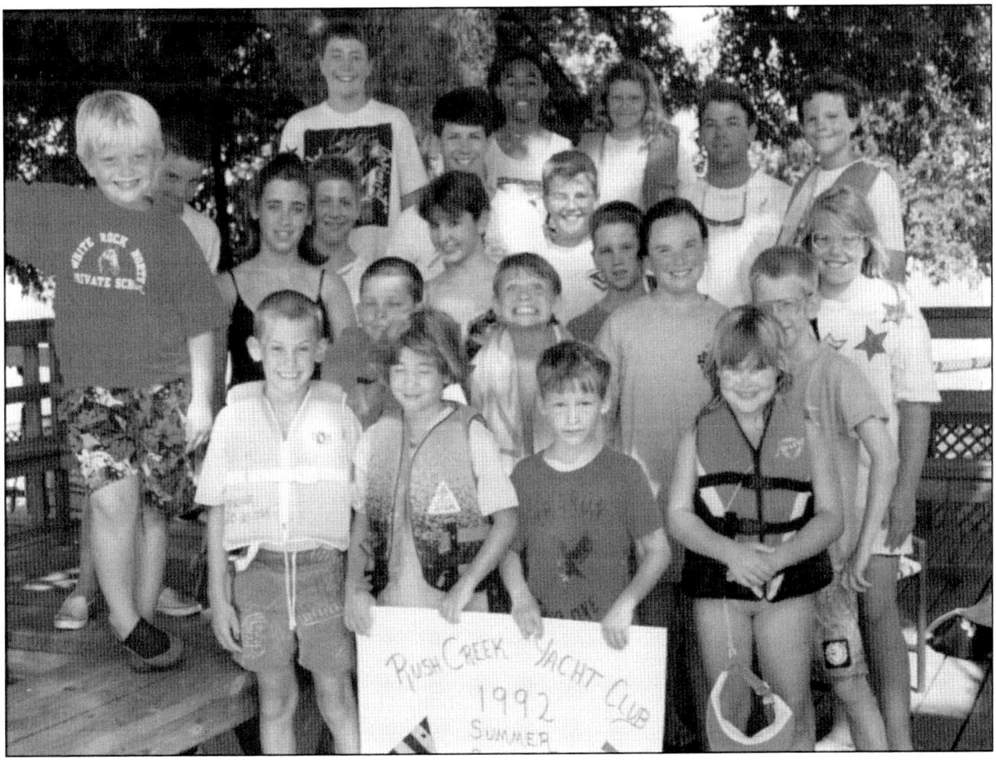